INSTITUTIONAL ECONOMICS

VOLUME TWO

INSTITUTIONAL ECONOMICS

Its Place in Political Economy

VOLUME TWO

John R. Commons

with a New Introduction by
Malcolm Rutherford

Transaction Publishers
New Brunswick (U.S.A.) and London (U.K.)

Fourth printing 2009

New material this edition copyright © 1990 by Transaction Publishers, New Brunswick, New Jersey. Originally published in 1934 by the Macmillan Company.

This book is printed on acid-free paper that meets the American National Standard for Permanence of Paper for Printed Library Materials.

Library of Congress Catalog Number: 89-32259
ISBN: 0-88738-831-0
Printed in the United States of America

Library of Congress Cataloging-in-Publication Data

Commons, John Rogers, 1862-1945.
    Institutional economics : its place in political economy / John R. Commons; with a new introduction by Malcolm Rutherford.
        p. cm.
    Reprint. Originally published: New York: Macmillan, 1934.
    Bibliography: p.
    Includes index.
    ISBN 0-88738-831-0
    1. Institutional economics. I. Title.
HB99.5.C65   1986   89-32259
330—dc20   CIP

ISBN: 0-88738-797-7 (v. 1)
ISBN: 0-88738-831-0 (v. 2)
ISBN: 0-88738-832-9 (2 vol. set)

TABLE OF CONTENTS
VOLUME TWO

CHAPTER   PAGE

CHARTS

TABLES

INTRODUCTION TO THE TRANSACTION EDITION

This reissue of J. R. Commons' major work, *Institutional Economics: Its Place in Political Economy,* is particularly timely as interest in Commons' work has never been greater. At least fifteen substantial articles dealing exclusively or largely with Commons' ideas have been published in the last six years alone, and many more are either forthcoming or currently in preparation.[1] In contrast, the secondary literature on Commons prior to this was both relatively sparse and episodic in character. Even as recently as the period between 1970 and 1980, when the secondary literature began to grow, a single special issue of the *Journal of Economic Issues* accounted for almost half of the significant output.[2] It is also noticeable that whereas virtually all of the secondary literature used to be produced by institutionalists for institutionalists, the more recent work on Commons includes papers written by noninstitutionalists and directed at noninstitutionalist audiences (see particularly Endres 1985; M. Perlman 1986; and Vanberg 1988).

This growing and broadening interest in Commons is undoubtedly due to the general revival of concern with the role of institutions in economics, and, more particularly, to the rapid growth in the attention being given to issues such as the importance of property rights, the behavior of courts and the evolution of common law, the behavior of legislatures and the determination of statute law, the evolution of organizational forms, and the use of the transaction as a basic unit of analysis. All these issues were among Commons' central concerns but did not figure largely in the work of the other leading early institutionalists. Commons is quite alone among the major writers in the American institutionalist tradition in the extent of his interest in law and organizations and their evolution, and it is exactly this that gives Commons' work its considerable contemporary relevance.

The fuller recognition of Commons' work and its present-day importance is, however, hindered by a number of widely held beliefs. It is accepted by many that Commons, like some other institutionalists of his time, produced work that was almost entirely descriptive and lacking in theoretical content. Commons has also been accused of taking a "naive," "collectivist" approach to institutions, conceptualizing them entirely as the intended outcomes of processes of deliberative collective decision making (Seckler 1966; 1975), and this claim has often been repeated (Schotter 1981; Langlois 1986). As more and deeper readings of Commons' work have appeared these two conceptions have been repeatedly challenged. Commons' work does contain a conceptual and theoretical framework (although not one that lends itself to making exact predictions), and his approach to institutions, although emphasizing the collective processes through which conflicts are resolved and particular rules enforced, is neither "naive" nor inconsistent with the idea that social customs and common practices can arise in an unplanned and spontaneous fashion (see Rutherford 1983; Chasse 1986; Vanberg 1988; Biddle 1988A).

Perhaps more serious, because it is not as possible to refute, is the view of Commons' writings, and particularly of *Institutional Economics*, as difficult, obscure, full of unfamiliar terminology, and requiring great effort to understand. Right from the very first appearance of *Institutional Economics* the book was assailed as "ponderous," "curiously disorganized, and filled with vagueness, clumsy terminology, rambling digressions and tedious repetition" (Bye 1935, pp. 201–2). Its length, organization, and style make it quite daunting, and most of its potential readership, particularly among more orthodox economists, have probably never even opened its pages, being dissuaded by its awful reputation alone. Yet, as Frank Knight argued in his 1935 review, "if they will take it in the right spirit, minds trained in orthodox economic theory and devoted to clarity, definiteness and 'system' are the very ones to read it with great profit" (Knight 1935, p. 805).

This introduction attempts both to underline the continuing relevance of the ideas contained within *Institutional Economics* and to increase their accessability. Some analysis of the place and organization of the book will be provided first, to be followed by a discussion of some of the major themes in the book and their role in Commons' overall conceptual framework. Introductions such as this usually devote considerable space to biographical information, but this will not be done here. The relevant details of Commons' life are already well known and easily available elsewhere (Commons 1934B; S. Perlman 1945; Harter 1962).

THE PLACE OF *INSTITUTIONAL ECONOMICS*

In order to fully understand *Institutional Economics* it is important to comprehend its place in Commons' work in relation both to Commons' other theoretical writings and to his many empirical investigations and vast practical experience. Commons is often regarded as a simple empiricist, deriving his more theoretical ideas directly from his own experience. Commons himself encouraged this view, opening *Institutional Economics* with the words: "My point of view is based on my participation in collective activities, from which I here derive a theory of the part played by collective action in control of individual action" (p. 1). This is a little misleading. From the very beginning of his career Commons was concerned with the development of conceptual and theoretical ideas, and one can trace an intellectual evolution in Commons' work that operated through the *testing* and subsequent modifying of his ideas in the light of his practical experiences. This evolution begins with *The Distribution of Wealth* (1893), and proceeds through *Proportional Representation* (1896), *A Sociological View of Sovereignty* (1899–1900), to *The Legal Foundations of Capitalism* (1924), *Institutional Economics* (1934A) and, finally, to *The Economics of Collective Action* (1950) published five years after Commons' death.

Commons' first major book, *The Distribution of Wealth*, attempts to combine marginalist notions concerning value and distribution with historicist ideas and reformist concerns. It reveals the pervasive influence of R. T. Ely in its emphasis on property rights and institutionalized monopoly advantages and privileges. It is clear that the attempt to expand economic theory to include extensive consideration of the role of property rights was a goal that Commons adopted from the outset and never abandoned. In *The Distribution of Wealth* he argues that "the place of law in Political Economy is a subject which has received from English economists no attention at all commensurate with its far-reaching importance." The "English economists have taken the laws of private property for granted, assuming that they are fixed and immutable," but such laws are "changeable," have a "profound influence upon the production and distribution of wealth," and are therefore in need of close examination (p. 59). It is in this broad sense that it is true that *The*

Distribution of Wealth "contains the foundations of Commons' economics" (Dorfman 1963, p. xv).

More specifically, Commons was concerned with the conflict between labor and capital and particularly with the position of labor, and this was a concern that persisted throughout Commons' career. Commons discussed the problems of low wages and unemployment and contrasted labor's position with the ability of businesses to generate and capitalize rents out of patents, copyrights, trade names, franchises, monopoly and "good-will." The issues of monopoly rents and good-will were developed later into his extensive discussions of intangible property, but his more immediate response to the problems faced by labor was to suggest the creation of a "right to employment" secured by government. At this point in his thinking Commons looked to direct government regulation and action to bring about institutional change although he believed that this was unlikely to occur given the then current form and composition of government. Commons, therefore, turned his attention to political reform, notably proportional representation, and to the development of a theory of the sociological basis of sovereignty.

In his essay *A Sociological View of Sovereignty* Commons analyses two historical processes. In the first, "the state gradually deprives other institutions of the right to use violence," while, in the second, "new groups force their way into the coalition controlling the state" (Chasse 1986, p. 761). The state is thus "an accumulated series of compromises between social classes, each seeking to secure for itself control over the coercive elements which exist implicitly in society with the institution of private property" (Commons 1899–1900, p. 45). These ideas are retained and developed in Commons' later works, but at this time proportional representation was the institutional adjustment that Commons thought would best continue the historic process of compromise between social classes. Commons' view was that territorial representation resulted in weak candidates who concentrated on not making enemies. What was required was a government consisting of individuals representing identifiable interests groups and who could argue and negotiate for those groups. Related to this was Commons' critique of traditional "log-rolling" activities among legislators and his concern that courts and commissions might be taking over legislative functions (Chasse 1986, pp. 762–63).

Between the turn of the century and the publication of his next major theoretical work in 1924, Commons was heavily involved in the empirical investigation of labour unions, in collective bargaining and mediation, in the work of bodies such as the U.S. Industrial Commission, the Industrial Relations Commission, the Wisconsin Industrial Commission, the Federal Trade Commission, and the National Monetary Association, and in the study of law and the basis of court decisions. These experiences deeply affected his earlier views—not on the importance in economics of property rights, nor the "fundamental vision" outlined in *A Sociological View of Sovereignty* (Chasse 1986, p. 762)— but on how particular institutions functioned and how the needed compromise between social classes could best be accomplished. His many "experiments in collective action," as he called them, gave him a very different view of legislatures, log-rolling, and the potential of courts and commissions. As Chasse has said: "From sweeping legislative changes, he turned to more flexible devices—commissions with insulated staffs, the courts, and independent outside interest groups affecting the state through 'the device of collective bargaining'" (Chasse 1986, p. 766).

Commons' mature views are presented in his three major books, *The Legal Foundations of Capitalism, Institutional Economics,* and *The Economics of Collective Action,* of which the second is by far the most important. It represents Commons' last major and most complete "research statement" (Parsons 1985). *The Legal Foundations* concentrates more narrowly on the history of court decisions and the concept of reasonableness as used by the courts. *Institutional Economics* both incorporates and refines this analysis and seeks to bring it together with a discussion of the evolution of economic ideas and the nature of a fully "rounded out" political economy. It is Commons' most complete attempt to incorporate legal institutions within economics. By contrast *The Economics of Collective Action* is a simplified exposition of his main ideas and not itself a major research treatise (Parsons 1950, p. 10). Thus, despite the later work, *Institutional Economics* stands as Commons' *magnum opus* (Coats 1983), the intellectual culmination of his extraordinary career as both theorist and practical experimentalist.

THE PURPOSE AND ORGANIZATION OF *INSTITUTIONAL ECONOMICS*

Institutional Economics is a difficult book in part because of its complexity of purpose and the way in which Commons organized his material. Commons' overall objective in the book was to give institutional economics—by which he meant the study of "collective action in control of individual action" or the "proprietary economics of rights, duties, liberties, and exposures" (pp. 1, 8) — its proper place in "the whole of a rounded-out theory of Political Economy" (p. 6). However, this involved neither a simple substitution of institutional for other types of economics, nor (as in his earlier *Distribution of Wealth*) a simple coupling of institutional concerns onto existing economic analysis. Existing types of economic analysis often masked the role of institutions within their basic conceptual frameworks. The problem was to reinterpret existing economic concepts, to tease out their hidden meanings and in this way to "include and give a proper place to all the economic theories since John Locke" (p. 6). Thus, in the preface to *Institutional Economics* Commons states that: "Each idea here incorporated is traced back to its originator, and then the successive modifications of that idea are developed and the earlier double or treble meanings of the idea are separated, until each, as a single meaning, is combined with the others in what I conceive to be the Science of Political Economy as it is developing since the last Great War" (p. v). Similarly, in the introduction, Commons writes that "institutional economics consists partly in going back through the court decisions of several hundred years" and also "in going back through the writings of economists from John Locke to the Twentieth Century, to discover wherein they have or have not introduced collective action" (p. 5).

An added complication is that *Institutional Economics* is a book that also deals at length with Commons' own experiences, his "years of experiment" (p. 9), so that the complete expression of his objective is found in his statement: "What I have tried to do is to work out a system of thought that shall give due weight to all economic theories, modified by my own experience" (p. 8). These experiences and their results sometimes take up lengthy sections of the book, for example thirty-three pages deal with his efforts in setting up unemployment and accident insurance programs (pp. 840–73), but throughout the book Commons is making references to his wide experience — from his involvement in the Pittsburgh-Plus case to his investigations of the Federal Reserve System.

Organizationally, *Institutional Economics* is deeply affected by the nature of Commons' objectives. On one level the book is organized around the central concepts of "Method," "Efficiency," "Scarcity," "Futurity," and "Reasonable Value." However, running through and around these themes is Commons' discussion of the history of economic thought. The chapter entitled "Method" starts with a discussion of Locke but then moves into a detailed outline of Commons' own views on transactions, his basic unit of analysis. The history of economic thought theme is picked up again in the next five chapters entitled respectively "Quesnay," "Hume and Peirce," "Adam Smith," "Bentham versus Blackstone," and "Malthus." These chapters deal with a variety of issues including matters of method, particularly Commons' pragmatism, the role of scarcity and conflict in economics as opposed to a presumed harmony of interest, and the importance of custom and common law as opposed to individual pleasures and pains. A more generalized treatment and elaboration of some of these issues is provided in the first six sections of the next chapter "Efficiency and Scarcity." The last four sections return to the history of thought with a more explicit discussion of the efficiency and scarcity theme in connection with Ricardo and Malthus, Marx and Proudhon, and Menger, Wieser, Fisher and Fetter. The next chapter on "Futurity" covers an astonishing two hundred and fifty-nine pages and deals with many and various aspects of incorporeal and intangible property and with Commons' profit margin theory of business depressions. The first part of the chapter contains a lengthy treatment of the work of Henry Dunning Mac-Leod. The writings of Sidgwick, Knapp, Hawtrey, Cassel, Wicksell, and Bohm-Bawerk are also discussed. The next chapter on "Reasonable Value" is almost as long and opens with a critical discussion of Veblen, particularly his treatment of intangible property. It then proceeds into a discussion of the behaviour of legislatures and courts in bringing about a reconciliation of conflicting interests and, notably, a limitation of the use of economic power to reasonable levels. The final chapter "Communism, Fascism, Capitalism" deals more briefly with Commons' views on how best to avoid totalitarian solutions to society's conflicts.

In overall terms, it is particularly important to understand the exact purpose of Commons' extensive discussions of the history of economic thought. In line with his philosophical pragmatism "Commons did not want to passively reflect the ideas of the past, but to engage in a dialogue with them — using them as raw material to be blended with his own experiential knowledge and shaped into tools for understanding and solving present-day problems" (Biddle 1988B, p. 6).

Main Themes in *Institutional Economics*

Institutional Economics is a book far too vast in scope to summarize adequately. Instead some of the major themes in the book will be outlined, concentrating on those points of greatest interest to modern economists concerned with institutional questions.

Method

Commons has often been regarded as following a holistic, as opposed to an individualistic, methodology (Gruchy 1947; Ramstad 1986). It is true that Commons was especially concerned with "whole-part" relationships, including the relationship between individuals and institutions, and that this relationship presents a problem that all of those concerned to deal with institutions in economics must face. Approaches to the problem have usually been divided into the individualistic and holistic. Individualistic approaches give primacy to the individual, emphasizing that individual actions create institutions and that institutions are to be analyzed as the intended or unintended outcomes of individual actions. In this, little attention is given to the role of institutions in shaping individual goals, preferences, and values. Individualism often entails a *reductive* or *psychologistic* approach that takes as its ultimate objective the explanation of social phenomena by theories of individual action alone, that is, without reference to other social phenomena as givens. By contrast, the holist gives primacy to the social and institutional and tends to stress the socialization of the individual. The individual is seen as having internalized the norms of the society he is born into and inhabits. This may be taken to the extreme of arguing in a way that suggests that collective or social phenomena are autonomous entities with distinct functions, purposes, or wills of their own. However, even if the argument is not taken to that extreme the holist would certainly reject the reductivist program of attempting to reduce all social phenomena to the outcome of the actions of noninstitutionalized individuals.

That Commons' approach emphasizes the role that institutions play in shaping individuals seems clear. Commons talks of the individual as an "Institutionalized Mind" and argues:

Individuals begin as babies. They learn the custom of language, of cooperation with other individuals, of working towards common ends, of negotiations to eliminate conflicts of interest, of subordination to the working rules of the many concerns of which they are members. They meet each other, not as physiological bodies moved by glands, nor as "globules of desire" moved by pain and pleasure, similar to the forces of physical and animal nature, but as prepared more or less by habit, induced by the pressure of custom, to engage in those highly artificial transactions created by the collective human will. ... Instead of isolated individuals in a state of nature they are always participants in transactions, members of a concern in which they come and go, citizens of an institution that lived before them and will live after them (pp. 73–74).

Commons' reference here to the "collective human will" might suggest more than an emphasis on the institutional and the adoption of that extreme holism that runs in terms of autonomous social entities. This would be a mistaken interpretation. Commons repeatedly refers to the "collective will," but all he means by this is the overall outcome of individual and collective, governmental and judicial, decision-making processes. The collective will is simply what emerges from the decisions of individuals. This brings up the role of the individual in Commons' work. The individual may be an "Institutionalized Mind," but he is also an actor with his own intellect and volition. Choice may often be made on the basis of custom and habit, but choice may also be "rational or scientific" and "sagacious" (p. 306). Such choices occur most often when some novel situation or new problem is met with. Indeed, habit is presented by Commons as something that frees the mind for dealing with "what is unexpected." Habit looks after the routine, while "the intellectual activity is concerning itself with the limiting factors or strategic transactions" (p. 698).

There is a clear link between the notion of a "strategic transaction" and Commons' discussion of institutional change. An existing rule or practice, or, for that matter, the lack of an established rule or practice, may become a key constraint, a limiting factor, to use Commons' terminology. This leads individuals or organized groups to attempt to establish some new rule or practice, a strategic transaction. This effort may take place on a variety of levels. The rule or practice in question may apply just to some particular group or organization. Such new practices or rules may spread to become common practices and social customs. Alternatively, the courts may be involved in litigation over some existing rule or common practice or in deciding a conflict over alternative rules or practices. Finally, the attempt to change social rules may involve political efforts, or attempts to exercise pressure on political parties, in order to affect legislation. Commons' analysis, thus, is quite consistent with the individualistic view that institutions emerge and change only through the actions of individual decision makers. Individuals, not autonomous social forces, determine the nature and evolution of institutions.

Commons' methodology, then, represents neither an extreme, reductive individualism, nor an extreme holism. In Commons' work it is quite clear that institutions deeply affect individuals, particularly in the form of their "habitual assumptions." Commons' notion of the institutionalized mind is *not*, however, inconsistent with an analysis of the evolution of institutions that runs in terms of the actions of individual decision makers. This combination of ideas has more recently been christened "institutional individualism" (Agassi 1975). It gives ultimacy neither to the social whole nor to the individual, but it instead conceptualizes institutions and individuals as involved in a continual process of mutual interaction.

Shortcomings of Existing Economics

For Commons, virtually all other writers in the history of economics (with the possible exceptions of MacLeod and Veblen) had failed to take adequate account of the institutional element. He offered a number of reasons for this widespread blindness to institutional questions, the most important of which were a tendency to focus on a natural abundance and harmony instead of scarcity and conflict and the resulting need to *create* a degree of harmony through institutional constraints; a tendency to substitute psychological propensities for custom and institutions; and, finally, a deep and broad confusion of concepts relating to material goods with concepts relating to ownership and property *rights*.

Commons' discussion of Locke, Quesnay, and Smith deals at some length with the first theme. Of most interest is his analysis of Smith. In Commons' view Smith's world was one of abundance, and in such a world the exercise of self-interest cannot injure others: "If there is abundance of nature's resources, no person can injure any other person by taking from him all he can get, if he does this by exchanging his own labour for that of the other" (p. 161). Each party has an "abundance of alternatives" and can freely choose without coercion. Also, any choice made will not negatively affect the alternatives available to others (p. 161). Self-interest here is constrained not by institutions but by a "sense of propriety," a "divine instinct of mutuality of interests" (pp. 161–62). This focus on abundance and divine beneficence diverted Smith's attention from the fact of mutuality as a "historic product of collective action in actually creating mutuality of interests out of conflict of interests." Had he concentrated on this actual historic process Smith would have seen not the "invisible hand" but the "visible hand of the common-law courts, taking over the customs of the time and place, in so far as deemed good, and enforcing these good customs on refractory individuals" (p. 162).

On the other hand, "the first of the economists to make conflict of interests universal in economics was David Hume in his theory of *scarcity*" (p. 6). In this Hume was followed by Malthus, and Malthus, in turn, provided the foundations for the evolutionary thinking of Darwin and Wallace (p. 246). The notion of scarcity leads to the idea of the prevalence of conflict and the need for institutional constraints. The acquisition of scarce things must be regulated by "the collective action which creates the rights and duties of property and liberty without which there would be anarchy" (p. 6).

Related to the above issue is the second problem mentioned by Commons, the tendency to substitute psychology for institutions. This can be seen in a wide variety of ways. In Locke and Smith individuals are divinely endowed with given psychological propensities that provide a substitute for an institutional analysis. Locke's state of nature, for example, is populated by "intellectual beings like himself." Locke "projected backward the practices, to which he was accustomed and which he wished to see perpetuated, into an eternal reason binding upon men henceforth without change" (p. 50). In Smith, the instinct of sympathy, truck and barter, and the sense of propriety "take the place of all collective action in economic affairs" (p. 166).

An even more complete substitution of psychology for institutions is found in Bentham. Bentham's individuals are noninstitutionalized, responding only to pleasure and pain. His concept of the community is a mere aggregation of individual atoms, not a concept of "membership, citizenship, or participation" or of "both individual and concerted action, governing and being governed" (p. 243). In addition, Bentham does not merely ignore the common law processes of resolving disputes but wishes to replace them with legislative acts based on the greatest good for the greatest number. Bentham's ethics are based on individual desires, and this completes the "dualism of individual and society" (p. 225).

In terms of the work of the "psychological economists from Jevons to Fetter" (p. 439), Commons argues that their psychology deals only with man's relationship to materials. The psychology of diminishing marginal utility, time preference, etc., may well be universal but it neglects and deflects attention from institutional issues of *ownership*. Its starting point is individual psychology where there are no social conflicts of interest. What is of more concern to institutional economics is the "social psychology of negotiations and transactions, arising out of conflicts," which requires "enforceable rights and duties" (p. 440).

This raises the last issue mentioned above, the conflation of materials with ownership that Commons found so pervasive in the history of economic thought. In classical and "hedonic" economics, property has a "corporeal" meaning only, and in this way property is made "equivalent to the material thing owned" (p. 5). The corporeal meaning given to property and the lack of any clear distinction between materials and ownership of materials gave rise, in Commons' view, to such numerous confusions as those between wealth and assets, output and income, efficiency and scarcity, use values and scarcity values. In each case there is a confusion of material output, of the augmentation of material wealth by greater output or efficiency, with income concepts related to ownership and the ability to withhold. Thus: "Output is a service rendered to other people regardless of the price; income is the price received by the owner, based on his right to withhold service from others in the proprietary process of bargaining or waiting until the others will pay a satisfactory price. *Income* is the proprietary acquisition of assets; *output* is the engineering augmentations of wealth" (p. 257).

To overcome these confusions, what is required is not the development of new concepts so much as a clear separation of the various double meanings of the older concepts (p. 424). The proprietary meaning associated with ownership and institutions must be distinguished from that of material goods. Such a distinction allows for the explicit recognition of the institution of property and its gradual evolution from a purely corporeal concept to incorporeal property (debts) and, most importantly, to intangible property (future profit). This, in turn, provides the basis for the development of a truly institutional economics:

> Not until it became vaguely felt by the heterodox economists in the middle of the Nineteenth Century — such as Marx, Proudhon, Carey, Bastiat, MacLeod — that ownership and materials were not the same thing, were the beginnings laid for institutional economics. These economists were vague in that they had the older idea of "corporeal" property (even yet retained by economists), which identifies ownership with the materials owned, or distinguishes only "corporeal property" from the "incorporeal property" which is contract or debt. Hence, it was not until the new idea of "intangible property" arose out of the customs and actual terminology of business magnates in the last quarter of the Nineteenth Century that it was possible for Veblen and the Supreme Court to make the new distinctions which clearly separate from each other not only the ownership of materials and the ownership of debts, but also the ownership of expected opportunities to make a profit

by withholding supply until the price is persuasively or coercively agreed upon. This ownership of expected opportunities is "intangible property" (p. 5).

The expansion of property from corporeal to incorporeal and intangible property also makes the dimension of time, or futurity, as Commons calls it, more explicit. Incorporeal property involves the right to a future payment. Intangible property involves the right to the future income obtained from a particular source or opportunity. Even an exchange involving corporeal property does not necessarily involve the immediate delivery of the physical objects involved. Property of all types involves the rights to the *future* ownership of physical objects.

Transactions and Working Rules

Commons' basic unit of analysis is the transaction. This notion is used by Commons to overcome the various problems outlined above. The transaction is a relationship *between* individuals, and what is transacted is the *right* to property of various kinds. The transaction highlights the conflicts of interest between the various transactors and the potential roles of negotiation, persuasion, coercion, and duress. The concept of a transaction directs attention to the institutional context of defined property rights and defined abilities to exercise legal and economic power. The institutional context within which transactions take place consists of what Commons calls the "working rules," including custom and law, that define what each party to the transaction can, cannot, must or must not, and may do. Transactions "are the alienation and acquisition, between individuals, of the *rights* of future ownership of physical things, as determined by the collective working rules of society" (p. 58).

As is well known, Commons distinguishes between rationing, managerial, and bargaining transactions. A bargaining transaction is between legal equals, while managerial and rationing transactions are between a legal superior and a legal inferior. In managerial transactions the superior is "an individual or a hierarchy of individuals, giving orders which the inferiors must obey." In the rationing transaction the superior is "a collective superior or its official spokesman," for example, a legislature, a court, an arbitration tribunal, or a corporation's board of directors (p. 59). Bargaining transactions *"transfer ownership* of wealth by voluntary agreement between legal equals," managerial transactions *"create wealth* by commands of legal superiors," rationing transactions "apportion the burdens and benefits of wealth creation by the *dictation* of legal superiors" (p. 68).

Examples of rationing transactions given by Commons include many of the activities of legislatures and courts: a legislature deciding on taxes or tariffs, or a judicial decision of an economic dispute. Also included are the decisions of a cartel concerning the output of its members (p. 68). Managerial transactions involve the relationship between "foreman and worker, sheriff and citizen, manager and managed, master and servant, owner and slave" (p. 64). It is within the sphere of managerial transactions that the problems of agency arise (p. 65). Both rationing and managerial transactions involve the use of legal authority, but such authority is not unconstrained by working rules. The rationing decisions of legislatures and courts are constrained by constitutional rules, precedent, and custom. Managerial transactions are constrained by "the law of command and obedience that has been created by the common-law method of making new law by deciding disputes that arise out of managerial transactions" (p. 66).

In contrast, bargaining transactions involve legal equality, but legal equality is not incompatible with the differential ability to exercise economic power. For Commons, economic power, or the lack of it, was determined by two main factors: the number of alternative opportunities available to the parties to the bargain and their respective abilities to withhold (bargaining power). The best available alternatives define what Commons calls the "limits of coercion" (p. 331), and the terms of the transaction will settle somewhere between these limits, exactly where depending on the bargaining power each party can bring to bear. Again, the working rules of society, particularly in the form of common law, affect the exercise of economic power, limiting it to levels considered reasonable by the courts. In this connection Commons discusses such issues as the evolution of common law on discrimination, unfair competition, inequality of bargaining power, and due process (pp. 62–63, see also pp. 331–48).

As one final point, it should be noted that working rules represent exactly that "collective action in control of individual action" that Commons defined as his subject. Working rules in the form of law and custom determine the nature of the transactions undertaken and the terms on which they will be undertaken. A change in working rules may shift a transaction from a rationing to a bargaining type or vice versa. It may allow greater or less managerial discretion. It may expand or restrict the ability to exercise economic power. Working rules, then, are more than just constraints. By controlling individual action, working rules may "expand" the "will of the individual" by enabling an individual to achieve goals that require the organization and direction of the actions of others. Similarly, working rules may "liberate" individuals from coercion or duress exercised by others.

Organizations and Going Concerns

Thus far, attention has been concentrated on the notion of working rules as general rules of conduct enforced by custom or by the sanctions imposed by the state. These rules can be seen as affecting the transactions undertaken by individuals and organizations. However, Commons was concerned to move beyond an analysis of individual actors, or organizations treated as individual actors, operating within collective controls in the form of general rules of conduct. In particular, he wanted to provide an analysis of "collective action" in a somewhat different sense, in the sense of the growth of collective organizations such as corporations, unions, political parties, and associations of various kinds. Such organized forms of collective action Commons called "going concerns," a going concern being a "joint expectation of beneficial bargaining, managerial, and rationing transactions, kept together by 'working rules' and by control of the changeable strategic or 'limiting' factors which are expected to control the others" (p. 58).

In this way the concept of working rules is applied by Commons to the internal rules and practices of particular organizations as well as to those more general rules of conduct discussed above. As Vanberg (1988) points out, there is much ambiguity in Commons' use of such terms as working rules and going concerns, with the result that the distinctions to be made between (i) the society and the general rules of social conduct, (ii) the state and the constitutional rules of the state, and (iii) private collective organizations and the internal rules and regulations of such organizations, are blurred. The lack of clear distinctions does create significant problems in Commons' work. On the other hand, and as will be seen below, Commons' system involves a considerable degree of interplay between these various levels of going concerns and working rules.

To return to the issue of particular organizations, there are two key points in Commons' argument. The first point is that "the working rules which determine for individuals" the limits of their "correlative and reciprocal economic relationships may be laid down and enforced by a corporation, or a cartel, or a holding company, or a cooperative association, or a trade union, or an employers' association, or a trade association, or a joint trade agreement of two associations, or a stock exchange or board of trade, or a political party" and that "these economic collective acts of private concerns are at times more powerful than the collective action of the political concern, the State" (p. 70). Individuals, then, are constrained not just by general social rules of conduct but also by the rules of those particular organizations of which they are members.

The second point of significance is that Commons argues that an organization should not be treated as if it were an individual but as a *coalition*, which depends for its continued existence on the continued "willingness of participants to make their respective contributions to the collective effort" (Vanberg 1988, p. 32). Organizations are created by individuals or groups to pursue particular objectives and operate in the expectation of joint benefit. Organizations come and go, rise and fall in the face of changing legal, technical, and social conditions, but while they exist their internal rules and procedures are shaped by the conflicts and disputes that arise within the organization. In the face of a dispute or conflict the "officers of an organized concern" must make a decision. Such decisions "by becoming precedents, become the working rules, for the time being, of the particular organized concern" (pp. 72–73). The evolution of an organization's own internal rules and practices, then, are deeply affected by the nature of the conflicts between the various groups that go to make up the coalition. This is a point that is insufficiently appreciated even in modern institutional economics.

Legislatures and Courts

The various levels of working rules outlined above represent different aspects of collective action in control of individual action. But Commons also saw the set of working rules evolving over time in what he called a process of "artificial selection." What is perhaps most interesting about Commons' discussion of institutional change is the interplay that exists between the practices of individuals and particular organizations, more general customary rules, and the common and statute law.

In Commons' view the state is a concern that has taken over the power to use physical sanctions. The state "consists in the enforcement, by physical sanctions, of what private parties might otherwise endeavour to enforce by private violence" (p. 751). Instead of private violence, a "form of concerted action, under the name Political Parties, has evolved" with the purpose of "selecting and getting control of the hierarchy of legislative, executive, and judicial personalities whose concerted action determines the legal rights, duties, liberties, and exposures involved in all economic transactions" (p. 751). Political parties "have become the economic concerns through which the sanctions of physical force are directed towards economic gain or loss" (p. 752). Other concerns also influence the political process through organized lobbying or pressure groups. Large organized groups can "employ lobbyists and politicians to control the legislatures and line up the voters" (pp. 889–90). Legislatures operate on the basis of vote-trading or "log-rolling." However, in *Institutional Economics* Commons does not "criminate" the process of log-rolling as he did in his earlier work. Rather, he presents the outcome of log-rolling "as nearly a reasonable reconciliation of all conflicting interests as representative democracy has been able to reach in parliamentary countries" (p. 755). Log-rolling "may be said to be the democratic process of agreeing upon the rationing of economic burdens and benefits" (p. 756). If the log-rolling process has problems they lie in the difficulties of attaining agreement and in the fact that not all interest groups are properly represented. Commons retains his argument in favour of proportional representation as the best method of ensuring representation of all major economic interest groups, but he is also uncomfortably aware that it can lead to many parties and deadlocked legislatures (pp. 898–900). Commons gives a hint of the argument he later develops in more detail in his statement that "in a sense the lobby is more representative than the legislature" (p. 898).

Commons' ideas on the operation of legislatures may be partly responsible for the notion that he conceptualizes working rules and changes in those rules as the intended outcome of political processes of decision making. However, Commons himself places much greater emphasis on the customs and common practices of individuals and concerns and the decisions of the common law courts in deciding disputes. What is noticeable here is that individuals and concerns will tend to develop new practices or rules over time in pursuit of their own objectives or out of the resolution of internal conflicts. Whenever an existing rule or practice becomes a limiting factor some effort will be made to develop a new rule or practice. New practices "arise out of existing customs, precedents, and statutes" (p. 707). Such practices may spread to become social customs. Customs arise out of "similarity of interests and similarity of transactions engaged in" (p. 699). This, of course, is quite consistent with the idea that customs arise spontaneously in an "invisible hand" fashion, but Commons was not willing to limit his analysis to such invisible hand processes. He was aware that many, if not most, social situations create conflicts over the rules to be followed. In Commons' work there is no presumption that the invisible hand will result in harmony over the rules to be followed, instead it is the court system that must decide disputes and *create* order, or a "workable mutuality," out of conflict.

When a dispute over some rule, practice, or custom reaches the court, the court will decide on the existing practices or customs. The court bases its decision on its own criteria of precedent, public purpose, and reasonableness, and approves what it considers to be "good" practices and eliminates what it considers to be "bad" practices. In this fashion a custom may be given legal sanction, or the practice of some particular concern may be generalized into a social rule: "A local practice becomes common law for the nation" (p. 712). This process of the courts taking over good practices and eliminating bad practices is one that Commons is constantly referring to. Commons talks of the development of labor law out of the conflicts brought about by union activity. For example, the 1842 decision holding that "a combination of workmen designed to benefit themselves...was not an unlawful conspiracy" (p. 770). Similarly, with the development and refinement of the concept of intangible property out of business practice, Commons traces the development of the court's distinction between a "reasonable" power to withhold (goodwill) from the unreasonable exercise of that power (privilege). Commons criticises Veblen's exploitation view of business as due to his "failure to trace out the evolution of business customs under the decisions of the courts" (p. 673). It is through this process of common-law decision making that collective action "takes over... the customs of business or labor, and enforces or restrains individual action, wherever it seems to the Court favourable or unfavourable to the public interest and private rights" (p. 5).

In *Institutional Economics* Commons expresses no concerns about the court system usurping the functions of the legislature, and it is quite clear that he regards the common law system of making law by deciding disputes as one of great strength and flexibility. Problems can arise if the "habitual assumptions" of judges are obsolete, and the judicial system is limited by only being able to decide disputes after the event, but Commons suggests that the common law method can be successfully extended to quasi-judicial bodies dealing with labor or commercial arbitration, and that judicial decision making can be supplemented by the experimental rule making of commissions.

In this fashion the legislature and the courts are engaged in the determination of the set of working rules that bear on the transactions undertaken by individuals and concerns. The courts are of particular significance as even the statute law has to be interpreted by the court: "The statute...enacted by Congress does not become a law until it is interpreted by the Court in a particular dispute" (p. 712). The overall process is one of the "evolutionary collective determination of what is reasonable in view of all the changing political, moral, and economic circumstances and the personalities that arise therefrom to the Supreme bench" (pp. 683–84). With the continuation and improvement of these political and judicial processes Commons saw a movement toward the resolution of the conflicts of labor and capital and the attainment of a "Reasonable Capitalism" (p. 891).

CONCLUSION

The foregoing makes it abundantly clear that throughout his career Commons was deeply concerned with the same broad set of theoretical and practical problems. For Commons, theory and practice should go hand in hand. His concern with how to alter economic theory so as to take proper account of the institutional factor and his practical concern with how to bring about a reasonable reconciliation of the conflicting interests of business and labor are simply different aspects of the same problem. *Institutional Economics* is a book that concentrates somewhat on the theoretical issues, but Commons' practical interests are never out of sight for long. That many of the particular practical issues discussed by Commons seem of less pressing importance today is in part the result of his many institutional reform efforts. In contrast, his theoretical concerns still remain.

There are many themes and ideas in *Institutional Economics* that have significance for any modern economist interested in institutional issues. Commons' methodology, his emphasis on transactions, his conceptualization of transactions as transfers of property *rights*, his concern with organizations as collective economic actors, his analysis of legislative decision making as log-rolling, the great attention he paid to the common law and the common law *method* of deciding disputes, and his overall emphasis on conflict of interest and the need for organized selection and enforcement of rules are all issues of considerable modern importance. *Institutional Economics* is a book that was intended to persuade economists to give these institutional issues greater attention. At the time of its original publication its impact on economics was limited, at least in part because of its style and organization, but with the benefit of hindsight many of Commons' arguments and concerns have become much more clear. His vision of an economics that gives the institutional element its proper place is one that has never lost its validity and one that has recently regained much of its former strength and vitality. Without doubt Commons ranks as "the most fascinating and, in the long run, the most obviously seminal of the great triumvirate of first generation American institutionalists" (Coats 1983, p. 149).

NOTES

[1] Published and forthcoming articles include Atkinson (1983; 1987), Biddle (1988A; 1988B), Carter (1985), Chasse (1986), Coats (1983), Endres (1985), Kanel (1985), McClintock (1987), Parsons (1985; 1986), M. Perlman (1986), Ramstad (1986; 1987; 1988), Rutherford (1983), Schweikhardt (1988), and Vanberg (1988). In addition, papers by Atkinson, Biddle, Richard Gonce, Ramstad, Rutherford, and Rick Tilman are due to be given at various conference sessions during 1989.

[2] It is not the intent here to give a full listing of the secondary literature on Commons. Prior to 1940 secondary work consisted primarily of commentaries by other institutionalists such as Mitchell (1924; 1935) and Copeland (1936). In the forties the main contributions came from Gruchy (1940; 1947) and Parsons (1942); in the fifties from Dorfman (1959), Harris (1952), and Hamilton (1953); and in the sixties from Harter (1962), Kennedy (1962), and Chamberlain (1963). The literature expanded substantially between 1970 and the early 1980s with major articles from Barbash (1976), Dugger (1979; 1980), Goldberg (1976), Gonce (1971; 1976), Isserman (1976), Liebhafsky (1976), Ostrom (1976), Randall (1978), and Zingler (1974). Of these articles, five were part of a symposium on "Commons and Clark on Law and Economics" in the December 1976 issue of the *Journal of Economic Issues*.

BIBLIOGRAPHY

Agassi, Joseph. 1975. Institutional Individualism. *British Journal of Sociology* 26 (June): 144–55.

Atkinson, Glen J. 1983. Political Economy: Public Choice or Collective Action. *Journal of Economic Issues* 17 (December): 1057–65.

———. 1987. Instrumentalism and Economic Policy: The Quest for Reasonable Value. *Journal of Economic Issues* 21 (March): 189–202.

Barbash, Jack. 1976. The Legal Foundations of Capitalism and the Labour Problem. *Journal of Economic Issues* 10 (December): 799–810.

Biddle, Jeff. 1988A. Purpose and Evolution in Commons's Institutionalism. Mimeo. Forthcoming in *History of Political Economy*.

———. 1988B. The Ideas of the Past as Tools for the Present: The Instrumental Presentism of John R. Commons. Mimeo. Forthcoming in JoAnne Brown and David van Keuren, eds., *The Estate of Social Knowledge*. Baltimore: Johns Hopkins University Press.

Bye, Raymond T. 1935. Review of *Institutional Economics* by John R. Commons. *Annals of the American Academy of Political and Social Science* 178 (March): 200–202.

Carter, Michael R. 1985. A Wisconsin Institutionalist Perspective on the Microeconomic Theory of Institutions: The Insufficiency of Pareto Efficiency. *Journal of Economic Issues* 19 (September): 797–813.

Chamberlain, Neil W. 1963. The Institutional Economics of John R. Commons. In *Institutional Economics: Veblen, Commons and Mitchell Reconsidered*. Berkeley: University of California Press, pp. 63–94.

Chasse, John Dennis. 1986. John R. Commons and the Democratic State. *Journal of Economic Issues* 20 (September): 759–84.

Coats, A. W. 1983. John R. Commons as a Historian of Economics: The Quest for the Antecedents of Collective Action. *Research in the History of Economic Thought and Methodology* 1: 147–61.

Commons, John R. [1893]. *The Distribution of Wealth*. New York: Augustus M. Kelley, 1963.

———. 1896. *Proportional Representation*. Boston and New York: Thomas Crowell.

———. [1899–1900]. *A Sociological View of Sovereignty*. New York: Augustus M. Kelley, 1967.

———. [1924]. *The Legal Foundations of Capitalism*. Madison: University of Wisconsin, 1968.

———. [1934A]. *Institutional Economics: Its Place in Political Economy*. Madison: University of Wisconsin, 1959.

———. [1934B]. *Myself*. Madison: University of Wisconsin, 1963.

———. 1950. *The Economics of Collective Action*. New York: Macmillan.

Copeland, Morris A. 1936. Commons's Institutionalism in Relation to Problems of Social Evolution and Economic Planning. *Quarterly Journal of Economics* 50 (February): 333–46.

Dorfman, Joseph. 1959. *The Economic Mind in American Civilization*, Vol. 4. New York: Viking.

———. 1963. The Foundations of Commons' Economics. Introduction to J. R. Commons, *The Distribution of Wealth*, New York: Augustus Kelley, pp. i–xv.

Dugger, William M. 1979. The Reform Method of John R. Commons. *Journal of Economic Issues* 13 (June): 369–81.

———. 1980. Property Rights, Law and John R. Commons. *Review of Social Economy* 38 (April): 41–54.

Endres, A. M. 1985. Veblen and Commons on Goodwill: A Case of Theoretical Divergence. *History of Political Economy* 17 (Winter): 637–49.

Goldberg, Victor P. 1976. Commons, Clark and the Emerging Post-Coasian Law and Economics. *Journal of Economic Issues* 10 (December): 877–93.

Gonce, Richard O. 1971. John R. Commons's Legal Economic Theory. *Journal of Economic Issues* 5 (September): 80–95.

———. 1976. The New Property Rights Approach and Commons's Legal Foundations of Capitalism. *Journal of Economic Issues* 10 (December): 765–97.

Gruchy, Allan G. 1940. John R. Commons' Concept of Twentieth-Century Economics. *Journal of Political Economy* 48 (December): 823–49.

———. 1947. *Modern Economic Thought: The American Contribution.* New York: Prentice-Hall.

Hamilton, David. 1953. Veblen and Commons: A Case of Theoretical Convergence. *Southwestern Social Science Quarterly* 34 (September): 43–50.

Harris, Abram. 1952. John R. Commons and the Welfare State. *Southern Economic Journal* 19 (October): 222–33.

Harter, Lafayette G. 1962. *John R. Commons: His Assault on Laissez-Faire.* Corvallis: Oregon State University.

Isserman, Maurice C. 1976. God Bless Our American Institutions: The Labour History of John R. Commons. *Labour History* 17 (Summer): 312–28.

Kanel, Don. 1985. Institutional Economics: Perspectives on Economy and Society. *Journal of Economic Issues* 19 (September): 815–28.

Kennedy, W. F. 1962. John R. Commons, Conservative Reformer. *Western Economic Journal* 1 (Fall): 29–42.

Knight, Frank H. 1935. Review of *Institutional Economics* by John R. Commons. *Columbia Law Review* 35 (May): 803–5.

Langlois, Richard N. 1986. The New Institutional Economics: An Introductory Essay. In Richard N. Langlois, ed., *Economic as a Process: Essays in the New Institutional Economics.* Cambridge: Cambridge University Press, pp. 1–25.

Liebhafsky, H. H. 1976. Commons and Clark on Law and Economics. *Journal of Economic Issues* 10 (December): 751–64.

McClintock, Brent. 1987. Institutional Transaction Analysis, *Journal of Economic Issues* 21 (June): 673–81.

Mitchell, Wesley C. 1924. Commons on the Legal Foundations of Capitalism. *American Economic Review* 14 (June): 240–53.

———. 1935. Commons on Institutional Economics. *American Economic Review* 25 (December): 635–52.

Ostrom, Vincent. 1976. John R. Commons's Foundations for Policy Analysis. *Journal of Economic Issues* 10 (December): 839–57.

Parsons, Kenneth H. 1942. John R. Commons' Point of View. Reprinted in John R. Commons, *The Economics of Collective Action.* New York: Macmillan, 1950, pp. 341–75.

———. 1950. Introduction. In J. R. Commons, *The Economics of Collective Action*. New York: Macmillan, pp. 9–18.

———. 1985. John R. Commons: His Relevance to Contemporary Economics. *Journal of Economic Issues* 19 (September): 755–78.

———. 1986. The Relevance of the Ideas of John R. Commons for the Formulation of Agricultural Development Projects: Remarks upon Receipt of the Veblen–Commons Award. *Journal of Economic Issues* 20 (June): 281–95.

Perlman, Mark. 1986. Subjectivism and American Institutionalism. In Israel M. Kirzner, ed., *Subjectivism, Intelligibility and Economic Understanding*. New York: New York University Press, pp. 268–80.

Perlman, Selig. 1945. John Rogers Commons, 1862–1945. Reprinted in J. R. Commons, *The Economics of Collective Action*. New York: Macmillan, 1950, pp. 1–7.

Ramstad, Yngve. 1986. A Pragmatist's Quest for Holistic Knowledge: The Scientific Methodology of John R. Commons. *Journal of Economic Issues* 20 (December): 1067–1105.

———. 1987. Institutional Existentialism: More on Why John R. Commons Has So Few Followers. *Journal of Economic Issues* 21 (June): 661–71.

———. 1988. The Institutionalism of John R. Commons: Theoretical Foundations of a Volitional Economics. Mimeo. Forthcoming in *Research in the History of Economics Thought and Methodology*.

Randall, Alan. 1978. Property Institutions and Economic Behaviour. *Journal of Economic Issues* 12 (March): 1–21.

Rutherford, Malcolm. 1983. J. R. Commons's Institutional Economics. *Journal of Economic Issues* 17 (September): 721–44.

Schotter, Andrew. 1981. *The Economic Theory of Social Institutions*. Cambridge: Cambridge University Press.

Schweikhardt, David B. 1988. The Role of Values in Economic Theory and Policy: A Comparison of Frank Knight and John R. Commons. *Journal of Economic Issues* 22 (June): 407–14.

Seckler, David. 1966. The Naivete of John R. Commons. *Western Economic Journal* 4 (Summer): 261–65.

———. 1975. *Thorstein Veblen and the Institutionalists*. Boulder: Colorado Associated University Press.

Vanberg, Viktor. 1988. Carl Menger's Evolutionary and John R. Commons' Collective Action Approach to Institutions: A Comparison. Mimeo. Forthcoming in *Review of Political Economy*.

Zingler, Ervin K. 1974. Veblen vs. Commons: A Comparative Evaluation. *Kyklos* 27 (No. 2): 322–44.

PREFACE

This book is modeled upon textbooks in the Natural Sciences. Each idea here incorporated is traced back to its originator, and then the successive modifications of that idea are developed and the earlier double or treble meanings of the idea are separated, until each, as a single meaning, is combined with the others in what I conceive to be the Science of Political Economy as it is developing since the last Great War. The originators of new ideas and theories have appeared before and after revolutionary wars, during what I call the War Cycle. Since I base my analysis on the Anglo-American common law, I begin with the English Revolution of 1689; then follows the World War of the French Revolution, 1789; then the American Revolution of 1861, an outcome of the suppressed European revolution of 1848; then the war of a dozen revolutions beginning 1914.

As I have explained elsewhere in my autobiography, I have been a part of two of these revolutionary cycles: the American, which abolished slavery, and the world revolutions of the past twenty years. My first book, *The Distribution of Wealth* (1893), was dominated by the theories prevailing during the last quarter of the Nineteenth Century; my *Legal Foundations of Capitalism* (1924) and this *Institutional Economics* (1934) are dominated by the theories emerging in the revolutionary cycle of which we now are a part.

Among the many students and assistants from whom I have derived much during the past twenty-five years, Mrs. Anna Campbell Davis has assisted me on legal and economic cases during seven years, and Mr. Reuben Sparkman on economic cases during four years. My colleagues in the Department of Economics have given me invaluable help, and other economists, including former and present students, to whom I have submitted manuscripts in my writing and rewriting, have picked out flaws and helped me over difficulties.

JOHN R. COMMONS

MADISON, WISCONSIN
August, 1934

xxxiii

CHAPTER X

REASONABLE VALUE

I. Veblen [1]

1. *From Corporeal to Intangible Property*

Two diverse theories of the modern intangible property have been developed since the year 1890. The one is the exploitation theory of Veblen, the other is the reasonable value theory of the courts. Each is founded on the new idea of property as the present value of future profitable transactions; but Veblen took as the source of his materials the testimony of industrial and financial magnates before the United States Industrial Commission of 1901, [2] and published it as his *Theory of Business Enterprise* in 1904. The judicial idea was developed slowly and can be found only in the decisions of the Supreme Court since 1890.

From the United States Industrial Commission's hearings and findings come such illustrations as follow: Andrew Carnegie had the strategic position in the steel industry in that his costs of production were the lowest and he owned iron and coal mines and the lake barges and railways needed to bring his materials to his furnaces and mills in Pittsburgh. He had not carried his product into the tinplate end of the industry; but he announced his intention of building such a plant with the latest improvements on the shores of Lake Erie. It became plain to all who knew Carnegie's methods of destructive competition that this new plant would drive them out of the market. J. Pierpont Morgan and Company and their lawyers were then called upon to construct a huge holding company which should take over all of the plants necessary to form an integrated whole of all corporations in all branches of the industry. It was necessary for this combination to buy all of Carnegie's interests, whose value as corporeal property was estimated on the basis of reconstruction cost at about 75 million dollars. But, owing to Carnegie's threatening position in the markets, he was

[1] Cf. Teggart, R. V., *Thorstein Veblen, a Chapter in American Economic Thought* (1932).
[2] *Report of the United States Industrial Commission*, I (1900), XII and XIV (1901), XIX (1902). Veblen, Thorstein, *Theory of Business Enterprise* (1904, 1927).

able to command 300 million dollars in gold bonds. This difference of 225 million dollars could not be ascribed, on the traditional theory of economics, as the value of the corporeal property. Nor was it incorporeal property since it was not a debt owed to Carnegie. The only other name that could be given to it was "intangible property," the name given by the financial magnates themselves. Veblen rightly interpreted this intangible property as merely an exploitation or "hold-up" value, because it arose solely from the need of all competitors to remove Carnegie from the price-cutting competition which it was known he would initiate.

As for all the other companies taken over by the holding company, they were willing to exchange their stocks for stocks in the holding company. The valuations given to them in terms of holding company stocks were likewise much in excess of the corporeal value of their property. So that when the United States Steel Company was finally organized it had a total capitalization of two billion dollars, including 300 million dollars debt owing to Carnegie and one billion seven hundred million dollars of common and preferred stock, whereas the value of the corporeal property at cost of reproduction was probably less than one billion dollars. This intangible valuation was eventually built up out of profits into a corporeal plant equal in value to the original intangible value. The excess original valuation of one billion dollars above the corporeal property value was given the name "intangible property," or "intangible value," because it was asserted that the increased prospective earning power of the holding company would justify that amount of valuation, which eventually proved true.

Veblen, in 1904, could properly say that this intangible value based on expected earning power was literally only a "pecuniary" valuation, and not the "industrial" valuation of the traditional economics which always held that value tended towards the cost of reproduction of the plant and commodities. The Steel Corporation was evidently not a monopoly. It should therefore come under the economists' competitive standard of cost of production, for the holding company purchased only the number of companies needed to round out an integrated industry. It was purely the exercise of the rights of private property, without monopolization, and this was so decided by the United States Supreme Court in 1920.

Hence Veblen distinguished "capital" as the value of the corporeal property; but he distinguished intangible value, or intangible capital, as the purely pecuniary valuations by business men, according to their strategic power of holding up the community and "getting something for nothing." In this he was correct.

Thus Veblen was the first who builded upon the modern concept of intangible property, which he derived directly from the customs of business men who used the term. Veblen practically disregarded the corporeal property of primitive society and of the classical, Marxian, and hedonic economists, as well as MacLeod's incorporeal property of debt. He rested solely on the new concept of intangible property as the present value of the future bargaining power of capitalists.

But he did not investigate the decisions of the Supreme Court. The Supreme Court of the United States, when cases arose, rested its decisions on this same new phenomenon of intangible property, not, however, on Veblen's exploitation, but on its own historic concept of reasonable value. In some cases this doctrine sustained the contentions of the capitalists, as in the United States Steel Dissolution Suit (1920). In other cases it greatly reduced the values contended for by the capitalists. In still other cases it gave a much higher value to the properties than the capitalists contended against. The court's valuation of intangible property, however bitterly fought on both sides, plaintiff and defendant—always contained a public purpose—while Veblen strongly contended that a science of economics, like other sciences, does not properly permit the introduction of purpose.

The beginning of the court's recognition of the new concept of intangible value was in the year 1899,[3] when the court declared that the reduction of railway rates by the Minnesota Railway Commission was a "taking of property," although it was taking, not the corporeal property, but the intangible property of power to fix prices. The court also declared that the taking of property was a judicial question, and not a legislative question, under the Fourteenth Amendment to the Federal Constitution which prohibited a state from taking property without due process of law. In the preceding similar case of Munn v. Illinois (1876), when the court's meaning of property was corporeal property, the court had held that the reduction of rates by a state legislature was not a *taking* of property, but was only a regulation of the *use* of property.[4] But in 1890 the lawyers of the railway company petitioned the court to reverse itself and to hold that taking the "value" of the property by reducing freight rates was also a "taking" of property under the constitution. They were correct in that what was now taken was not the corporeal property of the company but was the intangible

[3] Chicago, Milwaukee & St. Paul Railway Co. v. Minnesota, 134 U. S. 418 (1890) Commons, John R., *Legal Foundations of Capitalism* (1924), 15.
[4] Munn v. Illinois, 94 U. S. 113, l. c. 139 (1876). Commons, *Legal Foundations of Capitalism*, 15.

property of the right to charge such prices as the corporation wished and could. In other words, the lawyers were standing for Veblen's meaning of intangible property. The court accepted their contention to the extent that the taking of the newly defined intangible property was a judicial question to be decided by the Supreme Court and not by the state of Minnesota, and therefore the state rates were invalid.

In this way it was in the year 1890 that the first step was taken toward changing the meaning of property from corporeal property to intangible property. With this change of meaning the Supreme Court usurped what had previously been considered the right of the states, acknowledged in the Munn case, to regulate prices charged by public utilities.

The next significant step in recognizing intangible property as a value entirely different from the economists' meaning of corporeal property was in the case of Adams Express Company v. Ohio.[5] This was a taxation case, and the Supreme Court, against the protest of the corporation, raised the value of the property in question, for purposes of taxation in the state of Ohio, from $23,000 to $449,377. The corporeal property of the economists and the common law were the horses, wagons, safes, pouches, and similar tangible property. The intangible property was the whole market value of the stocks and bonds based on the expected earning capacity of the corporation as a going concern, of which Ohio's proper share among the states was $449,377. In this case the intangible property was eighteen times as much as the corporeal property. The court said, on rehearing, that "It is enough that it is property which though intangible exists, which has value, produces income and passes current in the markets of the world."[6]

In this case it will be seen that the court recognized precisely Veblen's distinction between "capital" as the value of corporeal property ($23,000)—corresponding indeed to the prevailing theories of economists—and the new phenomenon of the value of intangible property ($449,377). But instead of leaving the matter, as did Veblen, as a purely scientific hypothesis of economics about which nothing should be done, the court proceeded, under that rule of public purpose which requires equality of treatment in matters of taxation, to raise the reasonable value for taxation purposes from the older value of corporeal property to the 18-fold greater value of intangible property.

[5] Adams Express Co. v. Ohio State Auditor, 165 U. S. 194 (1897); rehearing 166 U. S. 185 (1897). Commons, op. cit., 172.
[6] 166 U. S. 219.

One more case will indicate a difference between Veblen's "scientific" treatment of intangible property and the court's public purpose treatment: The San Joaquin and King's River Canal and Irrigation Company had built an irrigation system which, on the principle of Veblen's intangible property, the Corporation had valued at $18 million. The state of California had furthermore authorized the company to charge rates for water at such amounts as would yield 18 per cent on this valuation. The United States Supreme Court, in the case on appeal from a lower court which had decided favorably to the company, reduced the value from $18 million to $6 million, and reduced the rate of return on this reduced intangible capital from the original contract rate of 18 per cent to the reasonable rate of 6 per cent. In other words, the court reduced the allowable earning capacity of the company about 90 per cent and ordered a corresponding reduction in water rates. So that, while recognizing Veblen's scientific observation of what the capitalist actually does to build up intangible capital, the Supreme Court deemed it extortionate in this case and reduced the earning capacity to what it thought was a reasonable earning capacity. The court said, in justification of its decision:

> "It is not confiscation nor a taking of property without due process of law, nor a denial of the equal protection of the laws, to fix water rates so as to give an income of 6 per cent upon the then value of the property actually used for the purpose of supplying water as provided by law, even though the company had, prior thereto, been allowed to fix rates that would secure to it one and a half per cent a month income upon the capital actually invested in the undertaking. . . . The original cost may have been too great; mistakes of construction, even though honest, may have been made, which necessarily enhanced the cost; more property may have been acquired than necessary or needful for the purpose intended." [7]

We can thus see the highly different conclusions reached by Veblen and the Supreme Court upon the newly arrived concept of intangible property which each of them was investigating at the same time after its recognition by the court, in the year 1890. The Veblen conclusion reaches a theory of exploitation, the Court reaches a theory of reasonable value. Veblen reaches it suddenly in a book; the court reaches it experimentally by investigation, by mistakes

[7] Stanislaus County v. San Joaquin and King's River Canal and Irrigation Co., 192 U. S. 201, 24 Sup. Ct. 241 (1904). Whitten, R. H., *Valuation of Public Service Corporations*, 59 (1912). The language of the Court in determining reasonable value was used in the Public Utility law of Wisconsin, 1907, drafted by the present author, and copied by other states.

and corrections according to the changing personalities on the bench.

If we look for the foundation of this remarkable difference in conclusions on the same phenomenon of the new capitalism, we shall find that it consists of a difference in the concept of science itself. Veblen's concept of a science was the traditional concept of the physical sciences which rejected all *purpose* in the investigation of the facts. The court's concept of a science was an institutional concept wherein the investigation must start with a public purpose as a primary principle of the science itself. It is the difference between physical science and social science.

Veblen's elimination of purpose from the scope of science was based on his interpretation of Pragmatism as then set forth by James and Dewey.[8] He does not seem to have known the Pragmatism of Peirce, which dealt only with physical sciences, nor the Pragmatism of the courts, which more nearly followed Dewey. When James and Dewey took over the name of pragmatism, James applied it to individual psychology, and Dewey applied it to social psychology. In this field they recognized that purpose was the dominant problem of a human science. Hence they were rejected even by Peirce himself[9] and likewise by Veblen. The latter considered that science is "matter-of-fact" science, arising from the modern inventions of machinery, wherein the scientist eliminates all of the older ideas of purpose or "animism" contained in the concepts of alchemy, or divination, and adopts merely the ideas of "consecutive change," or "process," which has no "causation" and no "final end" or "purpose." "Modern technology," he says, "makes use of the same range of concepts, thinks in the same terms, and applies the same tests of validity as modern science."[10]

If this is so, then there is no science of human nature. Science becomes only the physical sciences. When applied to human nature, therefore, according to Veblen, Pragmatism

> "creates nothing but maxims of expedient conduct," whereas "Science creates nothing but theories. It knows nothing of policy or utility, of better or worse. . . . Wisdom and proficiency of the pragmatic sort does not contribute to the advance of a knowledge of fact. . . . The mental attitude of worldly wisdom is at cross-purposes with the disinterested scientific spirit, and the pursuit of it induces an intellectual bias that is incompatible with scientific insight."[11]

[8] Veblen, T., "Why Is Economics Not an Evolutionary Science" (1898); "The Place of Science in Modern Civilization" (1906); "The Point of View" (1908). Reprinted in *The Place of Science in Modern Civilization and Other Essays* (1919).

[9] *The Monist*, 15:161 ff., 481 ff. (1905); 16:142 ff., 495 ff., 545 ff. (1906).

[10] Veblen, T., *The Place of Science in Modern Civilization and Other Essays*, 17.

[11] *Ibid.*, 19.

Yet in institutional economics it is exactly this bias which we investigate as a part of the whole economic process. Even when Veblen comes to a specification of these attitudes of worldly wisdom, which he assembles under the name of pragmatism, they turn out to be special cases of his general idea of institutional conduct, for, he says, the intellectual output of worldly wisdom

"is a body of shrewd rules of conduct, in great part designed to take advantage of human infirmity. Its habitual terms of standardization and validity are terms of human nature, of human preference, prejudice, aspiration, endeavor, and disability, and the habit of mind that goes with it is such as consonant with these terms." [12]

When we examine these terms of "worldly wisdom," we find that they are summarized in our concept not of a vague human nature, but of transactions and the working rules of going concerns wherein collective action controls individual transactions. In the field of jurisprudence these terminate in the theories of reasonable value and due process of law, always inspired by the collective purposes of the parties who make rules for a conflict of interest to be decided with the public interest in view. But, with Veblen, whose theories are not derived from judicial decisions but from the evident exploitation of capitalistic transactions when left unregulated by law, institutionalism becomes all of the exploiting devices which capitalists can invent and use.

In other words, we use the term "pragmatism" always in the scientific sense of Peirce as a method of investigation, but we consider that Peirce used it only for the physical sciences where there is no future and no purpose, while James and Dewey used it always for the human sciences, where the subject-matter itself is a pragmatic being always looking to the future and therefore always motivated by purposes. Thus, without leaving in the air all the enumerated special cases of exploitation, we collect them together in the general concept of all kinds of collective action in control of individual action according to the evolving working rules of the various customs and concerns. These rules and concerns can also be investigated by the pragmatic method of science, just as the technological rules of the physical sciences can be investigated; and they can thus be investigated as "matter of fact" in the evolving decisions of courts and arbitration tribunals, and in the changing meanings of reasonable value, as well as in the unregulated exploitations of Veblen.

[12] *Ibid.*, 19–20.

INSTITUTIONAL ECONOMICS

It is in the changes of these collective rules, including custom and going concerns, and all kinds of social philosophies, that we find, as does Veblen, the evolutionary theory of economics. No better demonstration of the reason why the orthodox economist could not develop an evolutionary theory has been given than Veblen's characterization of the faulty conception of human nature of the Austrian economists. This we have quoted above,[13] as being the same as Bentham's concept. But we avoid the faulty concept by making the subject-matter of economics the transactions of individuals and the going concerns of collective action.

2. *From Accrual of Wealth to Accrual of Ideas*

We have noted [14] the incoming of the idea of society in the decades of the 1830's and 1840's and the accompanying naïve and magic formulae of an infinite accrual of the social services of the past embodied in the material goods and fixed capital of the present. But, is it a physical accrual, when those embodied services of the past have long since been worn out, depreciated, and obsolete; when they must be continually replaced by new labor and improved by new inventions, giving rise to the concept of turnover? Is it not rather the accumulation of *embodied ideas* from the dawn of civilization to the present steam, gasoline, and wireless? The scientist, engineer, or mechanic of today is simply repeating the ideas of the lever of Archimedes, the gravitation of Galileo and Newton, the electricity of Franklin, and the thousands of ideas of scientists, engineers, and mechanics of the centuries of civilization.

Veblen, under the name "instinct of workmanship," substituted this evolutionary institutional process of ideas for the physical concepts of accrual of physical capital, and thus gave a proper setting for the turnover concepts of recent years.[15] His "instinct" of workmanship, however, we should name the custom and law of managerial transactions. It led to the orderly production of commodities and services regardless of quantities, prices, and ownership. But this custom and law, as we have seen, is controlled by the modern rendering of the original legal doctrines of *assumpsit, quantum meruit,* and the right of the owner to command the behavior of those whom he admits on his premises.

Veblen had seen the attempt of Karl Marx to separate the classical double meaning of wealth or capital, as material and ownership of

---

[13] Above, p. 218, Bentham.
[14] Above, p. 325, From Division of Labor to Association of Labor.
[15] Above, p. 294, From Circulation to Repetition.

the material, into two antagonistic entities—social labor-power and the collective capitalistic ownership of the materials which that labor converted into use-values. But Veblen perceived that the two entities which Marx thus constructed were only two metaphysical substances, the one derived from Hegel's dialectics, the other from the natural rights and natural liberty of the economists.[16] The Hegelian scheme was directed towards a predetermined goal which, on the spiritual side of Hegel himself, was the unfolding of the spirit until it should reach a German world empire of unity and liberty, but which, on the heterodox side (led by Feuerbach),[17] had become Marx's materialistic unfolding of modes of production until it should reach a world empire of the proletariat. Marx's essential interpretation was the foreordained decay of the capitalistic system of ownership and the revolutionary capture of that system by the unpropertied and unemployed class who all along, as Veblen interprets Marx, had had a natural right to the whole product of their labor.

Hence the Marxian scheme, according to Veblen, was pre-Darwinian, for the Darwinian evolution has no foreordained goal, but is a continuity of cause and effect without any trend, any final term, or consummation. It is "blindly cumulative causation." It is the rise and fall of civilizations and not the unfolding of any one civilization to Marx's foreordination of labor ownership. It may as likely turn out to be ultimate control by capitalists as control by labor, wherein Veblen foretold the possibility of Fascism as well as Communism. These variabilities would be the Darwinian evolution, not foreordained, and Veblen endeavored to work them out as mere process without a goal.

But Darwin had two kinds of "selection" among the variabilities: Natural Selection and Artificial Selection. Ours is a theory of artificial selection. Veblen's is natural selection.

According to Veblen, the Marxian theorists, on account of the Darwinian theory of "natural" selection then entering the field of economics, were reaching a period of doubt as to the inevitableness of the irrepressible class conflict, and the resort to force was deprecated by them. The leading Marxists were making concessions to patriotism, and to the changing international situations into which they were being thrown. Herein Veblen foretold their changed attitude at the opening of the World War, where patriotism overcame their ideas of class struggle and ultimate world domination by the proletariat.

[16] Veblen, T., *The Place of Science in Modern Civilization and Other Essays*, 411.
[17] See article on Feuerbach, L. A., *Encyclopaedia of the Social Sciences*, VI, 221–222.

To meet this new Darwinian idea of continuous change and its abandonment of a foreordained goal, Veblen simply substituted the idea of Process, without ascertainable goal. But in doing so he created an even greater antagonism than did Marx himself, between the labor process of increasing the nation's material goods and the capitalistic process of withholding, holding back and putting the laborers out of employment.

While Veblen rightly charged Marx with the pre-Darwinian concept of foreordained evolution derived from the metaphysics of Hegel, yet it is hardly conceivable that Marx could have built upon any other foundation, when he held only to the classical idea of corporeal property. If property was only the mere ownership of materials, and if the value of that property was merely the amount of socially necessary labor embodied in it, then the only concept of *change* that Marx could introduce was that of the augmentation of the materials produced by labor, paralleled, of course, by the augmentation of ownership.

But this is not the Darwinian process of minute changes, ending eventually in the different species. Hence Veblen could move from the metaphysics of entities, with foreordained goals, to the Darwinian idea of a process, only by changing from the Marxian and orthodox concept of corporeal property to the new and indeed post-Marxian concept of intangible property. The latter is a process itself of buying, selling, borrowing, lending, and augmenting the pecuniary value of property rights; while corporeal property has, in itself, no power of buying or selling, and its augmentation is only the increase of use-values by the labor process of working and invention.

Consequently if, according to Marx, this mere ownership of material things was being centralized in the hands of the few, ownership itself becomes a kind of entity entirely separate from the other entity, social labor-power. Veblen, when he changes from entities to processes, must change from corporeal property which contains no pecuniary process of buying and selling, to intangible property which is none other than the pecuniary process itself. Correspondingly, when he changes from Marx's social labor-power he must substitute an orderly process of the creation of material wealth, uncontrollable by the pecuniary process. This we name the expected orderly repetition of Managerial Transactions. Veblen named it the Instinct of Workmanship.

Veblen knew of the scientific management theories of Frederick Taylor only in their beginnings, when they had not reached the humanitarian content contained in the analysis of a managerial transaction which we have quoted from Henry Dennison.[18] Nor had scientific management yet reached the general social well-being as the goal of the managerial economists of recent years.[19] Taylor's idea of scientific management was solely the engineer's idea of measurement applied to labor as it had been applied to machinery. The manager determined by his superior position just how much and how the laborer should produce. Veblen in 1914 revolted against this idea and built up the contradictory idea of the idealized workman, whether manual, scientific, or managerial, carrying forward the traditions of good workmanship.

For these reasons Veblen became the intellectual founder of all the modern schemes which would place the engineer, instead of the capitalist, at the head of the social process.[20]

Veblen's theory here was again a substitution, in place of the orthodox static theories of equilibrium and harmony of economic facts, of an evolutionary theory of knowledge, science, arts, habits, and customs of the producers of wealth regardless of the sabotage of capitalistic ownership. Thus the material things themselves of the orthodox and Marxian economists, such as machines, commodities, natural resources, disappear as the subject-matter of economics, and reappear as the applied knowledge and acquired habits of the instinct of workmanship, headed by engineers.

Indeed, in this, Veblen is quite correct, for the material things of the older economists are only the use-values which appear, disappear, are renewed and invented by the continuous repetition, or turnover, of what we resolve into managerial transactions. But it is knowledge, habit, invention, that endure and reconstruct new materials, because these are the human abilities unfolding through the ages through instruction, tradition, experience, experiment, investigation. This knowledge is simply technological, and is, as Veblen says,

"the matter-of-fact knowledge of the physical behavior of materials with which men have to deal in the quest of a livelihood. . . . To say that minerals, plants and animals are useful—in other words, that they are economic goods—means that they have been brought within the sweep of the community's knowledge of ways and means." [21]

It is this that gives an institutional character to even the material things themselves which had formed the basis of orthodox eco-

18 Above, p. 64, Managerial Transactions.
19 The Taylor Society, *Scientific Management in American Industry* (1929).
20 See his *The Engineers and the Price System* (1921).
21 Veblen, T., *The Place of Science in Modern Civilization and Other Essays*, 325, 329.

nomics. It is the reason why we substitute "managerial transactions" for the physical concepts of "material" and "labor." The
material things come and go with a rapid turnover by depreciation,
obsolescence, and consumption; but that which keeps up their renewal and increasing efficiency is the traditions, customs, and innovations handed down from one generation to the next in the
evolving character of managerial transactions, but which Veblen, by
a kind of "reification," names "the immaterial equipment of industry, the intangible assets of the community." [22]   This "immaterial equipment" is inherited and transmissible, for it is "the
conscious pursuit of an objective end which the instinct in question
makes worth while."

For this reason Veblen gives the name "tropism," or "tropismatic
activity" for such animal or human behavior as is unreflective or
non-deliberative, and he reserves "instinct" for human volitions.
For this reason we name it custom, as he intended, instead of instinct. Such instinct, he says, is "a matter of tradition out of the
past, a legacy of habits of thought accumulated through the experience of past generations." It "falls into conventional lines, acquires the consistency of custom and prescription, and so takes on
an institutional character and force." [23]

These accustomed ways of doing and thinking are "sanctioned by
social convention and so become right and proper and give rise to
principles of conduct. By use and wont they are incorporated into
the current scheme of common sense." While thus the instincts
are not so much hereditary as educated, they are subject to variation, selection, and survival through competition and struggle, primarily as adaptations to meet the material requirements of life and
the cultural changes of civilization.[24]

The instinct of workmanship, or, as we should say, the custom of
workmanship, runs, according to Veblen, through all other proclivi-
ties, for it is the sense of fitness respecting the ways and means for
accomplishing any ultimate purpose. In the arts, "where the sense
of beauty is the prime mover," the instinct of workmanship provides
the technique; in religion it is the ritual; in courts of law it is procedure and legal technicalities; in industry it is the process of production and the organization of a force of employees. The business
man, too, shows the instinct of workmanship in his manipulation of
markets and of human needs for the purpose of obtaining a profit.
"So that this instinct may, in some sense be said to be auxiliary to

[22] *Ibid.*, 330.
[23] Veblen, T., *The Instinct of Workmanship, and the State of the Industrial Arts* (1914), 7.
[24] *Ibid.*, 16 ff

all the rest, to be concerned with the ways and means of life rather than with any one given ulterior end." "It involves holding to a purpose." It is concerned with "practical expedients, ways and means, devices and contrivances of efficiency and economy, proficiency, creative work and technological mastery of facts. It is a proclivity for taking pains." [25]

Thus Veblen is compelled to introduce *purpose* into his instinct of workmanship, and thereby to change from Darwin's "natural" selection to Darwin's "artificial" selection.

Veblen's second and complementary concept which converts physical capital into an evolutionary process is his concept of a going concern. His concept is, however, what we have named a technological "going plant," reserving the term "going concern" to include both the going plant and the going business. Veblen's "going concern," or rather going plant, is a turnover of materials, machines, buildings, operated and maintained by an organization of superintendents, experts, foremen, and workers turning out use-values. Karl Marx had given his attention to the physical materials and equipment of "embodied labor"; Veblen gave attention to the organization of workmanship within the plant, which we name the hierarchy of managerial transactions. Hence Marx expressed the concept in the passive and metaphorical terms of an "organic composition of capital," but Veblen expressed it in terms of a managerial process under the "foremanlike oversight and correlation of the work in respect of kind, speed, [and] volume," a "function of the foreman's mastery of the technological situation at large and his facility in proportioning one process of industry to the requirements and effects of another." [26]

This is "efficiency," and Veblen, although he rejects the term "purpose," parts with "modern scientists" who would reject such a word as efficiency because it is said to contain the metaphysical concept of "causation." Efficiency is, in truth, as we agree with Veblen, a concept of cause and effect, for it is the intentional control "exercised by the master-workman, engineer, superintendent," and it "determines how far the given material equipment is effectually to be rated as 'capital goods'." [27]

This we should certainly name purpose, and Veblen's physical capital becomes, not a quantity of things, but a changing process of usefulness directed by "prevalent habits of thought." The "physical properties of the materials are constant," and it is "the human

[25] *Ibid.*, 29–33.
[26] Veblen, T., *The Place of Science in Modern Civilization and Other Essays*, 345.
[27] *Ibid.*, 345.

agent that changes." Capital is not an accumulation of past products of stored-up labor—these are transitory and aimless—capital is a going plant of industrial knowledge and experience guided by the master-workman for the service of mankind. Capital is Henry Ford and his hundred thousand workers, and Ford's book, *My Life and Work,* is Veblen in action.

But Veblen and Ford recognized another instinct and had another meaning of Capital. This instinct might have been derived from Adam Smith's "propensity to truck, barter and exchange one thing for another," were it not that Smith saw in it the invisible hand of beneficence, while Veblen saw in it the malignant hand that disrupts the technical process in order to obtain "something for nothing." [28] This "pecuniary instinct" is Property. Property is Capital, and, just as Veblen's capitalist makes his pecuniary gain by the "right of abuse" rather than the "right of use," so Ford, as a result of the court's decision,[29] conforms to Veblen by buying out the stockholders and getting rid of their legal claims for profits and interest, in order to become in truth Veblen's "master workman" moved by the instinct of workmanship.

Adam Smith's concept of property, according to Veblen, belonged to the regime of handicraft and petty trade, before the machine process ripened, when the workman was the master-workman producing and selling his product, and when the merchant made his profit by adapting himself to changes in demand and supply of commodities, over which he had no control. But modern business property is an investment, not in commodities as they pass between producer and consumer, but in the mechanical processes of industry itself.[30] Smith's concept of property, we noted, went back to John Locke, who substituted a natural right of property and liberty, based on the worker's ownership of his own person and the products of his labor, in place of the authority of a superior based on prowess, service, and fealty running back from secular authority to divine authority.[31] In the time of Smith, economic life had become standardized "in terms of workmanship and price." Retaining, however, these ideas of natural right and liberty, modern business has abandoned John Locke's finding of the origin of property in the creative efficiency of the workman, and finds its basis in the capitalization of expected earning capacity. Property is not merely the ownership and liberty to dispose of what one produces; it is the present value

---

[28] Veblen, T., *The Vested Interests and the State of the Industrial Arts* (1919), 100.
[29] Dodge *et al. v.* Ford Motor Company *et al.,* 204 Mich. 459, 170 N. W. 668 (1919).
[30] Veblen, T., *The Theory of Business Enterprise,* 22, 80.
[31] *Ibid.,* 74–80.

of what is expected will be acquired from others who will produce. Thus property is the monetary capitalization of earning power, and this capitalization is modern Capital.

This is because the machine process has succeeded the handicraft process. The "machine process" is larger than the machine. It is a whole nation. It is procedure on the basis of a systematic knowledge of forces employed; agricultural and animal industries are also machine process. It is larger than the single plant, since none of the processes are self-sufficing but the "whole concert of industrial operations is to be taken as a machine process." Hence, summarizing Veblen, there must be adjustments within the plant, adjustments between plants and between industries, measurements of materials and appliances, standardized sizes, shapes, grades, gauges, not only of commodities and services, but also of time, place, and circumstance. It is a world-wide "comprehensive, balanced, mechanical process"—the engineer and not the capitalist.

So nicely is this process balanced that any disturbance at any point spreads quickly to other points and may bring down the entire process with idleness, waste, and hardship. Here, says Veblen, is where the business man comes in. "It is by business transactions that the balance of working relations between the several industrial units is maintained or restored, adjusted and readjusted, and it is on the same basis and by the same method that the affairs of each industrial unit are regulated." All of these relations are "always reducible to pecuniary" units, since the business man, as such, is interested not in the "plant" as an industrial equipment, but in the plant as pecuniary "assets." [32] It is to him an "investment," and investment is a pecuniary transaction whose aim is pecuniary gain in terms of value and ownership. He makes his gains, not by workmanship which is serviceable to the community, but by business which is not serviceable.

The distinction occurs in two kinds of assets, "tangible" and "intangible," the former being "peculiarly serviceable capital goods," the latter being "immaterial items of wealth, immaterial facts owned, valued, and capitalized on an appraisement of the gain to be derived from their possession." These intangible assets arise from the fact that ownership of the community's physical equipment makes the capitalist the *"de facto* owner of the community's aggregate knowledge of ways and means," that is, owner of the community's "immaterial equipment" as found in the technological abilities of engineers and workmen. But ownership gives to the capitalist not only the right of use of this technological capacity of the workers,

[32] *Ibid.*, 18.

but also the "right of abuse and of neglect and inhibition." [33]

Thus the legally prohibited "restraint of trade" is not the only form of abuse—the characteristic and all-prevailing abuse is that of making a pecuniary gain by "advised idleness of plant," by "charging what the traffic will bear," by "obstructive tactics designed to hinder the full efficiency of a business rival," by "freezing out" rival firms, by raising prices, so that, "under the regime of capital, the community is unable to turn its knowledge of ways and means to account for a livelihood except at such seasons and in so far as the course of prices affords a differential advantage to the owners of material equipment."

For "disserviceability may be capitalized as readily as serviceability." Not to mention naval and military establishments for protecting trade, or investments in race tracks, saloons, etc., or wasteful and spurious goods which involve "a perverse use of the technological expedients used," there is also the characteristic capitalization of intangible assets known as "good-will." This is Veblen's name for the capitalization of differential business advantages, including not only the original "kindly sentiment of trust and esteem on the part of a customer," but the more modern meaning of special advantages inuring to a monopoly or a combination of business concerns. It is these differential advantages over the community and over rivals, created by power to withhold supply, that constitutes the bulk of intangible assets, and this attribute furnishes us with the distinction to be drawn between tangible and intangible assets. Although both tangible and intangible assets are valuable on account of their income-yielding capacity to the owner, yet the presumption is that the former are potentially serviceable to the community, representing "materially productive work," which furnishes use-values, while intangible assets "in the aggregate, and on the average" are "presumably disserviceable to the community," since they furnish only money values to the owner.

The substantial difference lies in the fact that tangible assets are a capitalization of the technological proficiency of the community, that is, of the processes of production; whereas intangible assets are a capitalization of the adjustments or maladjustments, the differential control of supply, between industries and markets, that is, of "expedients and processes of acquisition not productive of wealth, but affecting only its distribution." Hence intangible assets are pecuniary privileges of business arising only from control of supply and power to withhold supply if prices are not satisfactory, and are

---

[33] Veblen, T., *The Place of Science in Modern Civilization and Other Essays*, 352 ff.

therefore exactly the opposite of productive efficiency of workers, which increases the supply.

Hence arises the distinction between "industrial" and "pecuniary" employments.[34] The classical division of factors of production as land, labor, and capital, proved inadequate, and a fourth factor, the entrepreneur, was introduced by economists as a peculiar kind of laborer with a peculiar kind of wage. At the same time, says Veblen, the original premises of a providential order of nature remained, with its theorem of a natural or normal equilibrium which worked out an "equivalence between productive service and remuneration." Profits, therefore, became, for the economists, the just equivalent of enterprise—as rent, wages, and interest had been the equivalent of land, labor, and capital.

Afterwards, a peculiar class of business men, called speculators, came into view, not having any "interest in or connection with any given industrial enterprise or any industrial plant." A half-century ago the business manager might have been construed as "an agent occupied with the superintendence of the mechanical processes." At that time the speculative function might have been considered inseparable from the industrial function, and therefore a distinction could be made between "legitimate" and "illegitimate" speculation, the former connected with "the successful operation of some concrete industrial plant," the latter furnishing no service to the community. But, in recent times, according to Veblen, the connection has been severed, so that a complete line of business or pecuniary employments has been separated off from industrial or mechanical employments. Hence "the line falls not between legitimate and illegitimate pecuniary transactions, but between business and industry," that is, between power to withhold supply and power to increase supply.

Business activities, Veblen continues, are "lucrative without necessarily being serviceable to the community." They include the activities of speculators in securities, real estate agents, attorneys, brokers, bankers, and financiers, who shade off "insensibly from that of the *bona fide* speculator who has no ulterior end of industrial efficiency to serve, to that of the captain of industry or entrepreneur as conventionally set forth in the economic manuals." Their characteristic is that "they are concerned primarily with the phenomena of value—with exchange or market values and with purchase and sale—and only indirectly and secondarily, if at all, with such mechanical processes." They are not concerned with production or consumption, but with distribution and exchange, that is, with the

[34] *Ibid.*, 279 ff.

institution of property, which is "not to be classed, in economic theory, as productive or industrial activity at all," since the function of private property is simply that of power to withhold supply.

Industry is, indeed, "closely conditioned by business," since the ownership of property means "the discretionary control of wealth." The business man decides what shall be produced and how much or little, but his object is not production or serviceability, but "vendibility." And he often gains as much or at least avoids a loss, by disrupting industry as by promoting it. In short, the gains from Veblen's pecuniary employments arise from power to obstruct and withhold production vouchsafed by the institution of property, whereas the gains from his industrial employments arise from increasing production vouchsafed by the instinct of workmanship.

It is these pecuniary gains that Veblen defined as vested interests. "A vested interest is a marketable right to get something for nothing." Vested interests are "immaterial wealth," "intangible assets." They are the outgrowth of three main lines of business, namely, limitation of supply, obstruction of traffic, and meretricious publicity, all with a view to profitable sales. They are "devices of salesmanship, not of workmanship." They are not, however, dishonest—"they are conducted strictly within the lines of commercial honesty." They are simply unearned incomes allowed by law. For this reason they are named "free income," in that they are obtained by their recipients out of the total mechanical production of the community, through power to withhold supply and opportunity, but without rendering an equivalent service through increasing the supplies of commodities and opportunities of employment.

What, then, are the objects with which pecuniary employments are occupied? The early physical economists, Quesnay, Ricardo, and Marx, eliminated money entirely or reduced it to a commodity, and represented rent, profits, and wages as quantities of commodities exchanged in a barter economy, with money as a mere unit of account not different from other weights and measures. But Veblen's modern business man is occupied solely with obtaining money itself, or rather with obtaining various legal instruments such as stocks, bonds, and checking accounts at the bank, which have the capacity of commanding commodities and labor in exchange. These legal instruments are evidences of ownership and not products of workmanship. They have no necessary connection with commodities, in fact are not commodities at all, but are legal instruments for controlling the supply of commodities. The oldtime workman or merchant brought actual commodities, previously produced, upon the market. But these modern intangible properties, taken as a whole, are, according to Veblen, titles or claims to something which has not yet been produced, namely, an expected net earning capacity, that is, differential advantages over and above expected outgo for wages, determined by the process of keeping up prices by restricting supply, and keeping down wages by restricting the demand and increasing the supply of labor. On this account, Veblen's intangible properties are claims to differential marketing advantages, which, when distributed among the claimants, take the form of profits, interest, and rent. They have no necessary basis in the mechanical processes of industry, and depend solely on rights of ownership and resulting control of supply.

In this respect, it will be seen, Veblen followed historical lines and made the same distinction which the United States Supreme Court finally made in the Adams Express Company case in 1896.[35] He has enlarged, as did the court, the definition of both property and capital from that of corporeal property to that of expected earning capacity. It is the buying and selling of this earning capacity that constitutes "traffic in vendible capital."[36] This vendible capital, as we saw in the Adams Express Company case, has no definite relation to the physical capital. It is, according to Veblen, a "fund of money values," and "bears but a remote and fluctuating relation to the industrial equipment . . . of the old-fashioned concept of industrial capital." The old basis of capitalization was "the cost of material equipment owned by any given concern. . . . The basis is now no longer given by the cost of material equipment owned, but by the earning capacity of the corporation as a going concern." In other words, "the nucleus of capitalization is not the cost of the plant, but the concern's good-will, so called."

And the meaning of "good-will" has been enlarged, says Veblen, to meet the requirements of modern business methods: "Various items, of very diverse character, are to be included under the head of good-will; but the items included have this much in common that they are 'immaterial wealth,' 'intangible assets'; which, it may parenthetically be remarked, signifies among other things that these assets are not serviceable to the community, but only to their owners." And he proceeds to itemize the constituents of good-will in what he considers its modern application.

"Goodwill . . . comprises such things as established customary business relations, reputation for upright dealing, franchises and

[35] Above, p. 52, From Corporations to Going Concerns.
[36] Veblen, T., *The Place of Science in Modern Civilization and Other Essays*, 380.

privileges, trade-marks, brands, patent rights, copyrights, exclusive use of special processes guarded by law or by secrecy, exclusive control of particular sources of materials. All these items give a differential advantage to their owners, but they are of no aggregate advantage to the community. They are wealth to the individuals concerned—differential wealth; but they make no part of the wealth of nations." [37]

If then, vendible, or immaterial, capital is identical with good-will, and good-will is but titles of ownership, what are the physical things that are owned? There must be a substantial basis of ownership. The primitive master-workman owned his building, materials, tools, and products, and the modern business man owns his physical plant but is not concerned with its technological properties. He owns "vendible capital," which, however, must also refer to something tangible which can be held and owned like a house, horse, or machine. Hence Veblen's corporeal concept of property, which led Fisher to assert that the business man owns his customers,[38] leads Veblen to assert that the business man owns his laborers.[39] Intangible capital, or good-will, is like physical capital or commodities, the only difference being that the owner of intangible capital owns his laborers, while the owner of physical capital owns buildings and tools. By owning his laborers, he owns the producing organization inseparable from the going plant, to which that producing organization is attached. This makes possible a quantitative difference, in that the traffic is vendible—that is, intangible capital—and is conducted on a much larger scale than traffic in physical products, and yields greater profits.[40]

We have seen the same figure of speech in the court's opinion in the Hitchman case,[41] affirming what became known as the "yellow dog" contract, where the term "good-will" was so defined as to give the employer a "right" of ownership in the services of his employees as against not only duress and coercion, but even against persuasion by a labor union. Veblen's concept is not far removed from the court's in that case.

Yet it must be remembered, from our formula of equal rights,[42] that the alleged ownership of consumers and laborers is not ownership at all, but is the liberty-exposure relation of buyer and seller.

[37] Veblen, T., The Theory of Business Enterprise, 139–140.
[38] Fisher, I., The Nature of Capital and Income (1906), 29.
[39] Veblen, T., The Place of Science in Modern Civilization and Other Essays, 346.
[40] Veblen, T., The Theory of Business Enterprise, 166; The Place of Science in Modern Civilization and Other Essays, 380 ff.
[41] Commons, John R., Legal Foundations of Capitalism, 296.
[42] Above, p. 78, Formula of Economic and Social Relations.

How is it that these mere rights of ownership or "vendible capital" have an earning capacity and therefore have a value apart from the value given to objects by the mechanical process of workmanship? Ownership, according to Veblen, in its modern form of "big business," has but one source of value, the power to *withhold* physical goods from producers and consumers. While workmanship *increases* the supply of goods, ownership withholds the supply. It is a power to stop industry at will, and this power compels producers and consumers to come to terms with the owners and to pay to them a price for the mere permission to use lands, machinery, and materials, besides credit. This permission to use has enormous value because it can be refused at will, and nothing can be done without it. Industry can be stopped and the workers dismissed at any moment if the price for permission to use is not forthcoming. But this again is the liberty-exposure, not the right-duty, relation.

Hence these mere permits for use can be bought and sold, borrowed and leased, like any physical object. They take on various names according to the purpose in hand. From the standpoint of the credit system they are stocks, bonds, debentures, bank deposits, which constitute a fund of claims to the expected earning capacity of these permits to use, known by Veblen as the "loan fund." But from the standpoint of the operations of industry itself, they are the differential advantages over and above what is paid as wages, the most inclusive of which is that intangible property known as "good-will."

It will be seen here that Veblen reproduces the same explanation of differential advantages that Karl Marx had introduced in explaining Ricardo's law of rent. But Veblen has extended it to all differential advantages and all net incomes. With Ricardo ground rent was due to the greater productiveness of labor on better land, but with Marx ground rent was due to private ownership of land. In either case the owner did not produce anything corresponding to the rent received. Rent, according to Ricardo, was a "transfer" of wealth, not a "creation of wealth." In this respect Ricardo, Marx, and Veblen agreed. But where Ricardo explained the unearned increment of land by the greater *productiveness* of labor employed on the better land, Marx and Veblen explained it by the greater power of the private owner to *stop production,* since he *owned* the instrument of labor's greater productiveness. Marx reached his conclusion by the Hegelian process of contrasting common property with private property. If all land were held in common, then differential *productiveness* would not yield a rent to any individual. The total product would then be averaged just as a farmer averages the total product of good and poor land within his farm. Marx likewise extended his averaging process to the total capital of the country; thereby he reduced profits, rent, and interest to an average rate of profit, and likewise extended it to the total social labor-power of the nation and reduced skilled labor to multiples of unskilled labor. Capital became, not individual capitalists, but aliquot parts of the nation's total power of ownership; labor became, not individual laborers, but aliquot parts of the nation's total power of production.[43]

Veblen, on the other hand, of course did not commit the fallacy of averages. He extended the principle of differential advantages from Ricardo's rent to include also the entire range of profits, interest, and rent, whether derived from good-will, patents, franchises, land, or any title of ownership. Where Marx had made capital the average power of acquisition, Veblen made it a host of differential powers of acquisition. In all cases it is, however, exactly like the Ricardian rent of land, namely, different degrees of power to obtain "something for nothing," or, as Ricardo would have said, different degrees of power to "transfer" wealth without "creating" wealth.

Thus Veblen exposed the dualism of materials and ownership inherent in the classical and hedonic definitions of wealth, previously attacked by Proudhon and Marx. In one direction this dualism leads to managerial transactions, in the other to bargaining transactions. We first consider the managerial transaction.

During the same years when Veblen was developing his theory of efficiency, Frederick W. Taylor, the engineer, was developing his time and motion studies.[44] Taylor, like Adam Smith, had one "postulate," the Harmony of Interests to be attained by greatly increasing the productivity of labor. He ran against the workers' doctrine of restriction of output, not in its organized form of unionism, but in its instinctive form of dread of cuts in piece rates and dread of unemployment.[45] He saw the conflicting customs of workers and employers, the use of force instead of persuasion, of bargaining instead of efficiency, and the gap between what the men actually turned out and what they comfortably could turn out. He saw the upper limit of fatigue and clumsy, wasteful methods of work. His chief interest lay in the physiological problem of fatigue and the engineering problem of maximum output. Previous writers

[43] Above, p. 267, Averages.
[44] Taylor, Frederick W., *Principles of Scientific Management* (1911); Copley, F. B., *Frederick W. Taylor*, 2 vols. (1923); Hoxie, R. F., *Scientific Management and Labor* (1918); Bulletin of Taylor Society; Clague, Ewan, *Theory and Measurement of Physical Productivity* (MSS). The following is mainly an abstract of Clague's dissertation on Taylor.
[45] Mathewson, S. B., and others, *Restriction of Output among Unorganized Workers* (1931).

had not got beyond a broad concept of productivity. Taylor had to find something that defined the problem narrowly enough to be amenable to measurement and universally applicable.

These limits were found in the engineering problem of improving human capacity and in the economic problem of inducing greater willingness. The former, for Taylor, was not different at all from any problem of mechanical engineering—the human being is, not a commodity, but a machine. But the economic problem was, in the words of Ewan Clague, that of "selling" scientific management to the workers.

"It should be perfectly clear," said Taylor, "that the greatest prosperity for the workman, coupled with the greatest prosperity for the employer, can be brought about only when the work of the establishment is done with the smallest combined expenditure of human effort, plus nature's resources, plus the cost for the use of capital in the shape of machines, buildings, etc. . . . The general adoption of scientific management would readily in the future double the productivity of the average man engaged in industrial work. Think of the increase, both in necessities and luxuries of life, which becomes available for the whole country, of the possibility of shortening hours of labor when this is desirable, and of the increased opportunities for education, culture and recreation which this implies. Scientific management will mean . . . the elimination of almost all causes of industrial dispute. What constitutes a fair day's work will be a question for scientific investigation, instead of a subject to be haggled and bargained over. . . . We do not bargain whether the sun rises in the East, we measure it." [46]

Thus economics is reduced to the engineering problem of man's relation to nature. Taylor, like Marx and Veblen, carefully excludes all so-called productive factors which confused the physical economists' notion of productivity, such as land, capital, machines. These are only tools. Productivity is a relation between output and labor, including management and the installation of the plant. It is the rate of output per man-hour. This is efficiency.

Increasing efficiency creates a surplus without increasing fatigue. The capitalist should share it with the laborer, but the latter is not entitled to it if he gets the going rate of wages. It is not a question of rights, it is a problem of management.

For the next step in the transition from Marx's metaphysical social labor-power, Veblen's' biological instinct of workmanship, and Taylor's mechanization of labor, to the social problem of managerial transactions, we turn to Henry S. Dennison, the employer-

[46] Taylor, F. W., op. cit., 11, 142.

owner-manager. Dennison's analysis has been reproduced above.[47] Dennison, like Ford, had bought off the claims of stockholders, and had gone further by making the election of directors and managers a function of the upper group of "worker-owners" instead of the "investor-managers." Here, management is not only the engineering science of Taylor, nor only the workmanship and authority of Veblen and Ford. It is a volitional process, a transaction between foreman and operative, where neither the worker chooses, nor the foreman chooses, but the choices are "joint devices."

3. *From Managerial Transactions to Bargaining Transactions*

Managerial transactions arise from the relations of a legal superior to a legal inferior. The psychological relation, at law, is command and obedience. But bargaining transactions arise from the relations of those who are legally equal. The psychological relation is persuasion or coercion. Just as Veblen's instinct of workmanship afterwards resolves into Dennison's "reasonable" managerial transactions of a going plant, so Veblen's pecuniary acquisitiveness resolves afterwards into the United States Supreme Court's reasonable values as they *would* be agreed upon by "willing" buyers and sellers in bargaining transactions of a going business. It requires the two to construct the concept of a going concern, each acting on the other—a producing organization, a buying and selling organization. And the two kinds of transactions may be made reasonable instead of oppressive, confiscatory, or exploitative.

Here it is that Veblen's instinct of workmanship, we must observe, is also an instinct of acquisitiveness and pecuniary valuation. The respectable line of disturbances created by Veblen's technological workers, such as strikes, boycotts, labor turnover, sabotage, and the bargaining by high-skilled workers for higher wages, suggests the idea that the same acquisitive instincts belong to both workmen and business men. His antithesis of efficiency and bargaining holds true—efficiency is the increase of supply, bargaining is the withholding of supply. Yet the instinct of workmanship does not go on producing goods regardless of wages. The power to withhold supply unless the terms are satisfactory is indeed Veblen's pecuniary motive and his rights of property. It also is an institutional, historical fact. It has also its evolving customs. The foreman or laborer does not find the materials and labor ready at hand, furnished by nature. He finds them held by owners of materials and owners of labor-power. Before he can use them he must obtain

---

[47] Above, p. 64, Managerial Transactions.

permission from the owner. It is for this reason, perhaps, that Veblen opposed trade unions just as he opposed combinations of capital. Each was collective restraint of trade. Each is a pecuniary instinct, and each is the intangible property of bargaining power. The difference between capitalists and workmen is not that the former have the pecuniary instinct and the latter do not, but that the power to withhold, vouchsafed by the laws and customs of property, is perhaps greater in capitalistic organizations than it is in labor organizations. But this is a question of degree, and questions of degree are questions of reasonableness. If they are questions of degree of power in managerial or bargaining transactions, then they can be dealt with on that basis, and there is no good reason for separating them into two entities, the idealized instinct of workmanship and the bedeviled instinct of acquisition.

The historical explanation of Veblen's cynical antithesis of business and industry is in the failure to trace out the evolution of business customs under the decisions of courts, as he had traced the technological customs. Such an investigation reveals the evolution of his "intangible property" which has consisted in making the distinction, not allowed by Veblen, between good-will and privilege, good-will being the reasonable exercise of the power to withhold, and privilege being the unreasonable exercise of that power. It is only in the analysis of a bargaining transaction that the economic foundation for this evolution can be found. Psychologically it is the distinction between persuasion and coercion; legally it is the distinction of rights, duties, liberties, and exposures; economically it is the three differences between free competition and fair competition, between equal opportunity and discrimination, between reasonable and unreasonable price, all of which are included in the evolution of the meaning of due process of law. These psychological, legal, and economic aspects are inseparable, as may be seen from our preceding formula of a bargaining transaction derived from the economist's concept of a market and the jurist's concept of legal relations.[48] These are true equally of laborers and capitalists, each of whom are acquisitive and pecuniary, as well as workmanlike. It is just because this fact of evolution in the decisions of courts is not observed by Veblen that he does not arrive at a concept of reasonable value.

4. *Flow of Time and Lapse of Time*

The distinction between managerial and bargaining transactions is the distinction between efficiency and scarcity. The evolutionary

[48] Above, p. 59, Bargaining Transactions.

fact, common to both, is the institution of property, developing out of conquest and custom into law. Management ranges from slavery, serfdom, peonage, master, and servant, to foreman and worker; bargaining from barter and money to credit, from individual bargaining to collective bargaining and stabilization. But there is another distinction between the two, the concept of Time.

It is the outstanding defect of physical theories from Quesnay, Ricardo, Marx, and MacLeod to Veblen, that they could not handle the distinction between a *flow* of time and a *lapse* of time. A "flow" is a moving point of time, without measurable dimensions, between the incoming future and the outgoing past. But a lapse of time is an interval between two points of time. The distinction underlies the difference between process and valuing, between managing and bargaining, efficiency and scarcity, profits and interest, risk and waiting, intangible property and incorporeal property.

None of the physical sciences requires this distinction between flow and lapse of time, because none of them deals with future time, whereas Time, for economics, as a volitional science, is solely future time. But the flow of time, for economic theory, is not only an expected flow of time, it is also an expected interval between a present point of time and a future point of time.

Veblen, in his truly scientific advance from theories of equilibrium to a theory of process, was, for that very reason, unable to go further and distinguish the human process from the physical process. His physical postulates could not possibly distinguish an expected lapse of time from an expected flow of time. This is the difference between incorporeal property and intangible property. This misconception of Time was, with him, as we have seen also with MacLeod and all the physical economists, a fundamental fallacy.

His "intangible property" does, indeed, look to future earning capacity, and it is properly named intangible, but that earning capacity is solely an expected *repetition* of business transactions along a risky *flow* of time, not an expected *postponement* of income during a *lapse* of time. His meaning of the term "lapse," which he uses, is really the meaning of "flow." This, we have seen, is exactly the difference between intangible and incorporeal property. Incorporeal property is waiting until a debt is paid; intangible property is the expectation that profits will be obtained from future transactions. Both are, indeed, "vendible capital," as seen in the distinction between stocks and bonds, and both profit and interest are inextricably interwoven in each. But they are the difference between an expected repetition of profitable transactions governed by the law of liberty and exposure and an expected waiting for income to be derived from the enforcement of a right and its equivalent duty.

The difference is doubtless subtle and its explanation is difficult for those who think in terms of modern physical science, or in terms of legal negotiability. The way in which Veblen rejected the distinction is seen in the foregoing double meaning of "lapse of time" and also in his contrast of "vendible products" with "vendible capital." Products, or tangibles, as well as intangible good-will and incorporeal debts, are each bought and sold, and the gains from buying and selling are profit or loss. The gains, he says, may in both cases "emerge under the form of a per cent per time-unit; that is to say, as a function of the lapse of time." "Yet . . . the business transactions themselves are not a matter of the lapse of time. Time is not of the essence of the case. The magnitude of a pecuniary transaction is not a function of the time consumed in concluding it, nor are the gains which accrue from the transaction." [49]

True enough. The terms of a selling-buying transaction are agreed upon at a point of time, when the minds meet and titles are transferred; but, if an *interval* of time is agreed upon between negotiations and the future performance or payment, then Lapse of Time is of the essence of the case. An increment of profit or loss occurs, in each transaction, at a point of time, and a succession of such increments is a *flow* of time. Hence an *interval* of time is not of the essence of profit. But if the product is bought *now* and sold 30 days from now, the interval of time is of the essence of interest.

The interval appears, indeed, both as risk and as waiting, and each has an effect on present valuation. But Veblen eliminates the waiting and attends only to the risking.

"The modicum of truth," he says, "in Böhm-Bawerk's proposition that 'present goods are preferred to future goods' . . . would appear to be better expressed in the formula 'prospective security is preferred to prospective risk'; . . . whereas the dictum that 'present goods are preferred to future goods' must, on reflection, commend itself as substantially false. . . . Even for the individual's own advantage 'present goods are preferred to future goods' only where and in so far as property rights are secure, and then only for future use. It is . . . present 'wealth,' not 'present goods,' that is the object of desire; and present wealth is desired mainly for its prospective advantage." [50]

By "present wealth" Veblen means present value of present property rights. But this present value has two dimensions, expected

[49] Veblen, T., *The Place of Science in Modern Civilization and Other Essays*, 379.
[50] Veblen, T., *The Instinct of Workmanship, and the State of the Industrial Arts*, 46 n., 47 n.

risk and expected postponement. Evidently a distinction is needed in the double meaning of Veblen's "lapse of time," corresponding to the difference between expected repetition, including variability or risk, and expected postponement of goods or of payment. Veblen furnished indeed a notable contribution to economic theory when he substituted "change" for "equilibrium." He thereby made Time an essential fact of economics. But he could not see the difference between *change* and *waiting*—which is the difference between a moving point of time in the ever-present, when change occurs, and an interval between a present point and a future point of time, when waiting occurs. The first may be named a flow, the second a lapse of time. The two go together, but it was Veblen's failure to recognize the distinction that permitted him to eliminate the incorporeal property of debt by identifying it with the intangible property of expected beneficial transactions. Not until Fisher's *Booms and Depressions*, in 1932, was the incorporeal property of debt given its proper place in economic theory.[51]

Thus it was that Veblen, the pioneer of institutional economics, next to MacLeod, did not, however, have the advantage of the conclusions which, during 15 years later, were being worked out experimentally by the courts and legislatures. His critical and constructive work covered the years 1898 to 1914; his writings thereafter were mainly expositions of what he had previously done with extraordinary insight. During his pioneering days the double meaning of wealth as materials and their ownership was just beginning to be broken down in a practical way by the court's transition from corporeal property to intangible property, but the administrative machinery for research in ascertaining reasonable value had not yet been set in motion. This did not begin until the powers of the Interstate Commerce Commission were extended in 1908, followed by hundreds of state commissions on fair competition, reasonable discriminations, and reasonable values, as well as by industrial commissions, after 1911, the latter to ascertain reasonable relations in the conflicts of capital and labor.

Also, the movement towards scientific management had only just begun, and a professional class devoted to ascertaining and installing reasonable conditions in all the parts of managerial transactions had not yet begun to find itself.

Other applications of the principles of intangible property, especially the stabilization of prices, had not yet even been thought of, much less the administrative machinery to be devised. And Veblen's exclusion from his system of the incorporeal property of debts, in-

[51] Above, p. 608, The Risk Discount—Overindebtedness and Depressions.

cluding differential rates of interest, made it impossible for him to lay the foundations (as his Scandinavian contemporary Wicksell had done) for a proposed regulation of this same intangible property by stabilizing prices through central control of discount rates and open market operations.

The problem set by Veblen of a dualism in economics between materials and intangible property has only recently been attacked by economists [52] whose work we epitomize under the terms transactions, going concerns, stabilization of prices, and reasonable value. Each transaction is a valuation, not of materials, but of Veblen's ownership of materials; each concern is both Veblen's going plant and the business man's going business; each fluctuation of general prices is Veblen's exploitation; each approach towards a better understanding of reasonable value reduces this exploitation. And these are scientific, not in the sense of Veblen's physical sciences, but in the sense of the human will in action.

II. FROM INDIVIDUALS TO INSTITUTIONS

Veblen ended in a cynical dualism of materials and ownership. Other outstanding economists in Italy, Austria, and America, whose span of life extends from the dominance of the hedonic man at the end of the Nineteenth Century to the collective suppression of hedonism in the post-war Twentieth Century, were also unable to reconcile the dualism. They abandoned, tacitly or openly, their earlier theory of individualism and went over bodily to the collective control of individuals in the conflict of interests, upon which institutional economics is builded.

Friederich von Wieser, the eminent Austrian economist, wrote in 1889 his *Natürliches Werth*,[53] and nearly forty years later *Das Gesetz der Macht* (1926). In the first book he revised and illuminated the great work of Menger. In the second book, after the World War, he went back to his own pre-war historical studies. The two books are as different as two worlds, and no attempt was made by Wieser, in his later book, to reconcile the two or to build a whole political economy giving to each its due place.[54] It turns

[52] Cf. Taylor, Horace, *Making Goods and Making Money* (1928) " . . . as time goes it is becoming increasingly necessary, in manufacturing industries, to make goods in order to make money." (Preface, vii.)

[53] *Natural Value* (tr. 1893). On the part played before the war by Tugan-Baranowsky, Oppenheimer, and others, see Takata, Y., "Macht und Wirtschaft," 7 *Kyoto University Economic Review* (1932), 136.

[54] In his *Grundriss der Sozialokonomik* (1914; tr. *Social Economics*, 1927), as a matter of contrast, he starts with the "simple economy" of a supposed isolated being and then passes, by contrast to "social," "state," and "world" economy, somewhat as we have done in passing from Crusoe to Going Concerns. But this is only illustrative and pedagogic;

out that the first book was individualistic, the second collectivistic. The first was a relation of man to nature, the second a relation of man to man. The unit of the first was a commodity that satisfies wants, the unit of the second was a moral, monopolistic, or violent force that collectively subdues the individual. One was the law of Value, the other the law of Might. In the law of value all individuals are alike, equal, and free, because they are isolated and have similar relations to nature; in the law of might the individuals are the passionate and stupid masses organized by astute leaders. In the law of value Wieser sought what is permanent and enduring under all historical and institutional changes. In the law of might he sought what was changeable and compulsory throughout the ages. In the law of value he found himself conforming to the individualistic schools. In the law of might he asserts that he cannot follow either the classic or hedonic individualism, or the organic analogies to the human body. He can take things only as he actually finds them in history, and he finds that history is the history of collective suppression of individuals. "Alle geschichthichen Bildungen sind Machtbildungen."

Quite similarly, and with a similar emphasis, does Pareto, the distinguished Italian economist whom Mussolini honors as the economic founder of Fascism, construct two antagonistic social philosophies. In his *Manual of Political Economy* (1909), society is a world of "molecules" acting upon each other; "utility" is the individualistic wants of these molecules, diminishing in intensity, which induce them to act; and out of these interactions comes Pareto's world-renowned contributions to the "equilibrium" doctrines of the mathematical economists.

But in his *Treatise on Sociology,* ten years later, Pareto expressly repudiates his own "molecular" concept of society. Instead of individual "utility" and individual wants, he substitutes "social utility" and "collective wants." "Social utility" is "non-logical," "non-mathematical," "immeasurable," exactly the opposite of his "individual utility." He finds it therefore used as a cloak for political and financial corruption which has changed modern democracy, notably in Italy, France, and America, into a "demagogic plutocracy." It degenerates into violence at home and abroad.[55]

Pareto's is indeed another Malthusian shift from the Age of

scientifically we start, as does Veblen, with a cross-section, at a point of time, of a process which has no beginning and no ending, and then proceed to the changing complexities of that process, somewhat as the accountant does in his balance-sheet at a point of time and his income statement for a period of time.

[55] Pareto, Vilfrado, *Manuel d'économie politique* (tr. from Italian, 1909); *Traité de Sociologie Générale* (tr., 2 vols., 1919), Chapter XII, "Forme Générale de la Société."

Reason to the Age of Stupidity. And it is for the very reason that social utility is non-logical, non-mathematical, immeasurable, stupid, passionate, and yet collectively dominates individuals that he calls for a Fascist dictatorship that will subordinate his "demagogic plutocracy." We have, in America, along with the Fascism towards which we are tending, the alternative problem of the formation and distribution of that social utility which calls for a social theory and practice of *Reasonable* Value.[56]

When we look for the ultimate unit of investigation on which the Fascist philosophy is founded, we find it in Othmar Spann, the recognized leading economist of Germanic Fascism. His "structure" of economy is built on the two foundations of *service* and *value* (Leistung and Wert).[57] When we analyze these foundations, as detailed by Spann, we find that they resolve into either Managerial or Rationing Transactions, which are the social relations of Superior and Inferior. If it be individual value for the private economy, then the relation is that of a Managerial Transaction. If it be social value for the national economy, then the relation is a Rationing Transaction.

In this respect the ultimate social unit of Fascism is the same as that of Marx's Communism; they differ only as to who shall be the managers and the rationers, whether the proletariat or the capitalists. There is neither in Pareto, Spann, nor Wieser, as there is not in Veblen, an analysis of bargaining transactions as they have, for example, been developed in Anglo-American decisions of the common law, the law arising from the customs of the people. Managerial and rationing transactions, based, as they are, on the legally Superior and Inferior, lead to a social philosophy of dictatorship and its social psychology of Command and Obedience. But bargaining transactions, based on the concepts of willing buyers and sellers, and therefore on an ideal of persuasion versus coercion between those who are deemed to be equal before the law, lead to a social philosophy of freedom of the will in non-discriminatory choice of opportunities, in fair competition and in reasonable bargaining power, under the protection of due process of law.

This latter Anglo-American aspect of the shift from the individualistic psychological to the collective standpoint is seen strikingly in the forty years' work of the American economist, Fetter. More than others he developed illustriously the psychological foundations of individualistic economics. But when he turns to practical eco-

[56] Below, p. 807, on Seligman's "Social Theory of Fiscal Science."

[57] Spann, Othmar, *Fundament der Volkswirtschaftslehre*, 75 ff. (1923, 1929). His basic philosophy of "Universalism versus Individualism," derived from Fichte, is summarized in his *History of Economics* (tr. from the 19th German ed., 1930).

nomics and the decisions of the courts, he writes heatedly his institutional economics on *The Masquerade of Monopoly* (1931), which is his equivalent to Pareto's demagogic plutocracy and to Veblen's capitalistic sabotage.

There are doubtless many economists who remain immune to these institutional changes, and those we have just now mentioned are doubtless in the minority. Yet they are types of what is being forced, avowedly or disavowedly, into economics by the massive collective movements of the Twentieth Century.

But is it necessary to abandon the older individualistic, molecular, and equilibrium theories in despair and disgust when they can readily be adapted to the newer collective theories of Wieser's *Macht*, Pareto's *Social Utility*, or Fetter's *Masquerade?* The waves of the water seek their equilibrium just as naturally when the water is raised ten feet by a dam or sunk ten feet by a drainage canal, as when the lake remains at its "natural" level. The difficulty with the older theory was in ascertaining how high up or low down the "marginal utility" was located. Wherever it may be located, the "equilibrium" and the "marginal utility" occur at that level. If labor organization raises the level of wages 100 per cent, then the capitalists, employers, and laborers adjust their individual competitions at that higher level. Or if the employers' organizations depress the wages 50 per cent, then the capitalists, employers, and laborers adjust their competitions to that lower level. Always there is a tendency towards equilibrium amongst the individual molecules, though collective action, or Pareto's demagogic plutocracy, the business man's demagogic democracy, depress or raise the level of social utility according to their power to dictate the rules of the game.

We find that the older molecular and marginal utility theories had extended an ethical doctrine of *equal opportunity* into an economic doctrine of *equal individuals*. There may be equal opportunity for all individuals, though some may have enormously greater capacity than others to use or enjoy the opportunities. And human nature is so adaptable that, no matter how high or low the level of those equal opportunities, the competitive adjustments can passably be made among individuals for considerable periods of time. It is not needful to repudiate the older theories of individual economics when all that is needed is to adjust them to the newer theories of collective economics.

III. From Natural Rights to Reasonable Value

The doctrine of Reasonable Value is superseding the doctrine of Natural Rights. The present writer, in his fifty years of experience, has seen it happen. The foregoing chapters may have given a premonition of this outcome. The doctrine of natural rights prevailed from the Eighteenth Century and the French Revolution to the American Civil War of the Nineteenth Century which was the true American Revolution. The natural rights doctrine continued its conflicting interpretations to senility in the opening years of the Twentieth Century. The single taxers founded their proposal on the natural rights of man to the gifts of nature; Quesnay had founded his claim to ownership by landlords on the natural order; the landowners had a natural right to the land which they had acquired; the business men had a natural right to run their business as they saw fit; the individual had all the natural rights to life, liberty, and happiness, later interpreted to mean property; the testator had a natural right to dispose of his property for generations after his dead hand. Natural rights were written into the Constitution by amendments and interpretations.

Many events had served to disqualify the claim of natural rights. Philosophers have questioned it and the literature is abundant. But philosophers conflicted and had no workable substitute. Not until subordinate classes organized, and not until the revolutions of the World War, was it brought home to the millions that such rights as we have proceed from national and other collective action, and are not "natural."

The preceding sections of this book brought us to the problems of Public Policy and Social Utility. These are the same as the problems of Reasonable Value and Due Process of Law. The problem arises out of the three principles underlying all transactions: conflict, dependence, and order. Each economic transaction is a process of joint valuation by participants, wherein each is moved by diversity of interests, by dependence upon the others, and by the working rules which, for the time being, require conformity of transactions to collective action. Hence, reasonable values are reasonable transactions, reasonable practices, and social utility, equivalent to public purpose.

The first idea usually suggested by the term Reasonable Value is the individualistic, subjective, and rationalistic idea, formulated by John Locke and transmitted to modern life through the Age of Reason of the Eighteenth Century: Man is a rational being and needs only to learn the truth in order to obey. Reason exists only in the individual mind, and reasonable value is what each individual thinks is reasonable. There are, therefore, as many meanings of reasonable value as there are individuals. This theory logically ended in the French Revolution and Godwin's anarchism.

But Reason differs from Reasonableness. Man is not a rational being, as the Eighteenth Century thought; he is a being of stupidity, passion, and ignorance, as Malthus thought. Hence Reasonable Value contains a large amount of stupidity, passion, and mistake. According to the historical analysis by Malthus, reason and moral character are a slow evolution out of overpopulation, conflict of interests, and the resulting necessity of having a government of law and order to regulate the conflict.

Yet, during all these years of the Age of Reason, the common-law courts were developing an institutional idea of reasonableness and reasonable value, in the process of deciding conflicts of interest and bringing order out of incipient anarchy. This institutional idea of reason and reasonable value has been collective and historical, whereas the rationalistic idea was individualistic, subjective, intellectual, and static. The institutional idea undoubtedly reaches its clearest evolutionary change in the common-law method of making new law by taking over the changing customs of the dominant portion of the people at the time, and formulating them, by a rationalizing process of justification, into working rules for future collective action in control of individual action. Since this process has reached its pinnacle in the sovereignty of the Supreme Court of the United States, the evolution of the idea of reasonable value requires, as its institutional background, an understanding of the historic evolution from executive to legislative, and then to judicial sovereignty.[58]

Still further back of this institutional development is the technological development from hand-work to machine-work and then the aggregation of machines into mass production, from the Digger Indian to Henry Ford. And along with this are the transitions from the agricultural stages of Feudalism to the marketing stages of Capitalism in its sequence from merchant-capitalism to employer-capitalism and world-wide banker-capitalism. Equally important is the closing-up of free land by conquest and overpopulation, which shut the outlets for independent spirits and reduced the margin for profit by nation-wide and even world-wide competition. This in turn proceeded from another technological process, the extension of markets and the market information by steam, electricity, gasoline, and wireless.

In each of these historical stages new concepts of rights and reasonable practices have rapidly impinged upon the old, until we reach the present contesting concepts of reasonable value in a world that inherits the old but is compelled by economic maladjustment to evolve a future *new* out of the obsolescent *old*.

[58] Below, p. 684, Sovereignty.

Much of the history that is written lacks the historical sense. It looks for causation of human activity in the preceding events. But if we place ourselves in the position of participants, as the modern biographical history does somewhat, and take their standpoint of negotiational psychology which requires us to imagine what the actors expected when they acted, then causation is in the future.[59] The actors are confronted by what they are induced to expect, whether it be the persuasions and coercions of bargaining transactions, the commands and obedience of managerial transactions, or the pleadings and arguments of rationing transactions. They take into account the personalities of those with whom they are dealing, whether it be their motives, their theories, their social philosophies, which have "loaded" their experience with expected consequences which they wish or fear. They take into account the alternatives open to self and others which afford the opportunities for freedom or unfreedom of choice, and many other circumstances which, at the time, set up the conditions within which they choose and act in all of their transactions. It is not a rational state of society that determines action, it is a marvellously irrational and complex set of expectations that confronts the participants in transactions. And it is a situation that changes from day to day and century to century. Within this changing complexity and uncertain futurity they must act *now*. It is out of these complexities and uncertainties that the concepts of reasonable practices and reasonable values emerge and change the institutions themselves from day to day and age to age.

The United States Supreme Court, in the case of Smythe *v.* Ames,[60] gave the perplexing definition of Reasonable Value, which, however, is the common sense definition under which all rational and semi-rational beings operate as best they can. It is the definition that coincides with the court's idea of due process of law with its many variations under different circumstances. The Court said, speaking of the many conflicting theories of value offered by disputants in a case of railway valuation, that each must be given its "due weight" under the circumstances. When once the Court, by this process of due evaluating, has finally decided a dispute, then that decision, under the institutional set-up of America, is the final word, for the time being, on Reasonable Value. To it all participants must conform under similar circumstances. Reasonable Value is the evolutionary collective determination of what is reasonable in

---

[59] A good example is Jacques Bainville's *Napoleon* (tr. 1933).

[60] Smythe *v.* Ames, 169 U. S. 466 (1898); see Commons, John R., *Legal Foundations of Capitalism*, 196.

view of all the changing political, moral, and economic circumstances and the personalities that arise therefrom to the Supreme bench. Natural rights lose their inflexibility and even begin to disappear in the determination of reasonable values. We can offer only a broad outline of the institutional and other changes which lie behind the historically changing concepts of reasonable value.

IV. SOVEREIGNTY

Sovereignty is the extraction of violence from private transactions and its monopolization by a concern we call the state. But sovereignty has been looked upon as an entity as well as a process. As an entity it is personified as The State, and seems to exist apart from the people. As a process it is the extraction of the sanction of violence from what had been considered to be a private affair, and the specialization of that sanction in the hands of a hierarchy of officials guided by working rules and habitual assumptions. Sovereignty, thus, is the changing process of authorizing, prohibiting, and regulating the use of physical force in human affairs.[61]

Three notable epochs of change in this process characterize the genesis of Anglo-American sovereignty, distinguishable as the periods of executive, legislative, and judicial sovereignty. The first began with the Norman Conquest of 1066, which made the King supreme over the hierarchy of officials; the second, with the English Revolution of 1689, which made the legislature supreme; the third, with the American Constitution of 1787 and the Fifth and Fourteenth Amendments (1791 and 1868), which, after judicial construction, made the Supreme Court of the United States supreme over federal and state officials.

1. *Executive Sovereignty*

In the early years of the first period there was no distinction between the physical and economic sanctions. Sovereignty was identical with property. The King was sole sovereign and sole proprietor. A grant by him of land to a tenant, or of a charter to a corporation, was a grant of sovereignty over sub-tenants on the land, or of sovereignty over persons who practiced the trade or profession. Latterly the distinction between sovereignty and property began to be made, and sovereignty, which now may be distinguished as physical jurisdiction over the bodies of subordinates, was taken away from these grantees, leaving to them only proprietary,

---

[61] For an earlier rendering of this subject see Commons, John R., "A Sociological View of Sovereignty," *Amer. Jour. of Sociol.* (July 1899 to July 1900).

or economic jurisdiction over their transactions. Cases of this kind may be cited, such as the grant of lands with power to set up courts having physical jurisdiction, or the grant of a guild charter which had both physical and economic control over persons within its jurisdiction.[62]

Survivals of these grants of sovereignty occur in modern cases in America where corporations obtain from the sheriff a deputy sheriff's license for their employees to use violence under the jurisdiction of the corporation.

2. *Legislative Sovereignty*

In the second epoch, beginning in 1689, property had already been distinguished clearly from sovereignty by a line of decisions similar to the foregoing in Bonham's case. The Revolution now placed a parliament of property owners superior to the King and his hierarchy of judicial and executive officials. This was certified by the Act of Settlement of 1700, which made the Judiciary independent of the Crown and paved the way for the appointment of all officials by a Cabinet that could command a majority in parliament.[63]

3. *Judicial Sovereignty*

In the third epoch, peculiar to the American Constitution, the definition of property and liberty was placed under the jurisdiction of the Supreme Court. The Fifth Amendment, as interpreted by the Court, gave the Court jurisdiction over Congress, and the Fourteenth Amendment, under judicial interpretation, gave it jurisdiction over the states as follows: "No State shall make or enforce any law which shall abridge the privileges or immunities of citizens of the United States; nor shall any state deprive any person of life, liberty, or property, without due process of law; nor deny to any person within its jurisdiction the equal protection of the laws."

By a "State" is meant certain officials of a state. Henceforth any private citizen is placed on an equality, before the law, with an official who exercises over him the physical jurisdiction of sovereignty. He can bring or defend a suit at law against an official, just as he can bring suit against any private citizen. The subject-matter now, however, becomes the exercise of physical force in

---

[62] Cf. Dr. Bonham's Case (8 Co. 113b, 114a, 77 Eng. Rep. 646), where physical jurisdiction of imprisonment was granted by Henry VIII to the physicians and surgeons, but was revoked by the court in 1608, leaving them only economic jurisdiction. Commons, *Legal Foundations of Capitalism*, 228.

[63] Commons, *op. cit.*, 50.

commanding obedience. Hence we have, in the stage of judicial sovereignty, the citizen Munn defending and appealing a suit brought against him by the State of Illinois; or the citizen Holden bringing suit against the sheriff, Hardy. The first assertion of what is meant by judicial sovereignty was made in 1803 in the case where Marbury, a private citizen, brought suit against Madison, the Secretary of State for the United States.[64]

It is in the light of this equality of citizens and officials before the law, on the issue of using physical force upon the citizen, that we interpret the meanings of the terms "privileges" and "immunities" as used in the Fifth and Fourteenth Amendments to the Constitution. It is evident, from the above reading, that privileges have a different meaning from immunities. *Neither* privileges *nor* immunities may be abridged. We conclude that these are two different relations between citizens and officials regarding the use of physical force by the latter upon the former.

There are only two such relations conceivable, namely a right and liberty. Each has its equal correlative. The right of the citizen is the duty of the official. In this case it is the right of the citizen to require the official to use physical force in his behalf. It is the right to require a policeman to arrest a thief and return the goods, correlative to the equal duty of the policeman to do so. Or, it is the right of the creditor to require the court to hear his case, to render a decision, to order the sheriff, if the decision is favorable, to levy execution on the goods of the debtor, and the subsequent right of the citizen to require the sheriff to carry out the court's order. This right of the creditor to require the use of physical force, if necessary, to collect the debt, is no greater nor less than the duty of the court and the sheriff to decide the case and to use that force in his behalf. The right and the duty are correlative and equal—they are indeed one and the same. If the duty cannot be enforced, the right does not exist. It is apparent, then, that by the word "privileges" as used in the Constitution is meant these rights of citizens to require officials to perform their duties to the citizens by using physical force on other people, if necessary.

But the terms right and duty usually imply the right of one citizen and the duty of another citizen, neither of whom is permitted to use physical force, except in self-defense. Only the public official is so authorized. Hence, since the use of physical force is the question at issue, and not the use of economic power, we infer that the term privilege is substituted for the term right, though the

[64] Munn v. Illinois (94 U. S. 113, 1876); Holden v. Hardy (169 U. S. 366, 1898); Marbury v. Madison (1 Cranch U. S. 137, 2 L. ed. 60, 1803).

term right might have been and often is used with the meaning of a right of a citizen against an official. Precision, however, would suggest that the term right should be used in the sense of a right, not against officials in their public capacity of using physical force, but in their private capacity of economic or other private transaction with other private citizens.[65.]

This interpretation is confirmed by the opposite meaning of immunities. Immunity, here, means freedom from the use of physical force by the official. In the case of Munn v. Illinois the state proposed to use physical force on Munn, if necessary to compel his obedience, and Munn appealed the suit, asking the court to enjoin the state officials from using that force. He claimed what he alleged had always been one of the immunities of citizens. So Holden, the employer, brought suit against the sheriff, Hardy, claiming immunity from the sheriff's proposed use of force to prevent him from running his business as he pleased.

But the term "privilege," as often used in legal terminology, has another meaning, equivalent to immunity. As such its meaning is the same as "no-duty," which in its economic meaning is liberty of action, indicated by such terms as free trade, free access to markets, and so on. Thus liberty is a "privilege" enjoyed by reason of the absence of duties.

This treble meaning of "privilege" requires us to make a choice, or else to substitute other words. Privilege means either a right, equivalent to a duty of officials, to use physical force; or an immunity from the physical force exercised by officials; or a liberty to engage in transactions with other citizens. The first meaning we express by the word Power, the second by Immunity, the third by Liberty.

By the first is meant Political Power, the power vested in the citizen to require the courts, executives, and legislatures to execute his will on others by using the concerted physical force of sovereignty. To "abridge" the privileges of citizens is to abridge their share of the political power by which they could otherwise require public officials to use force in executing their will on others.

By the second is meant immunity from the physical force of sovereignty. To abridge the immunities of citizens is to abridge the share of political power of *others* by which they otherwise could require public officials to use the physical force of sovereignty in executing *their* will on him.

By the third is meant Economic Liberty, the freedom of the citizen with reference to other citizens to buy or not buy, to sell or

---

[65] Above, p. 78, Formula of Economic and Social Relations.

withhold, to hire or quit, according to one's own inclinations, circumstances, and alternatives at the time.

Thus to the term Power is given the meaning which, under different ways of looking at it, has been known as Ability, Capacity, Freedom, Citizenship, or Membership. In the sense of Ability, or Capacity, or Power, it is the power of a citizen to set in motion the courts and other officials of sovereignty in enforcing what one claims as his rights or liberties. This is the same as Freedom, in the ancient meaning of "freedom of the city," freedom of the guild, freedom of the corporation—which meant, not liberty, the absence of duty, but included mainly a capacity to set in motion the collective force of the concern on one's own behalf. And this is the meaning of Citizenship and Membership. A citizen, or member of any concern, is one who has power or recognized "capacity" to call upon the collective force of the concern to protect and assert for him all the claims against others which the rules of the concern recognize and enforce. Power is the individual's share of collective power.

Consequently, the total lack of this power may be variously expressed as non-membership, non-citizenship, incapacity, or disability. The last term, Disability, comprehends the others. A disability is a denial of power to put in motion the collective physical force of sovereignty in one's behalf.

But this share of collective power would be meaningless if the officials did not recognize an equivalent duty. The broadest meaning of this duty of officials is Responsibility. But this term is too broad. It leaves to the official himself the decision, according to the accidents of his sense of honor or duty, his indifference, favoritism, or even caprice. There is needed a higher authority, having superior political power, to compel the official to act. This higher power is the Supreme Court. The term fitted by economic and legal usage to indicate what this higher authority will be expected to do to the official, if he does not act, is Liability.

Hence, the correlative and equivalent of Power is Liability. The citizens' power to require the official to act is no greater and no less than the liability of the official to be compelled to act by the Supreme Court.

It follows, therefore, that the correlative of Disability is Immunity—not the immunity of self, but the immunity of other people against whom the physical force of sovereignty was claimed. He, whose legal disability is total, has, by the same word, no power to call upon the courts to command the physical force of sovereignty to be used against others in his behalf. Their immunity is his disability. He is a non-citizen, a slave, or alien.

The Thirteenth and Fourteenth Amendments to the Constitution of the United States confirm these meanings of words. The Thirteenth Amendment (1865) liberated the slaves but did not make them citizens. The Fourteenth Amendment, three years later, made them "citizens of the United States and of the State wherein they reside." It changed their political disability into political power. It changed the immunity of other people into liability, by imposing on all state officials the liability to be compelled, by the physical force of the Federal government, to use their physical force on behalf of the now-enfranchised citizens.

But since the Fourteenth Amendment also required "equal protection of the laws" it follows that all citizens, in this relation to officials, have, under similar circumstances, the same relations of power, liability, disability, and immunity. From this equality there results reciprocity, which may be indicated by the following formula.

SUPREME COURT

Citizen	*Issue*	*Official*
Power		Liability
Disability	Physical force	Immunity
Immunity		Disability
Liability		Power

The foregoing relates to MacLeod's "rights of action," which we now distinguish from economic rights. A right of action is simply "the right to enforce one's demands in a court of law." It is a "Power," rather than a "right." But economic "rights" are the rights to enforce one's will on others in their economic transactions. Economic rights are, indeed, equivalent to rights of action, for only in so far as the citizen has power to bring an action in court does he have a right that has security of economic value.

Thus the duty to pay a debt is the creditor's right of action. For this reason it has economic value and can be bought and sold. Likewise, when Holden brought suit against the sheriff Hardy, the economic issue was whether the sheriff had constitutional power to enforce an eight-hour law upon the mine owners of Utah. The Supreme Court decided against Holden and in favor of the sheriff. Translated into terms of the foregoing formula, the court decided that Holden, the employer, was under a disability in that particular exercise of his will, and the sheriff enjoyed therefore immunity from damages or imprisonment if he should enter upon Holden's property and enforce the law. But, reciprocally, the court decided that the sheriff possessed the constitutional *power* and therefore Holden was under the correlative *liability* of the sheriff's forcible entrance on his premises if he violated the eight-hour law. The economic consequences were that Holden's disability was equivalent to "no-right" to require more than eight hours' labor. Economically, we name this an Exposure. The decision also meant that the correlative immunity of Holden's employees from action by the sheriff in evicting them from the premises was equivalent to "no-duty" to work more than eight hours; this no-duty is, economically, their liberty. Thus Holden's disability was the sheriff's immunity, and this, economically, was Holden's exposure to the liberty of his employees.

Had the court's decision been the reverse, then Holden's *power* to call on the Supreme Court would have been the sheriff's liability to damages due to Holden, or imprisonment for contempt of court, if he trespassed on Holden's property. The economic consequences in this case would have been that Holden had the right, of his own free will, to require his laborers to work more than eight hours, and they, correlatively, would have been under the legal duty to obey the will of Holden if they entered and worked upon his premises.

Other applications of the foregoing analysis might be made, and can be made in any of the court decisions on constitutional law. The significance of the analysis is discovered when we observe that legal rights and liberties play a part in economic transactions only to the extent that the citizen can get a hearing in court and a decision ordering executive officials to enforce the court's opinion.[66] The hearing and decision are merely listening to pleadings and arguments and giving a meaning to words; and it is by the changing meanings of words that rights, liberties, duties, and exposures are changed in the changing economic conditions. For the court proceeds, in these disputes between citizens and officials, as it had done in disputes between citizen and citizen, by the judicial process of weighing practices, customs, precedents, statutes, and constitutions in the light of changing conditions and conflicting habitual assumptions. This process has required changing definitions of all the words of the Fifth and Fourteenth Amendments to fit the economic and ethical changes of the past sixty years. The process of change

[66] The foregoing meanings of words would doubtless be disputed by lawyers as not coming within the technical meanings current with the profession. But when lawyers attempt to organize their terminology into a consistent logical system, they differ so greatly among themselves that the economist may be permitted to dissect the meanings and organize them, provided he does so by showing, not abstractions, but what the courts *do*, and thereby fitting the terms to the economic consequences. For the principal differences among lawyers, see the publications by Hohfeld, Cook, and Kocourek, referred to in Commons, *Legal Foundations of Capitalism*, 91 ff. Kocourek has organized his terminology in his *Jural Relations* (1927). In their discussions only private law furnishes the subject matter. We are dealing with Constitutional law, wherein the officials of government are placed on an equality with private citizens under the judicial sovereignty of the Supreme Court.

is still going on. Further changes cannot be predicted, but the more important in the past, for the science of economics, have been the changes in meaning of the words: person, liberty, property, due process, and equal protection.

For the meanings of all these terms arise out of the practices, customs, and habitual assumptions of the people and judges; and the changes that occur in these practices, customs, and assumptions bring with them changes in the meanings of the words. Then, when conflicts arise between citizens and officials, the court itself must change the meanings of the terms as found in precedents, statutes, and constitutions in order to arrive at their application to the new disputes arising out of the change in conditions and assumptions. The court does so, not by trying to formulate academic or scientific definitions that shall be good for all time, but by the experimental process of "exclusion and inclusion," which is the universal process of the human mind by which language itself changes. By "exclusion" a former meaning of these terms is deemed not to be applicable to the present dispute. By "inclusion" the issue in the present dispute is brought within a former meaning which had not hitherto been deemed to include it. Thus constitutions, statutes, and even precedents change in process of time through the gradual but universal process of human speech which excludes old meanings and includes new meanings in order to fit the language to the changing practices and customs which require language to reach agreements.

The process goes on quietly in the pleadings, briefs, arguments, and opinions of lawyers and judges, and it is not until several years have passed that the change can be formulated in a "leading case." [67] For the United States Supreme Court has in its hands the exercise of the two powers of sovereignty that create, revise, or enlarge the rights, duties, liberties, privileges, and immunities of persons and associations of persons. These are, in popular language, the mandatory and injunctive powers, or the mandamus and the injunction. The mandatory power is the power to command what individuals, associations of individuals, and officials of government *must* do. The injunctive power is the power to command what they *must not* do. They *must* pay their debts. Courts and sheriffs *must* enforce the payment of debts. They *must not* interfere with other persons. It is these commands that constitute the rights, liberties, privileges, and immunities of persons and associations. They extend, by the Constitution, to legislatures and executives, as well as

---

[67] An instance is the case of Mitchell v. Reynolds (1711) which rationalized the cases of 300 years preceding into the subsequent law of fair competition. See Commons, *Legal Foundations of Capitalism*, 265.

individuals. If the legislature *must not* interfere with a holding company, then the company has immunity in doing as it pleases within the limits of non-interference laid down for the legislature by the court. This process may be seen in the changed meanings of words brought about to fit the changes in economic conditions and habitual assumptions of the past sixty years.

It is evident, however, that the above analysis of powers, liabilities, disabilities, and immunities applies to the working rules of any going concern which sets up a judicial system to decide whether the executives of the concern shall or shall not enforce obedience upon its members who are subordinate to the concern. It applies to voluntary commercial arbitration, to voluntary labor arbitration, to ecclesiastical organizations, to the judicial committees of stock exchanges and produce exchanges, or to any form of collective "voluntary" action which uses the economic or moral sanctions with or without recourse to the physical sanctions of sovereignty. While the ethical relations of members in their dealings with each other in all concerns are expressed by the terms rights, duties, no-rights, and no-duties, and while the corresponding status of the members is expressed by the terms security, conformity, exposure, and liberty, the relations of the superiors to the inferiors are expressed in the terms power, liability, disability, and immunity. The latter terms signify the use of the physical, economic, or moral sanctions of collective action which enforce the approved relationships of security, conformity, liberty, and exposure between individuals in their private transactions.

4. *Analytical and Functional Law and Economics*

In our preceding formula [68] of legal, economic, and volitional correlation we have distinguished legal relations by the terms, right, no-right, no-duty, and duty. These may be designated as the functional relation between law and the corresponding economic relations of security, exposure, liberty, and conformity. Hence, these legal terms are semi-economic and semi-governmental. But if law is entirely separated from economics, and each is analyzed for its own field, then back of the semi-legal relations are the pure relations of sovereignty itself, in its control of individuals. In the American system especially, this comes about because the officials of government are brought, before the courts, into an equality with all citizens who do not have official authority. It is this that makes necessary a different set of terms indicating the relations set up in public or constitutional law.

[68] Above, p. 78, Formula of Economic and Social Relations.

It is this public law that sets up the relations between citizens and officers, that furnishes the physical sanctions without which individuals would not have the private rights and duties previously noted. These relationships are indicated by the terms "privileges and immunities" of citizens, which must not be taken from them without "due process of law," *i.e.*, without judicial decision. They may be correlated by taking, for example, the constitutional relation of the lowest public official who actually uses force, and the citizen upon whom the force may or may not be exercised. This is one type of managerial transaction—the relation between sheriff and citizen. But it may be expressed as a continuation of the formula of rights, duties, etc., in the preceding formula. The same formula would apply to all other officials under jurisdiction of the Supreme Court.

DUE PROCESS OF LAW

CITIZEN			SHERIFF	
Public Law	Private Law	Transactions	Private Law	Public Law
Power	Right	Opportunity	Duty	Liability
Disability	No-right	Competition	No-duty	Immunity
Immunity	No-duty	Bargaining	No-right	Disability
Liability	Duty	power	Right	Power

The two relations here distinguished may be named Force and Scarcity. The term "transaction" indicates, as we have already shown, the outgrowth of the relations of relative scarcity between individuals. The terms right, duty, with their opposites and reciprocals, indicate the intermediate relations between force and scarcity. But the terms privilege and immunity, as previously said, are two terms used in the Constitution, which, if drawn out to include the official and the citizen, would be equivalent to Power (privilege), Disability, Immunity, and Liability. It is the latter set of terms that, although differently used by jurists, we find are logically the correlative and reciprocal terms applicable to the sovereignty of the Supreme Court over all officials and citizens.

From these terms is worked out analytically the whole system of due process of law; while functionally they are the rights, duties, no-rights, and no-duties which impinge on the economic relations between individuals in their transactions. We may say that these constitutional terms, entirely separated from economics, apply to the purely analytic science of Force, and that (though the analytic lawyers speak of the rights and duties of sheriffs, as though they were private citizens and are subject to the court like private citizens) the sheriff has, as an individual, two sets of relations: the ordinary relation of a private citizen to other citizens, and the extraordinary relation of sovereign to a citizen, where there is no bargain whatever, but only the managerial relation of superior to inferior. It is this purely managerial relation which we express by the terms power, liability, immunity, and disability. In this case of sovereignty they are the managerial transactions that are the sanctions of the organized Force of the community.

(1) *Force.*—We have designated rights, duties, etc., as the present expectation of future control of materials and other natural forces for the production, delivery, and consumption of wealth. But a right is also equivalent to the auxiliary verb "can," in the sense that the individual can call upon the state to enforce his right. It is this word "can" that means he has the power to call, by "process of law," upon the sheriff to execute his will upon the opposite party burdened by the duty.

Hence the terms "power" and "liability" also are in the future, and the right which the citizen claims will, in the future, be of no effect unless he has the "power" to get the sheriff to exercise *his* sovereign power of force.

Neither will the opposite party be, in reality, subject to a duty unless the sheriff can be induced to perform *his duty,* which, however, we name his *liability* if he does not compel the citizen to perform his duty. The other opposite and reciprocal relation can be worked out analytically by the chart. The one who claims a right may find that he has *no-right,* and the legal reason is that he has no power to call upon the sovereign force—in other words, his relation to the sheriff is "disability," and the opposite party—who, correlatively, has no duty in the particular issue—enjoys "immunity" from the physical force of the sheriff. And so on for the reciprocal relations between sheriff and citizen. The sheriff enjoys immunity when he refuses to use force, if the citizen has no duty.[69]

The organization of government from which the sheriff derives these powers, liabilities, immunities, and disabilities, moving downwards from the Supreme Court through lower courts, are summarized in the one term "due process of law." The science which investigates this organization and its powers, disabilities, etc., applying to individual officers is analytic jurisprudence. It is the social

---

[69] See title "Sheriff" Bouvier's *Law Dictionary* for itemization of these powers, liabilities, immunities, and disabilities. See also Crocker, J. G., *The Duties of Sheriffs, Coroners, and Constables with Practical Forms* (1890).

relation of force of the community, specialized in the hands of a hierarchy of officials. Analytic jurisprudence properly includes military science and political science. It has its historical evolution, from tribal organization to conquest and order; from diplomacy, standing armies, constabulary, police, sheriff, for the maintenance of order and execution of the laws.[70]

This so-called "power" of analytic jurisprudence, which is simply an authorization to set the physical force of sovereignty in motion, goes further than a suit asking for a penalty or compensation, distinguished as Remedial Powers. It also includes authorization of the citizen to issue specific commands or instructions *changing* the legal relations of himself or others, which commands are then enforced in the future if necessary as though they were the general commands of the sovereign himself. These may be named the Substantive Powers of the citizen: When a citizen accepts an offer and thus creates a contract, or when he makes a will or appoints an attorney or agent, he thereby issues instructions to the courts and officers to use in the future, if necessary, the physical force of the community to enforce the contract, to recognize the appointment, to transfer the title, or to execute the will after he is gone. This substantive power of instructing the sheriff what to do eventually, is correlative to the liability of the sheriff so to do; this is the reality that creates rights and duties of citizens. Similar analysis holds for Disability and Immunity. Disability creates economic exposure, immunity creates economic liberty, which together we name free or fair competition.

This relation of law to economics we name functional jurisprudence. It will be seen how impossible it is to separate the functional aspect of jurisprudence from strictly analytic jurisprudence. Sovereignty does not stand alone in its analytic nakedness. It is an organized instrument of physical force which individuals endeavor to use in order to enforce their own wills on others, or to prevent others from using their will on the individuals.[71]

It is sometimes objected that this "functional" view of jurisprudence seems to present sovereignty as all-pervading in its activity, a kind of "big stick" always in use, whereas actually it is not used in by far the majority of transactions. More extensive, it is

[70] Various books on jurisprudence, such as Holland, T. E., on *The Elements of Jurisprudence*; Hohfeld, W. N., *Fundamental Legal Conceptions as Applied in Judicial Reasoning and Other Legal Essays*, ed. by W. W. Cook (1923); Austin, John, *Lectures on Jurisprudence* (1832).

[71] Cf. Heilman, Raymond J., "The Correlation between the Sciences of Law and Economics," *California Law Review*, XX (May, 1932), 379; "Bases of Construction of Systems of Legal Analysis," *Illinois Law Review* (April, 1932).

said, are the economic, ethical, or other social inducements in determining human behavior.

This objection, we consider, misses the point upon which all human inducements operate—the expectations of the future. The all-pervasiveness of force does not signify that the physical force of sovereignty is actually employed in all transactions—that would be either anarchy or slavery. It does signify that force has been brought within certain rules of procedure, and that confidence in these rules permits individuals and groups to go ahead without fear of the sheriff, if they behave themselves according to the rules in their economic transactions.

The test of this all-pervasiveness is simple enough—let the state with its courts and sheriffs and similar officials disappear. Then, of course, all economic, social, and ethical inducements will be different. The all-pervasiveness of sovereignty is simply the human function of futurity, guiding the transactions of the present upon the expectations of the shape which force will take in the future. It is futurity that correlates law and economics, each as parts of the whole economic society.

(2) **Scarcity.**—Analytic economics has to do solely with the function of scarcity, just as analytic jurisprudence has to do solely with the function of force. Its highest isolation has been that of the so-called "economic man," which is an abstraction of scarcity, just as the jurisprudential man is an abstraction of force. Each is abstracted, not only from the other, but from all functional relations to the other.

The analytic economists of the classical school (Smith, Ricardo) took scarcity for granted, and it was the hedonic school (especially the Austrian school) and the "neo-classical" school, especially Marshall, who analyzed and perfected its formula. They extracted, specialized, isolated, and organized the scarcity relation of wants and of quantities wanted by equals, leading up to the equilibrium of a market, just as the analytic jurists did for the force relation of superior and inferior, leading up to a modern court of law. While the analytic economists eliminated all "friction," in order to develop a "pure science" of economics—on the assumption that all individuals were perfectly free, infinitely intelligent, and absolutely equal—the juristic analysis assumed that there were sovereigns superior to inferiors.

It is therefore evident that a functional relationship must be worked out between law and economics, wherein neither of the two is merely analytic in its own fields of force and scarcity but wherein the two are combined functionally with each other. This can only

be done when the factor of time and especially futurity and expectation are introduced into the relationship. This factor always implies
the expected consequences which will follow from present transactions, whereas the analytic method has no time nor futurity—it
is pure static relation, without activity and expectation. Futurity
becomes the ever-expected power, liability, immunity, and disability
which the individual may take for granted if the community exercises force under orderly working rules. Scarcity becomes the
present opportunity, competition, and bargaining power in which the
abilities of the individuals are exercised. The terms right, no-right,
duty, and no-duty are the functional intervening relationships between the exercise of the will by the citizen in the present towards
an expected economic production or consumption, and the expected
sovereign powers that will or will not give effect to the expectations.

V. HABITUAL ASSUMPTIONS

For these reasons it is more important to know who the men are
on the Supreme Court bench than to know what the law is. The
Constitution is not what it says it is—it is what the Court says it
is. All economic investigations are investigations of people in their
economic activities. In order to understand *why* they act so and
so, it is necessary to discover the assumptions which they take for
granted as so familiar that they are not formulated in words. It is
these assumptions that we consider to be equivalent to the meanings
of many words in the history of ethical and economic thought, such
as beliefs, divine rights, natural rights, the natural order. These
meanings are fixed beforehand not in nature but in the customs and
habits of participants in transactions.

Each individual occupies a superior or inferior position in a concern, either temporarily or continuously. If he has had experience
with many concerns or with only one concern, he has acquired ways
of looking at things when making his decisions, choosing his alternatives, and dealing with others in his transactions. These ways of
looking at things we name his habitual assumptions; his "mind"
thus equipped we name, from Jordan, the "institutionalized mind." [72]

When a new worker goes into a factory or on a farm, or when a
beginner starts in a profession or a business, everything may be
novel and unexpected because not previously met in his experience.
Gradually he learns the ways of doing things that are expected from
him. They become familiar. He forgets that they were novel when

[72] Jordan, E., *Forms of Individuality* (1927), 172, a work of unusual insight. See criticism by John R. Commons, *Amer. Bar Assn. Jour.*, XIV (1928), 561. On the social purpose of custom in primitive societies see Brown, A. R., *The Andaman Islanders* (1926).

he began. He is unable even to explain them to outsiders. They
have become routine, taken for granted. His mind is no longer
called upon to think about them. In the extreme case of modern
machinery, where he performs but one or a few operations, inter-
views with such workers reveal that they usually do not think of
their work as monotonous. Their physical and mental framework
has become automatic, and their minds run off happily to a world
of memory, imagination, day-dreaming, or what not.

We speak of such minds as institutionalized. But all minds are
institutionalized by whatever habitual assumptions they have
acquired and they take for granted, so that they pay no attention to
them except when some limiting factor emerges and goes contrary
to what they were habitually expecting.

Hence, not only the physical framework of the body, but also the
spiritual framework of the mind, becomes institutionally habituated
to the dominant ways of doing things in the concern where the
worker gets his living. If it were not so, as is well known, the mind
could not have a free field for dealing with what is unexpected. In
general, the habitual assumptions are fitted to the complementary
factors, or routine transactions, of his environment, while the intellectual activity is concerning itself with the limiting factors or
strategic transactions. If the factors are continually changing, then
the intellect must be lively to control the strategic ones; but if they
run along as usual, then habitual assumptions are enough to take
care of the complementary and routine factors.

But this cannot be depended on if habits do not conform to custom. For custom is not merely collective action in control of individual action—it is collective opinion in control of individual
opinion. The individual opinions are the habitual assumptions, but
the collective opinions are the assumptions to which individual habit
must conform if individuals are to work together. Too much individuality of an unaccustomed kind is not wanted.

Yet opinion and action cannot be separated in scientific investigations, for action is opinion-in-action, and science measures the
action while inferring the opinion. Habitual and customary assumptions are read into habitual and customary acts. Here the process
of investigation is similar to psychoanalysis, but, instead of an individualistic science which investigates nerves or dreams as an explanation of individual behavior, social science investigates habitual
and cutomary assumptions as an explanation of transactions.

Habitual and customary assumptions may be classified as technological, proprietary, and ethical assumptions. The technological
assumptions relate to the production of use-values and they change

with changes in civilization, both as to the kinds and qualities and the customary means and instruments. He whose opinions do not fit the current opinions of what is useful, either as to the output or the methods and materials for producing output, cannot prosper or even survive. So it is with the proprietary assumptions that focus on the acquisition of profit, interest, rent, or wages. He whose assumptions do not conform to those customary with others cannot participate in bargains, and, when bargaining customs change, his assumptions must change. The ethical assumptions arise from the current customary procedure in deciding conflicts of interest. He whose opinions lead him to act in ways that do not fit these precedents finds himself disciplined.

Out of these ethical assumptions the ideas of right, wrong, duty, liberty arise. They involve, as do the other assumptions, a purpose and an instrument for accomplishing the purpose. Here we notice again the double meaning of "right," distinguishable as the ethical assumption and the transactional reality. The ethical assumption is usually described as the "adjective" meaning of right whose opposite is "wrong." But the transactional meaning, known usually as its "substantive" meaning, is the correlative of duty.[73] The transactional meaning may be right or wrong, according to what are the ethical assumptions, but it is nevertheless the meaning on which all business is conducted and on which disputes are decided.

To these technological, bargaining, and ethical assumptions, in so far as they are habitual and customary, Karl Marx gave the name "class consciousness" and Veblen gave the name "instinct." They are, indeed, characteristic of the differences in habits and customs among different classes. Marx had special propaganda reasons for limiting his term to two classes, but it may be subdivided into profit consciousness, job consciousness, wage consciousness, rent consciousness, professional consciousness, according to the similarity of interests of which the individuals are conscious. We choose to name it, however, habitual assumptions. The foundation is habit and custom arising from similarity of interests and similarity of transactions engaged in.

Supreme courts, like individual human beings, are dominated by these habitual assumptions arising from the prevailing customs of the time and place. Their opinions change by changes in judges, or by new cases which present old assumptions in a new light, or by changes in economic or political conditions, or even by revolutions. In the year 1771, the highest court in England, on the assumption that *liberty* could be read into the British constitution, set free a

[73] Blackstone, above, p. 218, confused the two and occasioned the attack by Bentham.

Negro who was claimed to be the slave of a lawful owner in Jamaica but who was temporarily held in England for transshipment. The court said,

> "The state of slavery is of such a nature, that it is incapable of being introduced on any reasons, moral or political, but only by positive law, which preserves its force long after the reasons, occasion, and time itself from whence it was created, is erased from memory. . . . Whatever inconveniences, therefore, may follow from the decision, I cannot say this case is allowed or approved by the law of England; and therefore the black must be discharged." [74]

In 1856, the Supreme Court of the United States, by a close majority and by reading into the Constitution the assumption of *slavery*, ordered a Negro, who had been temporarily in a free state, to be returned to slavery in the hands of an owner who claimed ownership under the laws of a slave state. The court said:

> "It is difficult at this day to realize the state of public opinion in relation to that unfortunate race, which prevailed in the civilized and enlightened portions of the world at the time of the declaration of independence and when the constitution of the United States was framed and adopted . . . in no nation was this opinion more firmly fixed or more uniformly acted upon than by the English government and the English people. . . . The opinion thus entertained and acted upon in England was naturally impressed upon the colonies they founded on this side of the Atlantic." [75]

The later emancipation of the slaves by executive sovereignty confiscated some four billion dollars of property-value. The idea of "natural" rights in 1856 became "unnatural" by the proclamation of 1863 and by the sovereignty of the Northern States expressed in the Thirteenth and Fourteenth Amendments in 1865 and 1868.

Thus customs change, and with them the habitual assumptions of judicial sovereignty. We have distinguished the inducements, which lead individuals to act, as individual and collective. We name the inducements by individuals to individuals simply inducements. We name the inducements by collective action to individual action, Sanctions.[76] Inducements are the individual persuasions, coercions, commands, which carry transactions through to their consequences. Sanctions are the collective inducements that require

---

[74] The case of James Sommersett, a negro, 20 Howell's State Trials, 1–82 (1771–72).

[75] Dred Scott, Plaintiff in Error, *v.* John F. A. Sandford, 19 How. 393, l. c. 407, 408 (1856). The Court had not noticed the Sommersett decision of 1771.

[76] Above, p. 218, Bentham.

individuals to conform their behavior to that of others. Each is founded on similar habitual assumptions. But the latter is the meaning of an Institution. An institution is collective action inducing individual action. While there is a great variety of institutions and sanctions, and these are continually changing in the history of civilization, the general principle common to all of them is custom and the derived habitual assumptions.

Custom sets up standards of two kinds, Standards of Measurement and Standards of Reasonableness. The standards are, at first, conflicting and uncertain. Eventually the legislature reduces the standards of measurement to precision as legal standards for the guidance of courts—such as the dollar or the bushel. But the standards of reasonableness are, for the most part, built up gradually by the courts in the decision of disputes. They are distinguishable as Standards of Transactions and Standards of Living. The former relate to managerial, bargaining, and rationing transactions in the production, marketing, and distributing of wealth. The latter are Standards of Consumption. The Sanctions are the collective inducements which lead individuals to conform to these standards.

Hence, the principle of Custom is the Similarity of Compulsion that induces individuals to conform to standards. That which is a "law of motion" in the physical sciences, or an instinct in animals, or a habit in individuals, is custom and habitual assumptions in a science whose subject-matter is conflict among the uncertain wills of individuals looking towards the future in their transactions and modes of living. They require standards of measurement and standards of reasonableness. The business man who declines to use the banking system which has grown up in the past, the laborer who refuses to come to work when others come, may be industrious, but he cannot live in industrial society. This is familiar enough and therefore not investigated. But when customs change, or when judges and arbitrators enforce a custom by deciding a dispute, or when laborers or farmers strike in order to modify a custom of business, or when a revolution confiscates slaves or other property of capitalists, or when a statute prohibits a customary mode of living, or when a holding company extends an old custom into new fields—then it is realized that the compulsion of custom has been there all along, but unquestioned and undisturbed.

The reason is Habit. Individuals do not start *de novo*—they start as babies, then continue as infants, then enter occupations, and are learning to fit themselves to custom. If their habits do not fit, then they cannot make a living of their own efforts, but are recipients of charity or punishment, or beneficiaries of the laws of inheritance. If they do fit, then the customs to which they adapt themselves give to them security of expectations.

The principle of custom, as we have seen, was eliminated from economics by Jeremy Bentham in his criticism of Blackstone during the year in which Adam Smith published his *Wealth of Nations*. Henceforth, economic theory was worked out on the three units of the Individual, the Commodity, and the State. On the one side this led to individualism, even to anarchism; on the other side it led to communism and dictatorship. But Custom is more powerful than the individual or even the State.

The word "custom" conveys different meanings to different minds, and therefore requires us to make two distinctions, the one relating to different *degrees* of compulsion on individuals, the other distinguishing the principle from its *justification*. As a principle derived from a variety of facts, custom is similarity of compulsion. It is simply a working rule. As justification or condemnation, it is anything wished to be accomplished or prevented by collective compulsion. When Bentham criticised Blackstone, his idea of Custom was "tradition" or "ancestor wisdom" which he thought the courts perpetuated as an obstacle to the Principle of Universal Happiness which he wished to be made the guide to legislation and judicial action. Henceforth law and economics were separated. Economists went off on the self-interest of individuals in seeking pleasure and avoiding pain, but the courts continued to follow Blackstone by deciding disputes on the ground of custom.

The difference turned on different views of human nature itself. Bentham and the early economists looked on human beings as rational creatures who could calculate the maximum of happiness in units of pleasure and pain, as business men calculate in dollars and cents.[77] But Malthus, in his *Essay on Population,* attacked this view of human nature after it had been taken over by the first great anarchist, William Godwin, and erected by him into a philosophy that proposed to abolish all compulsion on individuals.[78] Men are not rational beings, said Malthus. They are beings of passion and stupidity who do exactly the opposite of what their Reason advises them to do, else there would be no over-population, misery, wars, or sin. Consequently, men could not exist together without compulsion. This is, indeed, the justification of custom as well as

[77] Cf. Mitchell, W. C., "Bentham's Felicific Calculus," *Pol. Sci. Quar.*, XXXIII (1918), 161 ff.

[78] Godwin, William, *An Enquiry Concerning Political Justice and Its Influence on General Virtue and Happiness* (1793); above, p. 245.

sovereignty against anarchism. The human will is unreliable and must be coerced by custom or government.

At the opposite extreme from anarchism are those who, from Filmer to the present day, deify custom as the Voice of God.[79] On examination it will usually be found that what they mean is only a distinction between good customs and bad customs. A good custom is the Voice of God—a bad custom is the voice of the devil These are personifications of custom.

Somewhat similar is the use of such words as "nature" or "natural," when what is meant is customary. The "natural rights of man" are said to be the rights to life, liberty, happiness, prope y reputation, etc. But these are customs. Customs change, but if they change slowly, then the infancy of individuals is long enough to acquire habits and wishes fitted to the customs. Then they appear to be natural, unchangeable, inalienable, though they are artificial, collective, transitory, forfeitable.

More historical than these personifications and metaphors, is the theory that modern industrial society has passed from the Age of Custom and Status into the Age of Contract and Competition.[80] In archaic society, it is said, people remain in the status, or social class, to which they are born, but in modern Western civilization they voluntarily fix and terminate their positions in society by competitive contracts of buying and selling, hiring and firing, rent'ng, borrowing, etc.

But if the indication of a custom is its compulsion on individuals, requiring conformity, then contract, during the past three hundred years, is also a new custom. He who refuses to bind himself by contracts, as others do, cannot enter into, nor continue in, business or employment. Contracts have become customary and therefore compulsory.

What has happened, economically, is a change of custom from unreleasable debts to releasable debts. For, if custom is collective compulsion, it operates by imposing duties on individuals. Economic duties are debts, payable in services, or commodities, or purchasing power. And no individual is free to refuse to become a debtor if he obtains a living by obtaining control over the services, commodities, or purchasing power that previously belonged to others. In modern industrial society nobody obtains a living in any other way. The most powerful of sanctions, Scarcity, compels him to conform to the customs of the time and place which rate him as

---

[79] Carter, John C., *Law, Its Origin, Growth, and Function* (1907).

[80] Maine, Sir Henry, *Ancient Law, Its Connection with the Early Society and Its Relation to Modern Ideas* (1st American ed. from 2d London ed., 1870).

a debtor to those from whom he has acquired whatever, for him, was scarce.

When a judge or arbitrator looks for a custom as a guide to his decision, what he does is to give an added sanction to the enforcement of the custom. He may not even look to see if his habitual assumptions fit the custom. In commercial or labor arbitration the added sanction is the organized concerted action of those who have created the position of arbitrator and who expect to enforce the arbitrator's decision by the concerted economic power of the concern.

The same is true of a court of law. If the court, in deciding a dispute, looks for its standards to the customs of the neighborhood or of the class of people concerned, or takes "judicial notice" without formal testimony, or accepts the standards habitually, the court gives to that custom the additional sanction of physical force requiring that the transaction conform to the custom.

But the arbitrator or court goes further in seeking a guide to his decision in a dispute. He looks back to his own previous decisions, or to the decisions of other arbitrators or courts in similar cases, and then endeavors to make his present decision consistent with the preceding decision. This is Precedent. If there is no precedent, or if the precedents are conflicting, or if they are judged to be obsolete, then the arbitrator or court looks again for a custom, or for a principle which he derives from custom, to which, by the process of exclusion and inclusion, he may make his decision conform.

If he does not look to precedent or custom, then his alternative is to look to a statute, by-law, or constitution which, by deliberative action of those in superior authority, had modified the customs or precedents. But even so, these statutory laws are abstract and general, and, before they can be enforced in a particular dispute, they must be construed and interpreted as applicable to the dispute. This interpretation itself therefore goes back to custom or precedent, or habitual assumption, for guidance in applying the statute to the particular case. Hence even a statute, constitution, or by-law goes through the scrutiny of custom, precedent, exclusion, and inclusion, in the judicial process of deciding disputes. It may even be that custom or precedent, or habitual assumption, in this process nullifies or modifies statute law and constitutional law. When this occurs completely the law is a "dead letter." When it occurs incompletely the law is "construed."

Custom, precedent, statute, and habitual assumptions are, then, the process by which are formulated what may in general be named "working rules." Statutes differ all the way from edicts to administrative orders, legislative enactments, written constitutions, by-laws, and the trade agreements of collective bargaining, which we have seen in preceding pages. Precedents differ all the way from judicial to executive, administrative, legislative, and constitutional precedents. Customs differ all the way from feudal, agricultural, business, and industrial to the family and to religious worship. Precedent and statute are distinguishing marks of going concerns, but custom and habitual assumptions are the underlying principle of all human relations. Each may even be named a "law," not in the sense of a "law of nature," but in the sense of a law of human nature. For this reason we name them "working rules," indicating also thereby their temporary and changing character conforming to the evolution of economic, political, and ethical conditions.

They are a law of human nature in that they go to a fundamental and ultimate principle without which man cannot live in society—the principle of Security of Expectations. It is not justice, nor even happiness, that is fundamental—it is security, even the security of injustice and poverty. For insecurity is not so much the accidents resulting from the unintentional forces of nature as it is the insecurity of intentions, negligence, and caprice on the part of those having superior physical or bargaining power. The former insecurity can be, and has been, largely avoided by the technological improvements that bring nature's forces under control, but the latter insecurity can be avoided only by stabilization of the wills of those having authority. The extreme case of arbitrary will is slavery. In so far as new customs, precedents, and statutes restrain the wills and assumptions of slave-owners, in so far does liberty encroach on slavery.

The doctrine of precedent goes further. It is a doctrine of logical consistency and equality of treatment. If the arbitrator or court decides a present dispute differently from the decision in similar previous disputes, he is logically inconsistent, and he is treating one person differently from his treatment of other persons under similar circumstances. This is discrimination, or unequal opportunity. Hence, the doctrine of precedent is the threefold doctrine of security, liberty, and equality—Security, in that it leads to the expectation that disputes will be decided in the future as they have been decided in the past; Liberty, in that subordinate individuals will not be subject to the capricious will of superiors; Equality, in that all individuals of the same class will be treated equally under similar circumstances.

Thus the doctrine of precedent, as a restraint upon the arbitrary will of those in authority, goes to the three most fundamental wishes of mankind: security, liberty, and equality. It is universal for all mankind in all social relations. Even the child appeals to precedent when he complains that his parent treats his other children differently from himself, or treated himself differently yesterday and today. The laborer considers himself victimized when the foreman's friends receive favors which he does not receive. Civil service laws attempt to open up equal opportunity in the public service for all citizens, instead of leaving them to the friends of politicians. The business man appeals to precedent when he charges the railroad company with favoring his competitors by lower rates than those he is required to pay. The legal doctrine that the court is bound by precedent is merely a special case of the universal moral principle that everybody should be bound to treat others like himself and like each other under similar circumstances. Otherwise he is capricious, arbitrary, inconsistent. This would not be an evil if everybody were exactly equal in all respects, and if there were unlimited alternatives. The doctrine of precedent is the doctrine of treating equally those who are unequal. It is fundamental in all economic transactions, for it is the basis of security, liberty, and equality.

But the enforcement need not be the authoritative enforcement by the constituted authorities of a concern. It may be enforcement by competition. The modern custom of purchasing commodities and paying debts by means of checks on solvent banks is compulsory on individuals, for whoever persistently refuses to accept and issue such checks, although they are not legal tender, cannot continue in business or even get into business. Checking accounts are a custom, and custom is not contradictory to competition Competition is a means of enforcing custom. Those who enforce the custom are all individuals acting alike, but those who enforce precedents are the constituted authorities and agents of the concern, selected for the purpose. Hence, modern economic society has not passed from custom to contract—it has passed from primitive customs to business customs.

The foregoing will show how impossible it is to separate practices, customs, precedents, statutes, and habitual assumptions in the historical development of any going concern, whether the state, the economic, or the moral concern. They begin as optional practices with individuals, then become customs when individuals are compelled by customers and competitors to conform; then become precedents when disputes are decided; then statutes when formally declared by executive or legislative authority; then custom again when statutes are construed in particular disputes; and all along there are the changing, yet habitual assumptions when applied to particular transactions and disputes. They move along together. New practices arise out of existing customs, precedents, and statutes, while statutes themselves are effective only through the medium of practices, customs, precedents, and assumptions. In general it is precedents that are described as the "unwritten law," while statutes, by-laws, corporation charters are the "written" law. But the written law is only words. The "unwritten" law is written in the decisions of disputes which construe the written law in particular cases. It is practices, customs, and precedents—in short, this unwritten law —that is the living law. This is the common-law method of making law.

Certain technical, historical distinctions are made in Anglo-American jurisprudence between the common law, the law merchant, admiralty law, and equity. But these, from the social-economic standpoint, are special cases of customs, precedents, and assumptions. The technical "common law" originated from the customs of agriculture during the period of feudalism; the "law merchant" was taken over from the customs of merchants and thus enforced by the courts. So it is with the other kinds of law. All of them are alike in that they have grown up piecemeal from decisions of disputes through the process of looking to customs and precedents guided by habitual assumptions. The same is true of the working rules of all economic concerns. They also are both a mixture and a sequence of practices, customs, precedents, statutes (by-laws), and assumptions.

Hence, when we speak of the common law we mean, not the technical common law of the legal profession, but the Common Law Method of Making Law by Deciding Disputes. The method is not confined to courts of law. It is the method of commercial arbitration and labor arbitration, where the sanctions are not those of sovereignty. It is the method of making law in the family, the church, the labor union, the business concern. It is the method of precedent, choice of customs, unwritten law, and assumptions. Custom becomes common law by the common-law method of deciding disputes, thereby sanctioning what are deemed habitually to be good customs in the act of condemning or not enforcing what are deemed to be bad customs or obsolete customs. Hence, common law is the unwritten law of custom—unwritten because it is found in precedents and habitual assumptions.

Consequently, the alleged change from custom to contract is a change in the direction towards which the compulsion of custom is

708   INSTITUTIONAL ECONOMICS

exercised. The change may be momentous, but it is not because
custom disappears. Custom reappears as habitual assumptions under different forms, names, directions, and degrees of compulsion.

The degrees of compulsion on individuals are not clearly marked
off except in extreme cases, and they grade one into another, but
they may be distinguished on three principles of classification:
the kind of sanction, the precision and publicity of the standards,
and the degree of organization for enforcing the sanction.

(1) The *kinds of sanctions* are threefold: moral, economic,
physical. They are usually inseparable, but at the extremes they
may be distinguished, and, in the history of custom they become
actually differentiated and specialized. The moral sanction is the
compulsion of similarity of opinion. Its specialization is the Church
in those countries where the church has been separated from the
state and from its private property as used for business purposes.
Formerly the church was a great land owner or financier, with economic power, or was itself the state with physical power. Deprived
of these economic and physical sanctions the church rests only on
the compulsion of opinion, with its trials for heresy. Godwin's
philosophy of anarchism would reduce all business and government
to the status of churches, with only the moral sanctions in control.
The compulsion of custom then would be only the compulsion of
good and bad opinion, and government itself would be only public
opinion.

At the opposite of anarchism, and, indeed, not inconsistent with
it, are the physical sanctions of violence, whose specialization we
name the State and whose sanctions we name Sovereignty. For
collective violence, like collective opinion, is a custom. The evolution of the modern state out of feudalism is the process of ex-
tracting the inducements of violence from private transactions and
placing a monopoly of their use in the hands of a hierarchy of
officials, from constable and justice of the peace to president and
supreme court, differentiated from other persons for the purpose of
using and regulating violence.

Along with opinion and physical force are the economic sanctions
specialized in their control by corporations, trade associations, trade
unions, which are changing customs of employing the sanctions of
scarcity in its many forms of gain or loss, for the purpose of regulating economic transactions.

The three kinds of moral, economic, and physical sanctions are
inseparable, and it is difficult, except in extreme cases, to know
which is more powerful in sanctioning the individual to act or
not act.

(2) The precision and publicity of *standards of transactions* range from the least precise and well known and therefore least compulsory, which we name Practices, to a more precise and well known, which may be named Usages, to the most precise and well known and therefore most compulsory, which may be named Precedent. The *practices* of any individual, or firm or association may be variable and indifferent to others because not sufficiently imitated to induce general imitation, as when one person practices economy and another practices extravagance. But a *usage* becomes sufficiently imitated, so that, like language or bank checks, its use is practically compulsory on all who participate in transactions. A *precedent* has the peculiar binding force that it is a standard used in the decision of disputes and regulation of conduct by a higher authority having power of control. It may be derived from practices and usages but it rises authoritatively above them in that it makes them precise, public, and enforced by organized action.

It is these Practices, Usages, Precedents, and the habitual assumptions derived from them that we define as Custom. Custom is variable in the degree of compulsion which collective action exercises over individual action, from the least compulsory Practices to the more compulsory Usages, and the most compulsory Precedents. And it is practices, usages, precedents, and assumptions together that make up the common-law method of making law by deciding conflicts of interest.

(3) But there is another custom, the Custom of Association. This also is variable in its control over individual action by working rules, according to the *degree of organization* from loose to centralized. It is this custom of association and rule-making that we name Going Concerns, in their exercise of moral, economic, or physical sanctions. Formerly the corporation was looked upon as a creation of sovereignty, existing only in contemplation of law.[81] But charters of incorporation now are known to be only the more precise and formal addition of the physical sanctions of sovereignty to the universal custom of association. What were stigmatized as conspiracies become corporations or other lawful associations in manifold variety when the custom of association is sanctioned by officials who guide the use of physical force.

It is in these three directions of variability that Custom exercises greater or less control over individuals. It varies with the kind of sanctions, whether moral, economic, or physical; with the degree of precision and publicity, as practices, usages, and precedents; and

[81] The Trustees of Dartmouth College *v.* Woodward, 4 Wheaton 518, 4 Law Ed. 629 (1819).

with the degree of organization, from loose to centralized, in its power to decide disputes and enforce conformity.

What happens among all these variabilities is a choice of customs by those having power to choose and enforce; and the evolution of customs is like that artificial selection which, in the course of centuries, changes the wolf into the dog, or domesticates the cow. A new custom arises from older customs by way of new conflicts and disputes, and it is the totality of changing customs that is civilization.

Not until practices or usages are converted into precedents by the decision of disputes, do they become precise enough to be analyzed logically with regard to the direction of control over individuals. We have proposed a formula for this analysis for bargaining transactions in our chapter on Method. A similar formula applies to Managerial and Rationing Transactions.

There are, in the three types of transactions, the three relations of opposition, correlation, and mutuality. A dispute occurs and collective compulsion will decide. It can do so only by defining the duty. Having defined the duty, the right is the same as the duty but beneficial to an opposite person. On the one person the duty, economically, is the required conformity; this, as regards the subject-matter in dispute, is, for the opposite party, his security of expectations, the legal equivalent of which is a Right. It is this identity of relationship, but opposition of interests, to which the technical term Correlation is applied in jurisprudence. Right and duty are correlative and equal but the parties are opposing. A credit is a debit, a sale is a purchase, an asset is a liability, an income is an outgo, a payment is a receipt, a right is a duty, and a duty is a right. But they attach to opposite persons, and this attachment is their correlation.

The defining of a duty is defining the limits of the duty. If it is unlimited, then the right is unlimited, and custom compels the slave to conform to the unlimited will of the master. But if the duty is limited, even slightly, there is simply "no duty" beyond that point, and, of course, no correlative right. This, economically, is liberty for the one and exposure for the other to the gain or loss resulting from that liberty. To the extent that duty and right are limited, to that extent are liberty and exposure enlarged, until, in the philosophy of Anarchism, the only supposed relation between individuals is liberty and exposure.

But this is modified by the principle of mutual dependence. Exposure may be beneficial or onerous, like exposure to sunlight. The term Transaction itself implies mutuality. Each party does something for the other. Neither may be fully satisfied. Usually neither is. Yet a transaction is a "meeting of wills," and mutuality is not the same as equality or justice. It is reciprocity, indeed, because it is a degree of dependence on each other. But it may be very unequal or unjust if the parties are unequal, whether they be borrower and lender, buyer and seller, landlord and tenant, employer and employee. Who shall decide? Custom decides, by its practices, usages, precedents, and assumptions. It is the sanctions of custom that determine the degree of mutuality, equality, reciprocity, justice, or injustice.

Thus custom is a stabilizer of competition. The theory of perfect competition, as worked out during two centuries of economic thinking, was based on assumptions of perfect liberty, equality, and knowledge on the part of individuals. On these assumptions, each individual knows what are his own best interests. He is equal to others in ability, property, and freedom from compulsion. He is responsible only for his own acts, and he must take the consequences of his acts. These assumptions are proper enough and are the method of all science, which eliminates disturbing factors by assuming that they are constant, and then introduces changes only in the single factor investigated.

But these assumptions are not only a matter of pure theory—they are a matter of actual practice and experiment. A stock exchange, a produce exchange, a board of trade, or a similar organized market, attempts to do exactly that which economists assumed when they eliminated disturbing factors and "friction." These exchanges attempt to establish a market where there shall be as nearly perfect competition as possible. Their rules are directed towards establishing liberty, equality, and mutuality through publicity and precision. What they do is to eliminate practices and customs that are deemed to obstruct free competition, or deemed to tend towards inequality or concealment.

Each of these markets is a study in itself, but the general principles on which all of them are based may be seen from a case that reached the United States Supreme Court from the Chicago Board of Trade. The facts and opinion of a unanimous court may be summarized from the opinion stated by Justice Brandeis thus: [82]

The Federal Department of Justice had proceeded against the Chicago Board of Trade, endeavoring to set aside a rule of the Board which prohibited its member brokers from making practically secret sales and purchases during the hours when the Board was not in session. The question was, Did this rule come within the

[82] Chicago Board of Trade v. United States, 246 U. S. 231, 1 c. 235-241 (1918)

restraints of trade, all of which were explicitly prohibited by the anti-trust laws? The court decided that the restraint was reasonable and thus overruled the strict language of a statute. From the opinion as stated by Justice Brandeis we may generalize the following inferences:

(1) The common-law method of legislation by the Supreme Court builds up an "unwritten law" by deciding disputes between conflicting interests as they arise, but with reference to precedents and the customs of the same and similar associations. The court recognizes that it is making law for similar conflicts in the future.

(2) The statute (anti-trust law) enacted by Congress does not become a law until it is interpreted by the Court in a particular dispute and until this interpretation becomes a precedent for similar disputes. The statute is a "dead letter." Its life is practices, usages, precedents, and habitual assumptions. The letter of the statute is subordinate to the economic purposes to be accomplished.

(3) The Right of Association is the authority permitted by the Supreme Court to a private association to make rules having the effect of law upon the transactions of its members, enforced, however, by the economic sanctions of gain, loss, and exclusion from membership.

(4) The private purpose of those who make the rules becomes a public purpose when approved by the court. Not good intentions but good consequences are the standards. The rule in question took away from individuals what had been a valuable property right. But neither the individual nor the association decides as to the goodness of the consequences. A superior authority decides.

(5) The Supreme Court decides what is and what is not a public purpose by choosing between existing practices and customs. A justice interested in the immediate dispute does not participate. A local practice becomes common law for the nation because it eliminates what, under the circumstances, are deemed to be bad practices.

(6) The Court thus becomes an authoritative faculty of Political Economy for the United States. It is authoritative, if not authentic, for what its majority says is reasonable *is* reasonable for the time being. What is wanted is not truth but orderly action. The concern must keep agoing. The Court enters beneath the letter of the law and investigates the economic circumstances out of which the conflict of interests arises. Each dispute is a separate case with its own facts, although these facts may be brought within general principles and reconciled with particular precedents discovered in similar cases. The mental weighing of all the facts thus investigated, in view of these principles and precedents, is the process of

deciding what is reasonable under all the circumstances. The economic interests of all parties, immediate or remote, must be valued as a part of the whole public purpose.

(7) Competition is not Nature's "struggle for existence" but is an artificial arrangement supported by the moral, economic, and physical sanctions of collective action. The theory of free competition developed by economists is not a natural tendency towards equilibrium of forces but is an ideal of public purpose adopted by the courts, to be attained by restraints upon the natural struggle for existence. The economic terminology is "raising the level of competition by reasonable restraints of trade."

(8) Each decision of a dispute sets up standards of competitive transactions intended to make more precise the otherwise uncertain practices. The standards, in the Board of Trade case, related to the *time* and *place* at which transactions are permitted; the *class* of transactions and commodities to which applied; the *qualifications* of parties to the transactions; the *publicity* to be afforded.

(9) The purposes to be accomplished are good, as decided by the Court, in that they tend towards (*a*) publicity, or as nearly perfect knowledge of all the facts by all parties as the circumstances will permit; (*b*) equal opportunity, or equal access to markets by preventing monopoly, discrimination, and secret transactions off the market; (*c*) greater efficiency in marketing the product; (*d*) greater benefit to producers and consumers of the commodity; (*e*) more liberty of the right kind by more restraints on liberty of the wrong kind.

This American system of custom, precedent, and assumptions is with difficulty comprehended by European economists and jurists who operate under a system of codes constructed originally by dictators on the model of the perfected Roman law and changeable only by legislatures. It is even understood with difficulty by the British, whose legislature is superior to the judiciary.

Likewise, American economists and jurists can with difficulty understand the European economists and jurists. In America we think concretely according to the common-law method of individual cases and precedents, conformably to our judicial sovereignty; while the Europeans think abstractedly in deductive terms handed down from Justinian, Napoleon, Adam Smith, or Ricardo. If we generalize, as attempted in this book, we discuss only general principles, leaving their application to investigations of the particular cases. In this way has arisen the American common-law method.

With forty-eight states and a federal Congress enacting laws, and with the conflicting fields of the federal and state laws vaguely outlined by the federal Constitution, the United States Supreme Court becomes the final authority which determines uniformity of law throughout the nation. The Court therefore necessarily looks to something superior to all legislatures as its standard of uniformity, and this something may be broadly described as custom, precedent, and habitual assumptions. Even the Constitution itself, the supreme law, is interpreted according to the changing customs of business and industry, with their moral sanctions of collective opinion and their economic sanctions of gain or loss. Custom is converted into a new common law—common for all the states—by the decisions of disputes as they arise. Each decision is a precedent which may be followed or distinguished in what are deemed to be similar or dissimilar cases, and a minority opinion may in time become a majority opinion.[83]

An examination of the writings of continental jurists, who follow what Gény calls the "traditional method" of the French courts, reveals to an American a curious difficulty on their part in getting away from the dominance of codes and acts of the legislature.[84] Those writers seem to be apologetic if they introduce custom, or usage, or Gény's "free decision," or "free scientific research," as a source of law. A precedent seems to have no binding authority, and succeeding cases must come back to the code.

But these variations from statutes and codes give little or no trouble to the Supreme Court of the United States. Statutes are declared void as conflicting with the Constitution of the United States whenever they take property or liberty *without* what the Supreme Court declares to be due process of law. Even if not declared void they are so construed as to fit the Court's changeable meanings of property, liberty, person, and due process in the particular dispute at issue, and succeeding and inferior courts follow these precedents. In some cases dissenting justices have quite accurately named these decisions by the majority as a "nullification" of the statute, or "judicial usurpation," or "veto." In the French code the next decisions apparently do not go back to precedents— they go back to the code itself. French decisions, therefore, are not nullifications of the code.

Then, in America, these meanings themselves are avowedly

[83] A notable investigation of this process is found in Swisher, C. B., *Stephen J. Field, Craftsman of the Law* (1930). Field's habitual assumption on constitutional law in 1872 became, by a change in the meaning of "due process," the unanimous opinion in 1896. See J. R. Commons' review of Swisher's book, *Jour. of Pol. Econ*, XXXIX (Dec. 1931), 828–831.

[84] A summary and elaboration of these pages was made for the Jubilee Publication in honor of Dean François Gény, professor of Civil Law at the University of Nancy. Gény's classic treatment was in his *Methode d'interpretation et sources en droit prive positive* (1899)

changed from time to time by the gradual process of "exclusion and inclusion," so that the Constitution is itself amended in course of time by merely changing the meanings of the economic and juridical terms, property, liberty, person, and due process of law. Since there is no appeal from the Supreme Court, except by the extreme process of constitutional amendment, which requires a three-fourths vote of the states, or by civil war such as that of 1861 which freed the slaves in defiance of the Dred Scott decision, it follows that the court is continually making and remaking the law by the judicial process of deciding disputes. This, for Anglo-Americans, is the common-law method of making law. But in America it reaches a height of authority unknown elsewhere because the Supreme Court is the final authority, superior to legislatures, states, and executives wherever a difference is asserted by the Court itself between its meanings given to words and the meanings given elsewhere.[85]

It will be seen from the foregoing how urgent it is in the United States, more than it is in other countries, to develop fundamental theories of the correlation of economics, jurisprudence, and ethics. The state and federal supreme courts are final authorities on acts of legislatures in all regulations of property, liberty, and persons under the "due process" clause of the Constitution. The issue usually arises in a suit brought by a citizen or concern against the state or federal officials or legislatures before the Supreme Court, asking for a writ prohibiting the enforcement of the law, on the ground that it conflicts with the Federal Constitution and its Bill of Rights. The Supreme Court, then, on the basis of the findings of fact and the conclusions of the lower court, whether a state supreme court or a lower federal court, passes upon the legislative act or the administrative order, as to whether it conflicts with the superior law of the Constitution. Everything turns on the court's assumption of meanings to be given to property, liberty, person, and due process.

By the common-law method of making law, the highest courts are not bound, in fact, to follow precisely any former meanings which they have given to these terms, but they avowedly state that their method is one of "exclusion and inclusion." By this is meant that a meaning given in a former decision may have been too broad or too narrow to fit the issue in the case under considera-

---

[85] An excellent account of the way in which this has come about, and one that parallels Gény's interpretation of the philosophy of Rousseau embodied in the code, which is the same philosophy as the Bill of Rights in the United States Constitution, is the article by J. A. C. Grant (Columbia Law Review, XXXI [1931], 56), on "The Natural Law Background of Due Process." Grant concludes: "Under the guise of the Supremacy of the law, we have established the Supremacy of the judges."

716INSTITUTIONAL ECONOMICS

tion. If too broad, then the precedent from the former case does not apply and is not binding on the court. This is the process of "exclusion." If the former meaning is too narrow, then that precedent can be extended to furnish the rule for the present case, and this extension is binding on the court. This is the process of "inclusion." This, of course, is the fundamental process of analogy, clearly enunciated by Gény, and, as practiced in the common-law method of reporting cases, the courts devote much of their attention in their lengthy opinions to this mental process of inclusion and exclusion. It is by this process of analogy that the meanings of property, liberty, person, and "due process" have been gradually changed.

These opinions are always published as minority opinions along with majority opinions; hence it is possible to see how it is that the habitual assumptions of the individual judges lead them to different conclusions on the same statement of facts. The "personality of the judge" stands out clearly in any comparative study of these majority and minority opinions. Indeed, to expound fully the term "due process of law" is to expound a complete social philosophy.[86]

Only the lower courts are bound to follow the established law, established by majority opinions, although they often propose innovations which become new precedents if the Supreme Court affirms or permits.[87] But the Supreme Court of the United States itself is not, in fact, thus bound. It can and does create new law, and thereby follows out literally Gény's "method of free decision." Eventually it may happen, and often does happen, as in the Slaughter House Cases of 1872,[88] that the minority opinion becomes the majority opinion, as it did in that line of cases, in 1897. This happens by the simple process of changing the meanings of words by exclusion and inclusion.

With this documentary material to work upon, the American economists have given considerable attention to the Supreme Court's divergent and changing theories of Value which grow out of their changing meanings of property and liberty and which rest ultimately on their social philosophies and habitual assumptions. The Ameri-

---

[86] This was done, for example, in a leading case on due process of law, Hurtado v. People of California, 110 U. S. 516 (1884). See Commons, John R., *Legal Foundations of Capitalism*, 333.

[87] An illustration was the change in the meaning of "good-will" proposed by a lower court (Consolidated Gas Co., v. City of New York, 157 Fed. Rep. 849, 1907) and affirmed by the Supreme Court (Wilcox v. Consolidated Gas Co., 212 U. S. 19, 1909), although in doing so the Supreme Court reversed the same lower court which had followed former decisions of the Supreme Court. On these cases see Commons, John R., *Legal Foundations of Capitalism*, 191.

[88] 16 Wall. 36 (1872).

can federal and state supreme courts actually carry out what Gény appears to set up as the ideal of what the French courts *ought* to do. It may be named the Process of Reasoning and Valuing:

(1) "Intuitions" of what is relatively important in promoting justice and general utility. These we name habitual assumptions.

(2) Selection of facts by the process of exclusion and inclusion, which is the process of analogy, guided by these assumptions.

(3) Weighing the facts mentally in accordance with these assumptions of their relative importance.

(4) Classification of the facts in accord with this selection and weighting.

(5) Logical deduction from the habitual assumptions which guided the selection, weighting, and classification.

(6) The whole is guided by Gény's "practical common sense" which, however, is only another name for the habitual assumptions with which we started.

If this is the circular process, as it seems to be, not only of judicial but of all reasoning and valuing by people not judges, then the practical question arises as to Gény's search for something outside the habitual assumptions and deductive reasoning of the courts. His assertion of the need for "scientific investigation" arises from the changes in economic conditions from individualism to collectivism, from individuals to corporations, from older to newer ideas of human nature, which make the older assumptions perhaps inapplicable to the modern "going concerns." But courts are not so constituted, or do not have the agencies for making such extensive investigations as would be required. Hence some of the American legislatures and the Federal Congress have attempted to provide exactly this scientific investigation by the creation of commissions.

An illustrative case is the Wisconsin State Industrial Commission. The Commission has jurisdiction over most of the transactions of employers and employees. It has not only its staff of expert investigators, but it also has advisory committees of employers, employees, physicians, engineers, architects, economists, numbering some two hundred persons in all. The investigations, findings, and conclusions on health, safety, accident compensation, child labor, hours of labor, and, more recently, on unemployment insurance, are governed by the "due process of law" provisions as interpreted by the courts. Therefore, provision is made for review by the court, but in such review no new testimony is permitted that had not been submitted previously to the commission. If new testimony is offered, the court is required to refer the case back to the commission, giving to the commission opportunity to reconsider and revise its own findings, if the commission so determines. In this way the trial court, with its strict rules of legal evidence, makes no investigations and takes no testimony whatever. It listens only to arguments, and it passes only on the due process of law of the commission's procedure.

The theory back of these commissions is the legal theory of due process of law carried forward into the investigation of facts, to the effect that if all interests to be affected by the law are permitted freely to confer through their recognized spokesmen, then the resulting findings of fact on which they reach agreement will be reasonable, and the orders issued in conformity thereto will be reasonable commands of the state to its citizens, governing their transactions with each other.

In a similar way, following the opinions in Smythe v. Ames, above referred to, public service commissions, the interstate commerce commissions, and various marketing and trade commissions ascertain, by investigation and hearing of all parties, the reasonable values and reasonable practices of the participants in their various transactions. Then these findings, by operation of law, are to be accepted by the courts in disputes arising under the general or special rules proclaimed by the commission.[89]

These American commissions are spreading out so as to cover practically all the fields which Marx might have called "class conflict." But the conflicts are broken up into the conflicts of labor and capital, of buyers and sellers, of farmers and wholesalers, of borrowers and lenders, and different classes of taxpayers. The commissions are a device by which the traditional separation of legislative, executive, and judicial powers, although required by the written constitutions, is nevertheless attempted to be avoided by combining in one body a process which, in law, is neither legislative, executive, nor judicial. Commissions are sometimes described as quasi-judicial, or quasi-legislative bodies, but their function is that of investigation. The law merely gives effect to the commission's conclusions drawn from its findings and weighing of the facts, if the conclusions are found by the court to conform to the due process which requires a hearing of all parties concerned. In short, these commissions are the American discovery, during the past three decades, of a practical method of correlating law, eco-

[89] This procedure, which reduces somewhat the judicial sovereignty of lawyers by excluding the courts from "scientific investigation of the facts," has been called in question before the United States Court in an important case coming up from New York, Helfrick v. Dahlstrom Metallic Door Company, et al., 256 N. Y. 199, 176 N. E. 141 (1931), 284 U. S. 594 (1932). See also Crowell v. Benson, 52 S. Ct 285 (1932).

nomics, and ethics by means of Gény's "scientific investigation of the nature of things."[90]

While these investigations and findings are not "scientific" in the sense of the physical sciences, they are "reasonable" in the sense of the political and economic sciences, because they are based on the three circumstances, not found in physical sciences, of conflict of interests, mutual dependence, and the rules of order deemed necessary to keep industry agoing with due regard to public and private interests. They can be changed from time to time when new facts emerge from the technological, political, economic, and ethical changes. These call for changing meanings of Reasonable Value.

VI. Ideal Types

The foregoing discussion has led to the part played by scientific investigation in a science where Futurity plays the important part. The subject-matter differs entirely from that of the physical sciences whose materials do no forecasting. The method of investigation must therefore be different from that of the exact sciences because its outcome is the concerted but conflicting action of human wills in an historical evolution of determining what is workable within the changing economic, political, and ethical sequence. It is, how-ever, a special case of the part-whole relationship in all sciences, but it reveals itself in a social ideal of the future towards which the participants in existing concerns are more or less directing their transactions and regulations. We may get a clue towards this methodology by examining the theories of the German jurist-economist, Max Weber, whose work has had much influence upon succeeding economists of the institutional schools.[91]

The problem which confronted Weber was the dispute in Germany between the deductive and historical schools, represented mainly by

[90] Cf. Commons, John R., and Andrews, J. B ., *Principles of Labor Legislation* (3d ed., 1927), Chap. IX, "Administration."

[91] Weber, Max, "Die 'Objektivität' sozialwissenschaftlicher und sozialpolitischer Erkenntnis," *Archiv für Sozialwissenschaft und Sozialpolitik*, XIX (1904), 22. Weber builded on Rickert, H., *Die Grenzen der naturwissenschaftlichen Begriffsbildung* (1902). Stammler, R., and Weber, Max, " 'Ueberwindung' der materialistischen Geschichtsauffassung " *Archiv für Sozialwissenschaft und Sozialpolitik*, XXIV (1907), 94; Diehl, Carl, "The Life and Work of Max Weber," and citations there given, *Quar. Jour. Econ.*, XXXVIII (1924), 87; Schelting, Alex von, "Die logische Theorie der Kulturwissenschaft von Max Weber, und im besonderen sein Begriff des Idealtypus," *Archiv für Sozialwissenschaft und Sozialpolitik*, XLIX (1922), 623. The Weber method is used by Sombart, Werner, *Der Moderne Kapitalismus*, 6 vols. revised (1923), and by Tawney, R. H., *Religion and the Rise of Capitalism, a Historical Study* (1926). See Commons, John R., and Perlman, S., review of Sombart's *Kapitalismus, Amer. Econ. Rev.*, XIX (1929), 78 ff.; Commons, John R., review of Tawney's *Religion and the Rise of Capitalism, Amer. Econ. Rev.* XVII (1927), 63 ff

Menger and Schmoller.[92] Menger had set forth the extreme individualistic presupposition; he sought on the analogy of the older physical sciences, to abstract from all other phenomena the simplest "typical" trait and "typical" relation upon which an "exact" science of economics should be constructed. His typical traits were self-interest and utility, and his typical relation was that between the quantity of useful goods needed by an individual or society (*Bedarf*) and the quantity of such goods disposable at the time and place (*die verfügbare Güterquantitäten*). This typical relation gave to him the meaning of "economic" goods, distinguished from "non-economic" goods. On this principle Menger would build the "exact" science of Economics. In reality, it was the science of Scarcity which Darwin had builded for all organisms, and which, at Darwin's hands, we name Biological Scarcity, but which Menger, in transferring it to the human organism, converted to what we distinguish as Psychological Scarcity. Menger did not build upon that other aspect of scarcity which we name Proprietary Scarcity, derived from Hume.

But Schmoller contended that this abstraction of self-interest gave to us only "a shadowy phantom," an "imaginary Robinson Crusoe," abstracted from the complex historical, social, legal, and economic traits and relations required to reveal the whole truth of political economy. In fact, Schmoller might have gone further in his criticism of Menger's method. In order to get his "exact" science of individual psychology, Menger not only eliminated all such motives as ethical feelings of right, wrong, justice, duty, and not only eliminated all conformity to custom, all subordination to, or exercise of, coercion, but he also eliminated ignorance, and assumed infallibility and infinite knowledge, corrected, however, in practice, by an allowance for "error."

Yet Menger and Schmoller agreed not only that abstraction was necessary, but also that a great many abstractions were necessary in order to ascertain the whole truth. The jurist makes an abstraction of property rights, the biologist or economist of scarcity relations, the psychologist of feelings, intellect, or will, the chemist of atoms, etc. I see my table in my room. The older physicist abstracts the weight from the other qualities of the table; the chemist

---

[92] Menger, Karl, *Grundsätze der Volkswirthschaftslehre* (1871, 1923); *Untersuchungen über die Methode der Sozialwissenschaften und der politischen Oekonomie insbesondere* (1883); *Die Irrthümer des Historismus in der Deutschen Nationalökonomie* (1884); Schmoller, G., "Zur Methodologie der Staats- und Sozialwissenchaften," *Jahrbuch für Gesetzgebung, Verwaltung und Volkswirthschaft im Deutschen Reich*, VII (1883), 975. Concerning this issue see Commons, John R., "Das Anglo-amerikanische Recht und die Wirtschaftstheorie," in *Die Wirtschaftstheorie der Gegenwart*, III (1928), 293.

abstracts the chemical constituents; the biologist the organic structure; the modern physicist the electrons, protons, and voids; the jurist my property rights; the moralist the rights, wrongs, and duties that ought to be observed respecting that table; the economist the use-value, scarcity-value, and expectations of those who are related to that table; the psychologist the percepts, concepts, feelings, habits, volitions, of those interested in the table. For each of these concepts the attributes which the theorist abstracts are supposed to be *reality*. He can take these realities thus abstracted and then work each of them out separately into an exact, or nearly exact, science. The problem is, How can all of these abstract realities, after each has been worked into its own science, be brought together in a single science of my table as it stands there in my room?

Menger and Schmoller agreed, of course, in abstracting something different from what the biologist, chemist, or physicist abstracts. They agreed in abstracting psychology, ethics, habits, scarcity, usefulness, and so on, excepting property rights, which Schmoller included and Menger rejected; all of which, sooner or later, became each a separable abstract problem for economists. But even so, having separated themselves from the biologists and physicists, how shall they comprehend these quite diverse sciences of law, economics, psychology, sociology, ethics, etc., into a whole which shall contain the true reality for economic science?

On examination we find that each of them started with a psychological, and therefore subjective, abstraction to which he attached importance. Menger started with selfish desires for external physical objects and selfish satisfactions to be derived from those objects. Schmoller started with the ethical feelings of what *ought* to be the desires and satisfactions in view of the desires and satisfactions of others. Then Menger worked out his psychology into an exact science of diminishing and marginal utility, but Schmoller could only work his out into the descriptive evolution of customs, laws, and institutions. The effort, therefore, to combine the two in a comprehensive unit of a single reality that should be both theoretical in Menger's deductive sense, and empirical in Schmoller's historical sense, seemed hopeless, and the dualism went on between the deductive and historical schools, between economics and ethics, between theory and practice, between science and art.

Here Weber, following the philosopher Rickert, intervened with his "ideal-typus." He reversed the statement of the problem. It is not, How to combine different sciences *after* they have been worked out separately by abstraction; but, How to state the problem of combining them *before* they have been worked out separately.

This prior statement is the ideal-typus. How does it differ from Menger's "typical" traits and relations?

First, the ideal-typus is not a *reality*, or rather, is not a *copy* of reality. According to Menger, the reality was a certain thing or action that could be apprehended in idea as actually existing—say, the commodity, the individual dealing with the commodity to satisfy his wants, the quantity of commodities available, the quantity wanted—in short, Menger's typical trait and relation was as much a reality as a man riding a horse. And the "laws" worked out by Menger from these typical traits and relations into the marginal utility theory were also as much a reality as the attraction of gravitation.

Not so, replies Weber. That may be done by Newton because he was able to isolate a single principle of gravity which actually works in isolation. But the matter of self-interest is more complex. What Menger had done was to work out an "ideal-typus," not an idea of reality. His ideal type is not what *actually* works out, but what *would* work out if it were possible to isolate Menger's individualistic man from everything else. That is impossible, hence Menger's idea is, in fact, an abstraction, not an understanding of reality in all its complexity.

This we consider the heart of Weber's contribution. It converts the whole process of economic theorizing from a "theory," in the older sense of the logical consistency of reality, to the mere methodology of constructing intellectual tools to be used in investigation. There is no longer a question of antagonism between theory and practice, for a theory is only a tool for investigating practice, like a spade for digging up facts and converting them into an understandable system of agriculture. Indeed, a science is not a body of knowledge—it is just a method of investigation, and its theory is its method.

Second, this formulation of an ideal type is what every science does, and Menger is not to be criticized on that account. The criticism by Weber is that, in the social sciences, the parts cannot be isolated, and the ideal type should therefore include *all* of the traits and relations which afterwards are to be combined, and, since all of these can be ascertained only from history, the ideal type must be a historical concept.

Third: But not all of history is relevant to economic theorizing. Hence the economist must abstract from the empirical data of history only so much as is needed, but not less than is needed, to construct an all-round ideal type for the particular phase of history which, as economist, he is concerned with.

Fourth, even so, this ideal type abstracted from history will not correspond to the actual—it will still be an "utopia," a mental construction of what that historical institution *would* be if only the factors relevant to economics are abstracted as a whole in all of their idealized relations. Thus he constructed a purely idealized concept of a medieval borough or guild, or of a capitalistic corporation, or of a trade union, etc., to be used, not as a "theory" of what actually existed, but as a mental tool for trying to understand it.

Fifth, this ideal-typus of Weber is not an ethical ideal (*Endpunkt*) of what *ought* to be, but is only an investigational, or instrumental (heueristic) ideal which the scientist may use for research, selection of facts, and comparison with what he actually finds.

Sixth: Hence, the ideal-typus is not an "average," like a mathematical line running through the dispersion of empirical facts—it is strictly an "ideal" of what the facts would be if irrelevant facts were eliminated. Neither is it an hypothesis. It is a synthesis, which helps to formulate an hypothesis, for it sets up the following problem: What is the *meaning* of the activities in their relations to each other? And thus it suggests the kind of hypothesis needed to select the facts and weigh their relative importance. It is a synthesis of all the factors out of which we formulate an hypothesis. It differs from the theory of Menger as synthesis differs from analysis.

Seventh: This search for the *meaning* of human activities, formulated as an ideal-typus, can never be expected to yield an "exact" science, or even an approximation to the quantitative requirements of other sciences. Yet that is not what is wanted, anyhow. What the economist wants is *understanding*, and he wants *measurement* only as an aid to understanding. The subject-matter with which an economist deals is not a mechanism or organism whose motions the investigator cannot *understand*—it is human beings whose activities he can fairly well understand by putting himself "in their place" and thus constructing the "reasons," in the sense of motives or purposes, or values, of their activity under all the variable conditions of time and place.

This is the fundamental reason set forth by Rickert and Weber which separates social or economic science from the physical sciences. In the latter sciences the only questions asked are *How, What, How much,* simply because we cannot know the reasons. But in economic sciences we include the *Why*, because what we want is *understanding* of the motives at work.[93]

[93] The contradictory view is presented by Young, Kimball, "Social Psychology and Social Reform," *The Scientific Monthly,* XXXIV (1932), 252.

Eighth: The number of factors to be taken into account in the ideal-typus for social sciences is not predetermined—they include everything which the economist may find, upon investigation, to be relevant. Hence the economist cannot construct his ideal-typus without prolonged previous investigation. The whole range of civilization (*Kultur*) is open to him, but the various civilizations, on investigation, may arrange themselves in such a way that one may be compared with another by comparing the different ideal types, and, also, subordinate types similarly may be arranged and compared. Thus he can arrive at the ideal type of capitalism, of individualism, of feudalism, of mercantilism, which are special cases of the ideal-typus, and can develop hypotheses, to be tested by investigation, of the historical development from one type to another, or of the interrelations of factors within any particular organization to be investigated.

Weber has performed a significant service in thus constructing his ideal-typus. Yet we are convinced, by the way in which he and his followers make use of it, that it is a tool which must be cautiously analyzed before the germ of validity in it can be used in the scientific investigation of economic events. Its usefulness consists in clarifying our thinking on the social sciences, distinguishing them from the physical sciences. He leads us to inquire whether there may be an alternative method, or a special application of Weber's method, which—while being truly scientific in the sense employed in physical and organic sciences—yet distinguishes a science of human behavior from the non-human sciences by the same attribute of subjective value which Weber brings out, but which he thinks cannot be reduced to a science because *value* is essentially subjective, emotional, individualistic, and immeasurable. Thus he speaks of the "spirit of capitalism," the "spirit" of a medieval city, the "spirit" of a trade union. It is around these spirits that his ideal-typus is constructed.

We approach this problem by distinguishing four different meanings of the ideal type which emerge from the use made of it especially by Weber, Sombart, and Tawney. These we may distinguish as the ideal type for the four purposes of Pedagogy, Propaganda, Science, and Ethics. We shall designate these the pedagogical, the propagandist, the scientific, and the ethical ideal types.

1. *The Pedagogic Ideal Type*

As a pedagogical instrument, the ideal type is an intellectual construction by means of which the innermost soul or spirit of an historical situation or institution, or individual, may be so rationalized as to be understood in terms of the human motives that animate it. The need of such an instrument in economics and other social sciences arises from the fact of Valuation. Valuing is a strictly emotional process, differing for each individual and for the same individual at different times. It is not merely economic valuation, it is religious, sexual, patriotic—in fact it is the whole of the emotions aroused by a whole civilization which the Germans name *Kultur*—a term for which there is no English equivalent, since we think of civilization as a structure, rather than as something to be loved. Since valuation is thus an internal process of emotions, it cannot be reduced to the uniformity of repetition for all individuals, required by a science. Yet it is this very emotional process that must be appealed to if we are really to understand the reasons why people act as they do. This appeal can be made only by creating a mental picture revealing, not only *how* people act, but *why* they act as they do under the particular circumstances selected. This we name the "historical sense."

We do not say that this emotional process cannot be reduced to the uniformities of a science; but it belongs to the science of Psychology, with its art of Pedagogy, not to economics, either historical or deductive. Economics builds upon the emotional process, just as it builds upon jurisprudence, physics, chemistry. And, when Weber builds his ideal-typus upon it, he is indeed building on real foundations, but he is building a science and art of pedagogy, not of economics.

Yet his contribution is all the more important because it enables us to designate certain so-called economic theories, not as economics, but as pedagogy. Thus it is that Weber, by this meaning of ideal type gives a correct interpretation of Menger's emotions of self-interest operating under the circumstances of increasing supply. Menger's "diminishing utility," with its "exact" science of marginal utility, is not and never was either exact or a reality, and could never become real or exact. But it does give us an *understanding* of *why* people act with less eagerness in obtaining commodities which are abundant than they do when the same commodities are scarce, because it appeals to our experience of our own changing feelings under similar circumstances. Thus Menger's formula is not economic science, as Menger thought it was—it is, we should say, pedagogy, for it is an ideal type constructed to illustrate a certain aspect of human behavior. As such it is useful for pedagogic illustration, but since it never operates by itself, it cannot be used in a science which must take all factors into account. Therefore Weber would not reject Menger's analysis *in toto,* as the historical school did when Schmoller called it a caricature. Weber would retain it even though it is a phantasie, an utopia, simply because it helps us to understand one aspect of human behavior which must, however, be combined with other aspects before the scientific reality of the whole of human behavior can be understood. It is a useful utopia indeed, but for pedagogical purposes.

But the historical school of economics also has its utopias—its ideal types. Herein, we should say, Weber convicted them, also, of pedagogy instead of economics. The historical school constructs a picture of the Renaissance with Leonardo da Vinci as typical of that new spirit that came into Europe after the fall of Constantinople; or a picture of early Christianity with the Apostle Paul as its type. Here it is that the pure love of God and Man, without selfishness, working itself into the behavior of the converts, is the ideal type. These are just as unreal, for the whole civilization of the Roman Empire at that time, as Menger's "economic man." But, unless we create these mental pictures, abstracted from all the other phenomena of the Middle Ages or the Roman Empire, we could not *understand* the spirit of the Renaissance or of early Christianity.

These pedagogical ideal types are all of them mere utopias, mere phantasies, but they are exactly what we employ when we try to understand, or lead others to understand, the kind of behavior which we are examining; when we are, in fact, trying to place ourselves in the place of others and to obtain that "historical sense" which the economic theorist must have if he would interpret the economic behavior of others, not only in the past but also under circumstances other than his own in the present. We cannot possibly put ourselves in the place of a mechanism or an organism so as to understand its own "why" it acted so and so, because it has no emotions like our own. We do not know that electricity had any reason for hitting John Smith instead of Lily Lou. In fact, we *do* know that it had *no* reasons, because it had no emotions, in the matter. We do not know that a hen can explain to herself why she sits four weeks on ducks' eggs. In fact we know that she had no sense of values that we can understand. But we can understand what Benjamin Franklin was after, and why a farmer set the hen. It was his sense of Value, his feelings, emotions, purposes, curiosity, under all the circumstances of time and place. This is peculiar to the social sciences, including economics, and is unknown in the physical sciences. And it should be included in the social sciences, else they become only mechanistic.

Yet we hold that it is pedagogics, not economics. For the ideal type, with this meaning, is a mental tool which we construct in order to understand *why* beings, with emotions like our own, acted as they did. In the sciences of mechanisms and organisms we construct mental tools to answer only *what* and *how much* they did and what *we* may expect them to do. In the sciences of human behavior we do the same, but we go much further—we look for the values, the motives, the emotions, the purposes—in short, for the "why" and the "spirit." In other words, we seek to *understand,* not merely to classify, measure, and mechanize. This is the contribution of Rickert to social philosophy, and of Weber to institutional economics.

But the question still remains. When we seek to *understand,* in the sense employed by Weber, are we in the field of science? Weber correctly says, No, and constructs the ideal type as an utopia with the definite purpose of making clear his reason for saying No. If so, then the ideal type is not an instrument of science—it is an instrument of pedagogy.

It must now be observed that therefore the ideal type is simply the method of Personification, which is the bane of political economy. We personify, indeed, if we would understand in the intimate sense of emotions. In other sciences, this personification was astrology, alchemy, vitalism. That is to say, the astrologer, or alchemist, or vitalist, pictured himself with his feelings, will, intellect, reason—in short, with his ideal type—in the place of the observed motions, and asked *why* they so moved, instead of merely asking, as the astronomer, chemist, and biologist afterwards did, *how* and *how much* they moved.

We have already pointed out the two personifications that preceded the formulation of the scientific principle of scarcity. Ricardo personified scarcity as the resistance of nature to human labor. Thus "labor" became the personification of scarcity, and ended in the queer line of labor-theories, instead of scarcity-theories, through Marx, Proudhon, Böhm-Bawerk, Clark, the populists and greenbackers. They were trying to get rid of money, the scientific measure of scarcity, which tells us only *how* and *how much;* and they rested their case on Weber's utopia of *why*—a truly ideal type, an economic astrology.

The other personification of scarcity was in the diminishing utility theories of Gossen, Menger, Walras, and Jevons, rightly characterized by Weber as utopias under the polite name of ideal-typus. Where Bentham had personified economics and ethics by the ideal type of a parallelism of pain and pleasure accompanying the cost and income of commodities, these other hedonic alchemists appealed to well-known feelings of diminishing pleasure and its inverse, increasing pain. But, after all, it was a personification, put in the form of an utopian ideal type of that scarcity-relationship which we are actually measuring by the scarcity dimensions of money.

2. The Propagandist Ideal Type

The above personifications originated in the deductive or molecular economics of the classical, socialistic, anarchistic, and hedonic schools, by the elimination of money. A similar personification, from the historical aspect, is Weber's own "capitalist spirit," taken over by Sombart and Tawney. It is, now, a personification—not without money but with money—whereby is made possible the idea of unlimited accumulation of money values, but also with the same ideal type of Ricardo and Menger, namely, the acquisition of income for self without any regard whatever to duties or obligations owing to others. Contrasted with this is Weber's and Sombart's "handicraft-spirit" of the town-economy of the Middle Ages, where the manual workers and tradesmen adopted their guild rules designed to prevent a guildsman from getting rich at the expense of his fellow guildsmen.

What happens, in these cases, is the personification of capitalism and the personification of guilds and trade unions, each given its own peculiar ideal type, not because any such "spirit" actually existed apart from all its transactions, but in order that we, having similar emotions, can put ourselves in the place of the typical capitalist or typical trade-unionist and thereby "understand" him.

This is good enough, and much to be desired. But it must be noted that when we "understand" the behavior of others in this sense of fellow-emotions, we are necessarily understanding them in the sense of hating, deprecating, loving, admiring them. Hence our ideal type is likely to be constructed on the basis of our own emotions, as when Weber and Sombart overlook the violence and exclusiveness of guilds and unions towards outsiders, by selecting only their qualities of justice towards fellow-guildsmen or unionists; or when they overlook the conscientious payment of debts or the good-will services to customers, or other ethical attitudes of capitalists, and concentrate only on unlimited pecuniary self-seeking.

Consequently, the ideal type, since it is both pedagogy and personification, is the precise mental tool employed for Propaganda, either the attractive propaganda of advertising or the detractive propaganda of politics. The economist may, like Weber or Sombart, disavow that he is either a "labor" economist or a "capitalist" economist. Yet the fact that he selects for his ideal type of the handicraft spirit only that part of the whole spirit which looks towards justice between guild members, omitting that part which looks towards self-seeking and exclusion of outsiders; and the fact that he selects for his ideal type of the capitalist spirit only that part that looks towards unlimited self-seeking by the instrument of money, omitting the part which looks towards justice, equality, and good-will, must stamp the economist as building upon the foundations of propaganda while disavowing it.

Weber's disavowal of this propagandist bias is based on his distinction between the ultimate goal of what *ought* to be (*Endpunkt*) and the instrument or means by which any goal is reached. His ideal-typus is not a picture of what ought to be, such as the ideals of communism, anarchism, or individualism, nor is it a picture of what *ought* to be the ultimate state of mankind, whether the Virtue of the Intuitionists or the Universal Happiness of the Utilitarians. It is solely an instrumental ideal type taken from the factors deemed relevant to the working out of the particular process, regardless of what the investigator thinks should be the ultimate goal. He discovers this instrumental purpose objectively from the facts which he investigates. The capitalist "spirit," or the handicraft "spirit," or the "spirit" of early Christianity is not what the investigator thinks is right or wrong—it is what he finds, on investigation, to be the way that spirit would work if it were not hindered or aided by the working of any other spirit or circumstance. It is strictly an instrumental ideal type to aid the understanding, not a propagandist ideal type to convert or alienate anybody.

But we should note that the bias of investigators does not show itself only in differences of opinion as to the ultimate goal—it shows itself also in the differences in *weight*, that is, the relative *values* assigned to the different factors that go to make up the whole process. One investigator may attach greater weight to labor, wages, hours; another to investment, profit, interest; another to the long-run tendency of civilization; another to the immediate necessities of the short-run; another to humanity; another to business. These differences in valuing are, in fact, influenced by differences in the ideal of an ultimate goal, and cannot be separated from it. Hence Weber's "instrumental" ideal type, as well as his ideal *Endpunkt*, is also subjective and emotional. The differences in "weight" are differences in meaning and may be summarized as differences in those very subjective valuations which Weber intends to avoid. According to one's subjective valuations the investigator will not only *select* the factors which form his ideal type, to the exclusion of other factors, but will also give greater or less *weight,* or *value,* than other investigators to those factors which they might all agree in selecting.

Consequently, from the standpoint of that goal of all science which is the consensus of competent investigators, no agreement can ordinarily be expected in the formulation of their ideal types. They will differ both in the factors selected and in the relative importance assigned to each, as is seen in Weber's invidious contrast between the capitalist spirit and the handicraft spirit, or the trade-union spirit. This is bias and propaganda.

For this reason, apparently, the ideal type must be very elastic both in its selection of factors and in its relative weights of the factors, in order to get a consensus of investigators. This lack of voluntary consensus in Weber's ideal-typus is its weakness. It permits each participant to construct his own utopia by selecting and valuing, which may or may not fit the historical or contemporaneous facts, and may not work into collective effort to keep the concern agoing. A highly elastic ideal type is not perhaps hopeless in the science of economics. But it probably is not to be expected, since economists are not compelled to agree on a verdict, like a jury, nor to agree in a free country, and so they are at liberty to select whatever facts they choose and to assign whatever importance they wish.

But economic scientists are not the subject-matter of economic science. The subject-matter is human beings in their economic activities. These beings are both subjective and environmental—subjective in their emotions, motives, wishes, pains, pleasures, ideals —environmental in their transactions with others. All human beings have their subjective bias. In order to "understand" their activity, in addition to measuring the activity or its results, the investigator must "put himself in their place" and do, in imagination, what they do under their conditions of time and place. This is, however, the real service performed by Weber's ideal-typus. But, again, the investigator in formulating his ideal type, must do it in the form of motives or emotions of the capitalists or laborers, which he can presumably understand, the motives thereupon being considered to be the cause, or rather Weber's "value," for the capitalists and laborers, of their behavior. If he selects *one* of their motives, like self-interest, then he is in the position of Menger, with his typical trait and relation. And he cannot include *all* of their motives, for that would make him superhuman. He must select enough and no more than are necessary for economics. This puts him in the position of Weber.

But even here, in economics, the investigator does not have a workable ideal type, because it is too extensive. He must *distinguish* the motives—the motive of profit from the motive of interest, or rent, or wages, or production, or consumption. Thus, in creating the ideal type of Capitalism, as we have indicated, Weber, followed by Sombart and Tawney, constructs the motive of Capitalism, which he names the "capitalist spirit." The capitalist spirit "creates" capitalism. This is the reverse of Karl Marx whose capitalism created the capitalist spirit. With Weber the capitalist spirit consists, as indicated above, in the striving for unlimited profit in the form of an accumulation of money or money values, without any sense of obligation or duty towards others in the process. Opposed to this is the handicraft spirit of the guilds of the Middle Ages, which consisted in striving only for enough goods to satisfy needs without depriving others of their reasonable share. When the capitalist spirit comes to be restrained by rules and regulations, as the handicraft spirit was restrained by guild rules, then capitalism, as the ideal type, begins to "decay." Weber, of course, sees this already coming, as do his followers. The capitalist spirit is a striving for unlimited profits without a sense of justice, and the handicraft spirit—applicable also to the trade-union spirit—is a striving for justice at the·expense of profit.

Evidently, if this is the outcome of the method of ideal types, it sets up, after all, the bias of the investigator in selecting the factors which constitute his ideal type. This outcome arises, apparently, from trying to find a specialized motive fitted to each special type of behavior, and thus to treat each motive as though it might be pictured—utopia-wise—as working itself out in behavior as a separable ideal type itself.

This defect, apparently, might be corrected by creating an ideal type which should include *all* of the motives as shown in *all* of the behavior. But this would be the scientific ideal type—not the pedagogical, propagandist, or personified type. And it is this form of the ideal type which is useful in science. It is found in all words ending in "ism." Instead of the capitalist "spirit" as the motive for unlimited pecuniary gain regardless of the effect on others, this capitalist "spirit" would disappear entirely and only "capitalism," as a special historical stage, animated by all kinds of motives, emotions, and circumstances, would be the ideal type. There would then remain, indeed, great differences of opinion among investigators as to the emotions, the subjective valuations of capitalists, and as to the good or bad effects of capitalism. The question *why* would therefore not be answered, but there would be a nearer approach to the goal of all science, namely, agreement of investigators upon *how* and *how much*.

This meaning of ideal type is its scientific meaning. Two questions arise, however, suggested by the problem for whose solution Weber set out to create his ideal-typus. (1) Does this scientific method, eliminating the subjective altogether, reduce economics back again to the purely mechanistic science of the classical, communistic, and hedonic economists? What is the Scientific Ideal type? It is here that we shall find a method of investigation. (2) Does this scientific ideal type, thus ascertained, eliminate, as did those mechanistic types, the ethical aspects of economics which Weber endeavored to incorporate inseparably with the economic? What is the Ethical Ideal type? It is here that we shall find the meaning of Reasonable Value. We consider first the scientific ideal type.

3. *The Scientific Ideal Type*

The main contribution of Weber's ideal-typus is that it yields a principle of classification for a whole set of ideas, already in common use, to indicate vaguely the part-whole relation. This classification includes such terms as capitalism, trade-unionism, communism, socialism, business, the "economic man," the "law of supply and demand," etc. These concepts take their places as special cases of the universal concept of an ideal type which is set up, not as scientific instruments of investigation, but as various mental figments picturing to the imagination certain relations of parts to the whole which later are the subject-matter of detailed investigation. In order, then, that these vague and undefined concepts may be reduced to instruments for scientific investigation, we require to examine the reasons why they, as ideal types, are not fitted for science and how they may, perhaps, be changed into the mental tools which economic science can use. We name this kind of ideal type merely a Formula, as previously interpreted in our chapter on Method.

The ideal type, as formulated by Weber, can be corrected for the bias of investigators by being made sufficiently elastic for all investigators, instead of fixed by each for himself. It can be corrected for the subject-matter by being made primarily transactional and secondarily subjective in motives and emotions, instead of the reverse. Assuming these two corrections to be made, so that the ideal type is elastic and transactional, there still remains a third defect. The ideal type, as formulated by Weber and used by him and Sombart, even though it be made elastic and objective, is not yet transactional. Therefore it does not contain in itself the concept of Time with its main characteristics of motion, repetition, variability, and, especially does not contain, in itself, an objective formula of future time, which we conceive is what economists mean when they revert to psychology. The ideal type, as a part-whole relation, is formed by the investigator to be used as a guide in investigation, but it is *fixed in advance of investigation.* Hence if facts are discovered which do not fit the type, the type itself, as formulated by Weber, does not change to fit the facts; the facts are brought in as what he calls "hindrances" and "aids" to the pure evolution of the type. Yet these hindrances and aids are of the essence of the type, if the type be looked upon as a formula for the investigation of a moving, changing process, and especially if it be looked upon as a formula for expressing the uncertain expectations of the future which dominate the activity of human beings in the ever-moving present.

We must, then, ascertain the reasons for this time-defect in Weber's ideal-typus. First, the failure to start economic theory upon an *economic bond* which ties individuals together, such as transactions, debts, property rights—a bond which was supplied by the historical and socialistic economists in the form of non-economic bonds such as ethics, sovereignty, personifications, or analogies to organisms. Second, the failure to distinguish three separable ideal types of economics—the engineering and consumption economics, which are relations of man to nature; and proprietary economics, which is the economic relation of man to man. Third, the lack of theories of relativity of time and space, propounded only recently in physics. Fourth, a mistaken concept of custom as something that comes from the past instead of something that looks to the future. With the corrections suggested by these defects, the concept of futurity becomes objective and even measurable, and thereby completely displaces the need of looking inward for the unknowable emotions of individuals. Futurity becomes the scientific substitute for Weber's inward spirit.

If, then, we can construct, not an ideal type which may or may not fit the facts, but a mere *formula* as an instrument for investigation, which shall contain all of the variable factors which all investigators might include, but which can be weighted with highly variable importance of the several parts, according to time and place in the functioning of the whole—then it may be possible to combine in one evolving insight the fruitful method of research contained in Weber's ideal-typus. This we conceive to be possible if we start with an adequate and therefore complex formula of transactions, whose expected repetition, concurrence, and variability is a going concern.

Another fruitful contribution of Weber's ideal-typus is in its bearing upon the relations between theory and practice. The ideal type is not a theory—it is a formulation of the problem of relationship between the factors, which problem the theory attempts to solve. Yet it requires a preceding theory in order to formulate it. Hence it is simply a stage in the formulation of theory, which, at that stage, we name an hypothesis. An hypothesis is a statement of what we now *expect* from our present knowledge of the factors and our present understanding of their interrelations. And the form taken by this expectation may be named the scientific ideal type. But when, on investigation and experiment, we "try out" the hypothesis—our formula—and find that it does not exactly fit, then, if we are not pedagogic, dogmatic, or propagandist, we change the formula to get a better fit. Then this fit is another stage of a modified ideal type, and so on. Then, further, if we take into account the variability of the factors themselves and endeavor to construct a formula of a *process*, rather than a structure, we have another ideal type, this time of a moving, changing whole, which we must again repeatedly revise to fit the changes which research brings to light.

Instead, therefore, of a fixed ideal type which Weber names an utopia and which, indeed, becomes more utopian if it remains fixed as we proceed with our investigation, we have a changing hypothesis, taking in new factors or retiring older ones, always seeking to make less utopian the utopias which our minds construct. Thus theory becomes, not only a mental process for investigation of facts, but becomes also an interpretation, correlation, and expectation of facts. In short, theory becomes a different meaning of Weber's "understanding"—not the pedagogic meaning of fellow feeling, but the pragmatic meaning of insight on which we predict and act.

On account, however, of the novelty and complexity of the effort to understand the part-whole relationship, and in view of Weber's ideal type as a tool for investigating that relationship, we are required to make more precise the meanings, not only of our mental processes, but also of the environmental relationships to which such processes refer. This should give to us the mental tools, which, as John Locke intended, should enable us to separate our mental processes from the objects investigated—an equipment which is none other than that of keeping our personal bias out of our theory. We give, therefore, what we understand as the meanings of words for the purpose of expounding a theory of the scientific process of

arriving at an understanding of the part-whole relation to be obtained in economics.

First, as to the very starting point of our theory, the meaning of
a Fact itself. We pretend to base our theory on Facts. But what
are facts? A fact, in its beginning, is only a first impression from
the outside world, which we call an object, or a relation. Next, it
begins to have meaning, but only because we construct that meaning
out of our previous knowledge and experience, which we name
habitual assumptions. We read our own life history into the facts
and—we may be mistaken from the very start. At this stage the
fact is a Percept. It does not correspond at all to the whole of
reality—it corresponds only to a special attribute of the whole;
thus it is only a preliminary for us in approaching the next stage,
the stage of concept.

A Concept is a similarity of attributes, such as the concept use-
value, transaction, person, going concern. Is a concept, then, a
part-whole relation? Is it a Whole, of which the parts—that is,
the percepts—are constituent wholes? Here is the first double
meaning of the word Part—or rather a false meaning of Part. A
percept—that is, an object or relation—is not a part of which a
concept is the whole. A percept was only a special attribute—like
yellow, or a special complex of attributes, like a yellow flower—of
something that was unknown as a whole; and a concept is simply
another pragmatic convenience by which we summarize in one word
—a noun—a similarity of percepts.

Next, we distinguish Principles. While a concept was a similarity
of attributes, a principle is a similarity of motions. Here we distinguish the subjective from the pragmatic meaning of principle.
The subjective meaning is that of a cause, a reason, a law, compelling, as it were, the motions to be similar, as when I say, "This
is a law of nature," or "These are my principles which I will not
abandon." This subjective meaning was the source of Weber's
ideal-typus. But the pragmatic meaning of principle is nothing but
the expected similarity of action. With this latter meaning, each
motion, by itself, whether simple or complex, was a fact, a percept.
It was not a part-motion, of which the principle is the whole-motion.
A principle is a similarity of repetition of either part-motions or
of whole-motions. It is a convenience for summarizing similarities
in one word—but the other convenience of language makes it misleading by giving to it the name of a noun instead of a verb. Use-
value is a concept—a similarity of qualities; but using or valuing
is a principle—a similarity of motions. Transaction is a concept,
but similarity of transacting is a principle. Going concern is a

concept, but willingness is its principle, that is, its expected similarities of transactions. Adam Smith is a complex concept of a person, but Smithizing is a principle of a certain similarity of reasoning.

So it is with our concept of a "factor" as employed in the phrase "limiting and complementary factors." As concept, a factor is a unit, an individual, an object—say, potash or Smith; but, as principle, a factor is a broadcaster of similar activities. It is not potash that is the limiting factor in agriculture—it is the chemical, electric, or other activities of potash, operating with peculiar uniformity on the activities of other materials. And a person is not a noun—he is a verb of all the activities he is expected to radiate in dealings with nature or with other persons. It is these activities that are the limiting and complementary factors, the strategic and routine transactions, and their similarities are their principles.

We have, therefore, not yet reached the part-whole relation. Complexity is not a relation of parts to the whole. It is just complexity, and there is no understanding of how, or why, or what for. There may be similar complexities, like flowers, or similar simplicities, like yellow. In fact, that is what we mean by a hierarchy, or classification, of concepts or principles. A genus is a wide similarity of more simple attributes or motions; a species is a special case of more narrow similarity of attributes or motions. Animal is genus, man is species. The latter is not a part of which the former is the whole. The relation is, as Veblen would say, taxonomic, not functional.

In order, then, to proceed to the part-whole relation, we need another name for the mental process. We name it a Formula. A formula is somewhat like Weber's ideal-typus—it is a mere mental tool constructed for research and action, and it is a formulation of the relation of the parts to each other and to the whole. The parts are themselves wholes, requiring each its own formula, and so on down to the parts which we consider ultimate for our particular science.

But the question is, Is it a formula of concepts or a formula of principles?

Take the concept, Going Concern. Is it a formula of different similarities of individuals, of tools, machines, products, related to each other, or is it a formula of different similarities of acting and transacting?

Or take the concept of the individual himself who is a part of the concern. Is he the concept of Smith or the principle of Smithizing? Or take the concept of a transaction. Is it the relations of individual wills to each other or is it the relation of different kinds of similar volitional activities to each other?

Here, we may say, is the practical application of Weber's ideal-typus—it consists in the formulation of concepts and principles into a formula which shall be used, with modifications, as tools for investigation of facts. It is the familiar problem of definition. But definitions cannot be formulated without a theory of the functions to be played by all the parts in the final outcome. It is not enough to say that one definition is as good as another provided we use it always with the same meaning. Each definition must be fitted to the problem of research and action which we have in mind; then only is it to be, or can it be, used without changing the meaning.

We need to distinguish, however, first of all, whether we use it as a concept or as a principle, and whether we use it as a formula of interdependent concepts or interdependent principles. Take the five part-concepts on which we conceive that economic theory rests, and their relations to each other and to the whole which we call Willingness. Each is both a concept and a principle.

The concept of Scarcity above developed is that formulated by Menger. It is a concept of pure number existing only in the mind— a ratio existing between a quantity of things wanted and the quantity available at the time and place. As such a typical relation, or ideal type, it is a whole composed of two interdependent parts, each of which is itself another whole composed of its own interdependent parts. And the pure number—the ratio—is both the concept and the measure of the interdependence itself. But Scarcity is also a principle, when it is conceived to be the similarity, with variability, of the bargaining transactions of human beings relative to the quantities and prices of the things wanted. It is this principle—not the concept—that becomes a functioning part in the formula of the whole of Willingness.

Thus with Efficiency. The concept of Efficiency is again a concept of pure number, existing only in the mind. It consists of the ratio between two parts, the output and input during a unit of time. But the principle of Efficiency is the similarity, with variability, of the managerial transactions of human beings relative to, again, the chemical, electric, gravitational, or other motions of the instruments used and the products yielded.

The concept of Custom is that of the binding force which groups of individuals have over individual members; but the principle of working rules, guided by habitual assumptions, is the repetition, with variability, of the acts and transactions of individuals in so far as this binding force of the group continues to operate. The concept of sovereignty is like that of custom, differing in the rationing of physical power as the binding force; but the principle of sovereignty is the repetition, with variability, of the rationing transactions of superiors towards inferiors who are subordinate to their use of physical force.

The concept of Futurity is that of expected events, but the principle of Futurity is the similarity of repetition, with variability, of transactions and their valuations, performed in the moving Present with reference to future events as expected hindrances, aids, or consequences.

These five part-principles constitute, in their interdependence, the whole of the principle of Willingness. This, as concept, is the complex attributes of human beings. As principle, it is the expected repetition, with variability, of the total of all human acting and transacting within the limiting and complementary interdependence of the principles of scarcity, efficiency, working rules, sovereignty, and futurity. The functional relations are such because a change in one dimension changes all the others, and thus changes the whole transaction or concern. If efficiency increases, then scarcity diminishes; a variation of working rules occurs, as well as of expectations of the future, and perhaps of the use of sovereignty. In the formula of bargaining transactions it was noted that a change in any one of the dimensions of opportunity, power, and competition is a change in the other two. Changes in any one of its functional parts is a change in the whole of willingness.

Hence, we reach the concept of going concerns as the expected repetition of interdepedent transactions, the principle of which is Willingness, and the formula for which is the mental formula previously offered, of the changing interdependence of all its limiting and complementary principles.

This formula, we take it, fits Weber's concept of an ideal-typus, but we name it "scientific" instead of pedagogical, propagandist, or personified, because it is a formula including *all* of the factors instead of a few selected ones, and hence does not depend upon any selected subjective emotions for its formulation; and because it furnishes an elastic outline of the interdependence of all factors which must then be investigated both separately as part-whole relations in their own right and interdependently as limiting and complementary factors. Its claim for scientific availability as a mental tool of research rests upon the same distinctions as those made by Weber between philosophy or metaphysics, and methodology. It is solely an instrument of method, and its method consists in separating distinctly the science of human activity from the sciences of mechanism and organism. It is by means of this separation of the sciences that Weber avoids philosophy and metaphysics. For methodology is the logical structure of the concepts and principles in which each science formulates its own knowledge or its means of knowledge within its own field. The limits of methodology are the points where the particular science passes over into other sciences, and it is the attempt to pass beyond these limits that is the philosophical or metaphysical disturbance. When once it is perceived that these limits cannot be passed, in our present state of knowledge, then the problem of method does not get confused with the problems of philosophy or metaphysics. It is this distinction that enables us to define Willingness, Custom, Futurity, and Value pragmatically as we do, without metaphysical or philosophic implication.

For example, the problem of whether the Will is "free' or "determined" is a "metaphysical" problem from our pragmatic standpoint, and is therefore beyond the limits of the methodology of political economy. But it is not metaphysical from the standpoint of the sciences of psychology or neurology, which investigate, by means of their own peculiar formulae, the relations between mind and body. We take the will as we find it, namely the whole activity of human beings in their actions and transactions. Then we construct the concepts, principles, and formulae, which, it is believed on our present knowledge, will serve to investigate all the problems of political economy, without endeavoring to bring over the so-called metaphysical, but really psychological problem of freedom or determinism.

Here we recognize, however, that there can be no science of political economy if the will is free, in the sense of being wholly capricious and undetermined. This requires us to look for uniformities in the operation of the will, if we would have an economic science of Willingness. We look for such uniformities, not merely in the scientific sense of *how* and *how much,* applicable to physical sciences, but in the volitional sense of *why,* which we can "understand," in the meaning given by Weber. Yet we differ from Weber's *why.* He found that Value is a purely subjective, capricious emotion, subject to no logical rules whatever. This is undoubtedly true for individuals. In this respect it is the subjective will. If, then, we rest our science on subjective emotion, we can have no social science and must resort either to metaphysics or to a science which deals solely with individuals, namely, pedagogy. This was Weber's difficulty. He introduced into his methodology that which, for the purposes of social science, is an individualistic entity, subjective value, or the individual will. And this entity, as far as we know, whether "free" or "determined," is highly capricious, unaccountable, and especially individualistic. But if we rest our search for uniformity upon the transactions of many going concerns, instead of upon individualistic emotions, then we do have many similarities of which we can understand, in our own consciousness, *why* they are uniform—because they are similarities which we know by experience.

One of these uniformities is Custom. Although individual emotions, or subjective valuations, or the subjective will, may differ so capriciously that no scientific uniformity can be predicated upon them, yet we do find uniformities of action when we look to transactions, instead of emotions. Here, however, the metaphysical problem, or rather the problem of psychology instead of economics, sets a limit to the methodology of economic science. Psychology, or neurology, finds certain individualistic uniformities named Habit, and these uniformities, from the time of Hume, were not distinguished from Custom. But custom is merely similarity of many individual habits. Formerly, economic science took this as a presupposition which it did not necessarily investigate. But the methodology of recent economic science requires us to look further —indeed to set up an ideal type, or formula, of a social force or pressure which compels individuals to conform, in variable degrees of conformity, and which can itself be investigated in its own right, over and above the presupposition of habit.

Such investigation is historical, and its fruitful source of data is in the legal and arbitrational decisions wherein custom is converted into common law. Here it becomes the function of methodology to formulate a definition of custom, not on the psychological and individualistic basis of Habit, but upon the social pressure that compels uniformity of action by all individuals within the jurisdiction. Such a definition, drawn from such sources, indicates penalties or sanctions imposed on those individuals whose capricious emotions, valuations, or wills do not conform to that which we call the "working rule" of the custom. With such a concept of custom, economic science can and does operate as an instrument of investigation, and it serves to explain and understand.

But it does so because it brings in another principle peculiar to the social sciences which is not found in the older concepts of Habit, or Custom. This is the principle of expectation which we name Futurity. Habit is a repetition of acts, determined—if they be "determined"—by physiological processes that occurred in the past. But the binding, or "determining" force of custom is the similarity of expectations of gain or loss imagined in the future. This "futurity," while from the subjective standpoint it belongs to the individualistic science of psychology, yet, from the transactional standpoint, it is none other than the existing securities, conformities, liberties, and exposures based on social sanctions.

This principle of futurity furnishes also all that is meant objectively by the concept of value or purpose. Therefore, the capricious and lawless subjective value or will of Weber, which is incapable of the uniformities required by science, is displaced by those similarities of valuation and willingness which are the subject-matter of both jurisprudence and economics. But no science requires absolute uniformities in order to be a science. Even astronomy allows for variabilities, much more so economics. The very fact that we have a great complexity of forces—or rather, principles—operating together, prevents exact repetition of any one of them; and the difficult problem of economics is so to correlate the various principles in order tha. the variabilities may be explained and understood, not as unaccountable caprices of individual values and wills, but as changing interrelations of the several principles which constitute the whole of willingness. The variabilities may be said to be the, as yet, unsolved cases of functional interdependence of the factors.

4. *The Ethical Ideal Type*

Weber did not consider the ethical ideal to be an allowable meaning of his ideal-typus. But there is a double meaning of the ethical ideal. It may mean the *unattainable*, or it may mean the *attainable*. The latter, we hold, is the meaning of Reasonable Value. Reasonable value and reasonable practices are the highest attainable idealism of regard for the welfare of others that is found in going concerns under existing circumstances of all kinds, at a given historical stage of development. It may be named Pragmatic Idealism.

Weber rejected both the attainable and the unattainable *Endpunkt*, that is, the ethical goal. But, in the common-law meaning of reasonableness, only the unattainable idealism is rejected. The highest attainable ethical goal—which is the highest attainable regard for one's social responsibilities—is evidenced by the fact that it actually exists, and can be investigated and testified to as facts, in the practices of the best concerns that are able to survive in the then existing struggle for existence.

The ethical ideal type to be excluded from consideration is only the unattainable, such as, we may say, heaven, communism, anarchism, universal brotherly love, universal virtue, universal happiness. But if it is attainable, as shown by the best examples that survive, then a theory of the attainable is as much a scientific theory as is a theory of the attained. For it has already been both attained and maintained in the best individual or collective examples that can be discovered by investigation. An individual or concern that is "too good" may fail in business, and one that is "too bad" may fail because it is excluded by the then working rules of collective action. But a reasonable idealism is the highest practicable idealism, as shown, not by individual wishes, such as those of Bentham, but by investigation of those institutions that practice it, and yet survive. There are always individuals and concerns above the average, and the problem of social idealism through collective action consists in bringing the "average" and those below the "average" up to the level of those above the average.

In this investigation of those *above* the average, in their social regard for others, the same limiting factors must be investigated as in the case of those at the average or below the average. Such limiting factors are efficiency, scarcity, conflict, the existing working rules of custom and sovereignty, the habitual assumptions, etc., which place the upper ethical limits on what can be done at the time and place.[94]

Thus an economic theory of willingness, which takes into account both private self-interest and the social welfare, is a theory of the upper limit of what *has* been attained and therefore is a theory of the unfinished but attainable Future. When the Future is finished by becoming the Past, then the same theory of willingness becomes an historical theory of that which *has* been attained. The ethics of economic activity is the future, but history is the past, of the same principle—Willingness.

This theory of Reasonable Value—and of the Reasonable Practices which are such only because they terminate in Reasonable Values—may seem very disappointing to those idealists who picture in their own mind Weber's utopia. He definitely gives to his ideal-typus the name "utopia," because he considers it "non-existent.' But we consider it *not* to be utopian in so far as we can find it actually *existent* in the best practices of those concerns that actually maintain survival. The truly utopian is the unattainable, and we have seen too many utopists afterwards disillusioned and turned into pessimists and reactionaries, to warrant us in going further towards social idealism than what can be shown to be the best practicable. There is plenty of room for enthusiasms and propaganda in this

---

[94] Below, p. 840, Accident and Unemployment.

limited field, for the Malthusian passions and stupidity put up a desperate front against even a social ideal that can be demonstrated to be practicable.

This meaning of ethics, within the limits of the best that is practicable, is, nevertheless, an ideal type constructed for the purpose of investigating and understanding objectively the nature of transactions and going concerns. It must be distinguished, however, from that ideal type of subjective ethics which is capricious and individualistic. Our concept of the Ethical ideal type is based on a workable consensus, derived from investigation, of the best attainable welfare relations of all who participate in transactions. While it means what *ought* to be, contrasted with what *is* or *was*, it is not the subjective "ought" of capricious individuals. Most people, when they are confronted with the term, "reasonable value," think of it as an individualistic ideal in the subjective feelings which therefore differ as much as there are individuals. But our idea of reasonable value is the consensual idealism of those who work together and are dependent one upon another for the continuance of their coöperation. It is not what "I think" ought to be, but what "we think" ought to and can be attained, as a going concern.

Weber had in mind, when he rejected the *Endpunkt* or goal, what "I think," not what "we think" when acting together. The formula by which this ethical consensus of opinion is reached is, nevertheless, within the limits of the attainable, the similar ideal type of Weber's contrivance. It is found throughout all judicial reasoning. It consists in maxims, standards, fictions, personifications, analogies, and so on, constructed mentally for the purpose of rendering justice. Perhaps the most elementary ideal type, constructed during the past three hundred years and still undergoing reconstruction as new cases arise, is that ideal of a willing buyer and a willing seller, which is set up by the common law as the ideal type of economic relationships out of which a reasonable value ensues.

Likewise, that ideal type created in the Sixteenth Century of the common law, on which the greater part of the modern credit system is based: the *assumpsit* that "everybody is supposed to have undertaken to do what is, in point of law, just and right." This assumption may be merely an implied contract where there is no express contract, or it may be a pure fiction. Upon it is based the science of jurisprudence. In fact, practically all of the "fictions" which so incensed Jeremy Bentham, since they are legal assumptions that something which is or may be false is nevertheless true, are ethical ideal types for the purpose of adjusting old rules of law to new conditions. And they are based evidently on the experience of a similarity in the operation of wills, instead of capricious unknowable subjective wills. They are, therefore, strictly scientific.

The fiction of *assumpsit,* for example, as used in legal reasoning, whether it be that of an "implied" contract or a sheer outright fiction in the technical sense, is a fiction only by way of contrast with preceding notions of a capricious arbitrary will. This preceding notion was applicable to the preceding feudal or despotic period of violence, robbery, capricious and despotic government. But when peaceful industry began to come in, with its customs of merchants in buying, selling, and fulfilling their promises, then the observed similarities of these capitalistic transactions furnished grounds for implying that an individual plaintiff or defendant who was a party to a transaction did intend to do what could be implied from the principle of similarity of reasonable acts, no matter whether in his own mind he actually intended it or not.

No science other than the social sciences, especially economics and law, can be a science if it pretends that what is false is actually true. Physics and biology cannot read into electricity or a colony of ants, except by poetry, any purpose, intention, implied promises, or contracts, to do or not do anything. This is the solid foundation of the insight of Rickert and Weber in setting up their ideal type as peculiar to the social sciences, distinguishing them thereby from physical sciences. All that science requires for its methodology is certain similarities of motion. This is furnished, for economics and law, by the Anglo-American common law with its foundation on custom, which is none other than expected enforced similarity of transactions.

Economics or legal science could not read into the capricious subjective valuations or wills of individuals any dependable purpose to make a contract or to fulfill it if made. But if there has grown up a custom of merchants—which is nothing but a certain expected similarity of transactions—then hundreds of implications, assumptions, and fictions, based on that similarity, can be read into the minds of individual plaintiffs or defendants regardless of whether these implications were true or false respecting what went on in the subjective recesses of those minds.

The same is true in economics as in law. The fiction of the "economic man" is simply an assumption of a certain uniformity of the will. The defect of this fiction was that it was assumed to be the *only* similarity needed for economic theory, whereas it is continually modified by limiting and complementary factors, all of which, in so far as they are similar, we have named "principles." In fact, the economic and legal fictions and implied promises, purposes, intentions, motives, etc.—based on the principle of similarity, but inconceivable in the physical and organic sciences—are the only mental tools of investigation by the use of which economics or law can be made into a science. All of them may be generalized in the one concept, Weber's ideal type, whether it be the scientific aspect of that type when applied to what was or is, or the ethical aspect when applied to what ought to be within the limits of the best customary practice.

The most imposing use in America of the ethical ideal type is in the so-called "physical valuation" of railways and other public utilities. Here an alternative but non-existing going concern, based on the ideal of "cost of reproduction in existing conditions," is constructed in imagination by concerted action of engineers, accountants, economists, lawyers, and courts, for the purpose of bringing the actual concern of history into conformity with what is deemed to be the reasonable value of the capital invested. This extends to reasonable prices to be charged to the public, and to reasonable services to be rendered to the public.[95] Another ideal type is that of the stabilization of the purchasing power of money in so far as the same can be accomplished within attainable limits.

These and similar ideal types are based on Weber's significant contribution to the methodology of economic research. They are constructed, however, not on his rightly excluded individualistic emotions of value of a subjective will, all of which are widely different, capricious, and without any uniformity. They are constructed on the assumption of certain similarities of concerted willingness, for the express purpose of commanding, controlling, and bringing about a different valuation in accordance with what is deemed to be the ethical ideal type of what is already being done in that class of transactions. It is this kind of similarity which makes possible a theory of economic willingness, whether it be a scientific theory of what has happened, or is expected to happen, or ought to happen in the future.

The question now reverts to the point where we started: Does our formula of transactions or going concerns furnish an alternative to Weber's methodology, which, while being scientific in the sense employed in physical and organic sciences, yet also incorporates the peculiar quality of economic science which distinguishes it from them? The answer is that our formula is scientific in that it is not based on subjective capricious entities of magic, or alchemy, or value, or will, but is based on similarities of behavior, like all

[95] Glaeser, Martin, *Outlines of Public Utility Economics* (1927) 102–114, 468–475; Commons, John R., *Legal Foundations of Capitalism*, 143 ff.

science; and that it is economic in that it distinguishes from the physical and organic sciences by discovering economic similarities in the operation of human wills, whereas the other sciences discover similarities in the operation of physical bodies. These similarities, for economic science, all turn on the principle of Future Time, a principle not found in physical or organic sciences, and made possible in economic science only by the institutions of language, number, property, liberty, and working rules that maintain security of expectations.

It is doubtless true that, for pedagogical and propagandist purposes, these scientific principles need a different methodology, the method of Personification. But it is also true that personification is the very contradiction of science, and that the last science from which personification is being painfully eliminated is that in which the human will itself is the very subject-matter of the science.

Thus we reach what we consider to be the contribution of Weber, following his preceding philosopher, Rickert,[96] towards a science of political economy and its subject-matter, Reasonable Value. It is Analysis and Insight. The former method of economists, taken from the physical scientists, may be distinguished as the method of Analysis and Synthesis. This was a purely intellectual and mathematical process of breaking up the whole into its parts and then recombining them by correlation, coefficients, and so on. But Rickert distinguished Natural Science from Historical Science. In historical science the human will is at work. Hence, according to Rickert and Weber, historical science is not reducible to measurable quantities. It operates with a goal looking to the future. But, while this future can be measured, and actually is measured in a credit and debt economy, and, while all the parts of the entire moving process can be analyzed and then synthesized by the process of rationalization, yet this process never gives us a real insight of what is going on. The method of historical science, and therefore of economic science, is the process of analysis, genesis, and insight. We reach a better understanding by attaining a better analysis and a better knowledge of sequence. Analysis and genesis are the intellectual process of rationalization. But insight is the emotional process of reading life, will, purpose, cause, consequences, expectations, into the analysis and genesis.

Historically this process is not really different from the process of natural science, if by natural science we mean, not a body of knowledge, but a process of attaining control over the forces of nature by better knowledge of the ways in which these forces operate.

[96] References, above, p. 719.

But such is not the usual meaning of the word science. It is rather the meaning of the Art of Engineering. "Art" supposedly differs from "science" in that it means human control, whereas science means only human knowledge. If, however, the subject-matter of natural science is looked upon, not as a body of knowledge but as a body of scientists acquiring knowledge by experiment and investigation, then Rickert's distinction between natural science and the science of history is illusory. A case may be made out for this view, since chemical science, for example, has created some 200,000 products unknown to nature. Physical scientists have become restless on this subject, especially since Einstein and Eddington have reduced physics to the most extreme metaphysics ever imagined by the philosophers whom they had scorned since the days of Galileo.[97]

It would seem that their way out is to change the subject-matter of science from a body of knowledge to a body of scientists. If so, then natural science becomes the same as that which economists know as the "machine process," and the universe is no longer an infinite "mechanism" independent of the human will, but is a finite "machine" constructed by scientific investigators. Something like this may happen. It seems to be outlined by Dewey. He said, "Ideas that are plans of operations to be performed are integral factors in actions which change the face of the world. . . . A genuine idealism and one compatible with science will emerge as soon as philosophy accepts the teaching of science that ideas are statements not of what is or has been—but of acts to be performed." [98]

Meanwhile, accepting the usual meaning of physical science as a body of knowledge, its subject-matter has no future, no purpose, no ideal types, and therefore differs wholly from economic science. Hence, for the latter, we need not only analysis and genesis but also understanding of the human will at work.

If we base our methodology on these distinctions, then the subject-matter of economic science is human beings acting on three variabilities in their dealings with each other and in their control over the forces of nature and each other, namely, habitual assumptions, rationalization, and insight. Habitual assumptions arise from custom and can go on, and do go on, without much reasoning or insight. Rationalization is the strictly intellectual process, which can be distinguished but not separated from assumptions and insight. Insight is the emotional, volitional, valuing, intuitive, even instinc

[97] Nichols, Herbert, "A Crisis in Science," *The Monist*, XXXIII (1923), 390. Also references to Akeley above, p 619.

[98] Dewey, John, *The Quest for Certainty* (1929), 138.

tive, process—partly custom, partly rationalization, whose highest reach is the timeliness of strategic and routine transactions, in acting for the purpose both of control over and adaptation to the forces of nature and other human beings. The three aspects together constitute what we mean by Willingness.

There is nothing absolute or fundamental about this analysis of Willingness. We simply find that it is a useful formula in analyzing and understanding the behavior of individuals in their economic transactions. Since, however, it designedly includes the highly debatable and perhaps impassable gulf between psychology and economics, we have adopted the "two-language hypothesis" of psychology and economics. Applying this language to the analysis of Willingness, we are able to distinguish the double meaning, or rather double aspect, of several words. Thus, "capitalism" has the double aspect of the "capitalist spirit" (as set up by Weber, Sombait, and Tawney), and of business transactions as the measurable behavior of that spirit. Habitual assumptions have the double aspect of unthinking impressions, and of the customary repetition of transactions. Scarcity has the double aspect of scarcity-consciousness and of limited resources. Willingness has the double aspect of expectation and of the transactions expected. Purpose has the double aspect of intention and the effects intended. Responsibility has the double aspect of conscience and of consequences. Reasor has the double aspect of rationality and of reasonableness—the rationality of analysis displayed in theory and mathematics, and the reasonableness of behavior as understood in such terms as Reasonable Practices and Reasonable Values. Finally, the word Insight itself has the double meaning of Wisdom and Timeliness—Wisdom unmeasurable because subjective and futuristic, but Timeliness measurable by the degree to which the "right" thing was done at the "right" place, the "right" time, the "right" degree of force, and the "right" quantity of the subject-matter. It is in the modern investigations of Timeliness and its strategic and routine transactions that economics passes from the abstract rationalizing of Locke and Bentham to the realistic insight or lack of insight of those who participate in the operation of going concerns.

VII. Collective Action

For these reasons it is necessary to investigate and ascertain, if possible, the principles on which collective action itself operates, since the individual must operate within it. We distinguish this collective action as Politics, and the historical stages through which it passes as social-economic results.

1. *Politics*

(1) **Personality, Principles, Organization.**—By politics we mean concerted action within a concern, designed to get and keep control of the concern and its participants. The transactions are managerial, bargaining, and rationing. The concerns are moral, economic, and sovereign. The moral concerns are those without economic or physical power, and are, in modern times, such as religious, charitable, educational, fraternal, and similar associations in so far as they rely only on the sanctions of persuasion. The economic concerns are those, such as business organizations, labor unions, farmers' coöperatives, produce or stock exchanges, in so far as they rely on the economic sanctions of coercion by protecting gains or imposing losses, through participation in, exclusion from, or non-interference with, transactions. The sovereign concern, whether municipal, state, federal, or imperial, uses the sanctions of duress through physical compulsion. The politics of the concern, therefore, is the internal activities of conflicts and leadership designed to formulate the working rules and maintain jurisdiction over individuals through control of the sanctions available to the concern.

Within the concern itself, as with the concern as a whole, the politics of the concern is also based, as opportunity may suggest, upon one or all of the three sanctions of moral, economic, or physical force. And, according to which of these sanctions predominate in the effort to get control of the concern, the three corresponding names: persuasion, coercion, duress, are given to describe the inducements; while the terms: leader, boss, and chief indicate the corresponding types of leadership.

The leader, in this restricted sense, is one who depends solely on persuasion and propaganda to attract and lead his followers. The boss,[99] like the foreman, employer, or the Tammany boss, depends on coercion through control of the jobs, contracts, livelihood, or profits of the followers. The chief,[100] like the chief of police or the military leader, depends upon duress through his control of physical force. The three sanctions may or may not be used by the same person, but usually the successful chief is adept also in using coercion and persuasion. The boss, too, is adept in using coercion and persuasion. And the leader, by successful use of

[99] The word "boss" is a literal transfer from the Dutch *baas*, where it has the same meaning of economic control. The term first appeared in New York in 1836. See Commons, John R., and Gilmore, E. A., *Documentary History of American Industrial Society*, IV, 277 ff.

[100] From the Scotch *cheef* of a clan.

persuasion alone, may become boss or chief. Mass action, without leader, boss, or chief, is a mob. *With* leader, boss, or chief, it is a going concern.

Three additional terms, in common use to distinguish different combinations of these several sanctions by which leadership is attained, are: personality, principles, and organization. Personality differs in all degrees from the child to the man, from female to male, from the stupid to the dominating individuality. It is the combination of inherited and acquired characters, which, in the outstanding personality, fits the individual to become leader, boss, or chief according to the habits and assumptions of lesser personalities attached to him for the time being.

Principles likewise differ, but their differences are different policies which leaders formulate and set forth according to their judgment of the inclinations on which lesser personalities may be united in concerted action. In this respect we distinguish political principles from scientific principles. The latter are merely intellectually observed similarities of action or purpose, like the principles of the various sciences such as jurisprudence, logic, physics, electricity, gravity, or economics. But political principles are addressed to the will and are purposeful lines of action, such as free trade, protection, business ethics, trade union principles, religious or moral principles, patriotism, loyalty, and even economy and efficiency—according to which concerted action may be aroused towards a promised goal. Here the leader becomes such, because he can formulate in language what others feel but could not tell.

Finally, organization is distinguished from personality and principles in that, when it approaches perfection, it is a smooth-working, effective hierarchy of all minor and superior leaders, bosses, or chiefs —an hierarchy which, by analogy in some cases, has come to be known ʔs "the machine," because it goes on continuously though its membership changes, on the analogy of replaceable parts. No one person is indispensable, but individual leaders may rise within the hierarchy, or may be displaced by substitutes according to the methods of selection, t ansfer, promotion, and politics found to be workable. In the proportion to which organization reaches this smooth perfection we give to it, not the physical name "machine," nor the biological name "organism," nor even the indefinite name "group," but the social activity name. " going concern." The distinguishing character of a perfected going concern is its capacity to continue with changing personalities and changing principles, not depending upon any particular person or any particular principle. It adapts itself to circumstances, changing its personalities or its

principles to fit the changing inclinations, or the conflicting inclinations, of the various groups of people whose allegiance and patronage
are needed for the continuance of the concern. It acts, indeed, like
a person, and indeed is often personified, but latterly this metaphor
is materialized in the term machine; though the social term, without metaphor, is more properly: *going concern.*

Thus economic society is a changing complexity of personalities,
principles, and organizations which are inseparable in fact and are
united in the concept of going concern. It is to this complexity
within a concern that we give the name politics, in order to distinguish it from the former simplicities of economic theory which are
properly named individualism. Instead of assumed equal individuals we have the widely different personalities of leaders and led,
bosses and bossed, officers and privates. Instead of the former
simple assumption that every equal individual seeks his self-interest,
we have widely different and conflicting principles on which unequal
individuals seek a common interest. Instead of unregulated individuals, we have hierarchies which regulate them. The whole of
this complex activity is politics. And it is not Socialism or Communism that is the opposite of Anarchism or Individualism—it is
Politics.

The meaning of the word "politics" has usually been limited to
the activities designed to get control of what was deemed to be
the dominant concern, the State. But with the modern emergence
of innumerable forms of economic and moral concerted action, it
is found that the similar complexity of personalities, principles, and
organizations is found in all concerns. The fact that the sovereign
concern uses the sanction of physical force has seemed to give
dominance to it, as indicated by the word, "sovereign." But this is
illusory, since, as we have seen, sovereignty has been the gradual,
but incomplete, extraction of violence from private transactions, and
other concerns dominate the state.

For the State consists in the enforcement, by physical sanctions,
of what private parties might otherwise endeavor to enforce by
private violence. Consequently, instead of resorting to private
violence, a form of concerted action, under the name Political
Parties, has evolved as organizations within the sovereign concern
for the purpose of selecting and getting control of the hierarchy of
legislative, executive, and judicial personalities whose concerted
action determines the legal rights, duties, liberties, and exposures
involved in all economic transactions. For, the legal relations indicated by these terms are merely the physical sanctions of society
specialized for the purpose of control, distinguished from the "extra-

752   INSTITUTIONAL ECONOMICS

legal" sanctions of economic and moral power, which may even be more powerful than physical force.

Political parties, like other going concerns, have evolved through the variable combinations of personality, principles, and organization. In the early days of the American Republic, when personalities seemed to dominate, political parties were looked upon as "factions" whose unscrupulous struggles seemed to jeopardize the national unity of the hitherto independent colonies. But eventually it was found that such leading personalities as Hamilton and Jefferson stood for economic and political principles; and eventually, when these and other conflicting principles reached the stage of enduring organization, they actually and even unconstitutionally changed the method of electing the President from an illusory convention of distinguished citizens (the college of electors proposed by the framers of the Constitution), to the conventions of political parties designed to nominate and elect the electors.[101]

The original illusion of calm discussion by disinterested citizens arose from the naïve fallacy of the Age of Reason of the Eighteenth Century, that man was a rational being who needed only to see the right in order to do it. But political parties, like all concerted action, are founded on the passions, stupidity, and inequalities of masses of people, and they have the very practical purpose of getting and keeping control of the officials who formulate the will of the state. So that political parties, rather than the state, have become the economic concerns through which the sanctions of physical force are directed towards economic gain or loss. In other concerns (such as business organizations, labor organizations, farmers' organizations, bankers' organizations), these internal concerted struggles to get control of the concern pass under such different names as "syndicates," "insiders," "machines," "factions," "left-wingers," "right-wingers." Yet they have the similar phenomena of personality, principles, and organization—whose totality may be expressed by the one general term, the politics of the concern.

It happens, from the fact of division of labor within a concern, that leading personalities emerge as specialists peculiarly fitted by experience and success to guide certain special activities of the concern. The politician, as we have described him, is the specialist in psychology. By experience and insight he knows and works upon the passions, stupidities, inequalities, customs, habitual assumptions of individuals in such a way as to unite them in mass action. Just

---

[101] On Hamilton and Jefferson see especially Bowers, Claude, *Jefferson and Hamilton* (1925). On the origin of the Convention System see Bryce, James, *The American Commonwealth* (1921, 1929), II. See the discussions on Direct Primaries in Commons, John R., *Proportional Representation* (2d ed., 1907).

as the engineer is the specialist in efficiency and the business man is the specialist in scarcity, so the politician is the specialist in human psychology. This specialization has been overlooked by all utopias, as well as by business economists and managerial economists during the past hundred years. They would place the social philosopher, the "intellectual," the business man, the engineer in control of collective action. But "natural selection" places the politician there. It is he that has political sense.

Although the concerted action of politics within a concern is founded on passion, stupidity, inequality, and mass action, yet it can be investigated scientifically, like the complexities of all other sciences. We cannot tell in advance, for any particular situation, just what the complexity signifies. But, as in other sciences, we may construct, from observation or experiment, certain scientific principles, or supposed similarities of behavior, which then can be used in particular situations for purposes of investigation. This academic method, by which the scientific mind works in all investigations, we have described as the method of analysis, genesis, and insight.

The method of analysis consists in breaking up the complexity into all the supposed similarities of behavior, and then giving to each similarity a name which designates it as a proposed scientific principle to be tested by investigation. The method of genesis consists in the discovery of changes which have occurred in the past as explanations of why the present situation exists as it is. The method of insight consists in understanding the ways of leadership and followship.

We have already suggested this academic method in the distinctions, above, between personality, political principles, and organization. Each is a scientific principle, since it is a uniformity derived from observation, whose evolution is genesis and whose understanding is insight. But there are four other scientific principles with their subdivisions and subject-matter, discoverable in the analysis of the totality of politics, which in particular concrete cases, may be brought together in order to discover their relative importance in the analysis, genesis, and insight. These principles are Jurisdiction, Rationing, Stabilization, and Justification.

The subdivisions of the jurisdictional powers are territorial, personal, and transactional jurisdiction. The subdivisions of the Rationing process are "log-rolling," dictatorship, coöperation, collective bargaining, and judicial decision. The subject-matter of the stabilizing process is standardization of practices, prices, and employment. The subdivisions of Justification are propaganda and

754 INSTITUTIONAL ECONOMICS

habitual assumptions. Each of these is inseparable, in fact, from all the others, and all are properly included under the more general principle of politics, since all are different aspects of the general principle of concerted action within a concern designed to control the concern and therefore control individual action. They shade into each other; but they are distinguishable by the analytic process of taking extreme cases; by the genetic process of showing, historically, how they change from one to the other; and by the synthetic process of insight at the point where one or the other is a strategic factor and the others are routine or contributory.

(2) **Jurisdiction.**—By jurisdiction we mean the *scope* of the collective action which controls individual action.[102] It means some kind of authority which decides disputes between individuals by interpreting old rules or devising new rules; and it means some kind of penalty or sanction imposed on individuals for violation of the rules. The extremest penalty or sanction is the physical punishment imposed by sovereignty. But there are also the penalties of loss of wages, or loss of profits, imposed by modern economic concerns. And, if the economic government is not strongly organized, there is still the sanction of good or bad opinion of those on whom the individual depends for his living or profits. Jurisdiction is, therefore, collective action within a limited field, controlling the conduct of individuals by the sanctions of physical, economic, or moral force. We merely mention three aspects of jurisdiction—whose differences are understandable—by naming them Territorial, Personal, and Transactional Jurisdictions. The last named is the one which has mainly occupied our attention in the field of institutional economics.

(3) **Rationing.** *a. The Process.*—Rationing transactions are the process of exercising jurisdiction. They are distinguishable as "log-rolling," dictatorship, coöperation, collective bargaining, and judicial decision. The economic principle, common to all, is the formulation of rules which shall govern the transactions of subordinate participants in sharing among themselves the burdens and benefits of the production and enjoyment of wealth. Rationing transactions differ from managerial, in that the latter are the execution of the rules thus authorized; they differ from bargaining transactions, in that these are the agreements among individuals supposed to be equal, permitted by the rules and enforced by the executives.

These three types of transactions—rationing, managerial, and bargaining—in their various combinations cover the entire range of economic behavior. It requires historical analysis to distinguish

---

[102] See Commons, John R., on "Jurisdictional Disputes" in *Wertheim Lecture Series on Industrial Relations* (1928).

them, for they unfold from the simple conditions of primitive or frontier society, where they are not distinguishable, into the highly developed industrial civilization. They can here be distinguished, and can then be read back to their germs in the simple society.

Thus "log-rolling," a special case of rationing, may be distinguished as the principle of democratic concerted action. Though the term originated as American slang, yet, like such other terms as "job," or "boss," derived from the unlettered rank and file of the people, it enters learned literature when it is found to fit distinctions not otherwise provided in the language. While physical sciences take their technical terms from Greek or Latin, such procedure would be fatal to social science. In this case the term "log-rolling" indicates a primitive democratic process for which no other term is so precise in the effort to distinguish it from bargaining, managing, coöperation, and dictatorship. Fundamentally it is the process of reaching voluntary agreements of partnership among equals in sharing the benefits and burdens of a joint enterprise. The American pioneers agreed to help each other in rolling and raising the logs to build their log houses. Like many terms that finally get learned application, this term began with the physical process, then was expanded by analogy to include the legislative process of ' trading votes," where, however, it obtained inaccurately the invidious meaning of desertion from one's moral principles in order to get the votes of those whose morals were supposedly unprincipled.[103]

But this crimination of log-rolling confuses purpose with process. The process is universal; the purpose may be good or bad. When two persons fix up a partnership agreement to share the benefits and burdens of their common enterprise, or when the members of a legislature fix up a coalition agreeing to vote for each other's measures, it looks like collective bargaining, or coöperation; but it is not, if the meanings of words are to be made precise enough to fit the real differences. Log-rolling is not bargaining, though it is negotiation. In this respect it is like cooperation collective bargaining, or any transactions which also require negotiation respecting the terms on which agreements shall be undertaken. Negotiation is common to all transactions, but if they are classified solely according to this principle, then the social distinctions are blurred. The outcome of log-rolling, however, is as nearly a reasonable reconciliation of all conflicting interests as representative democracy has been able to reach in parliamentary countries.

Log-rolling is one extreme of which dictatorship is the opposite

[103] See Bryce, James, *The American Commonwealth*, II, 160 (1921, 1929).

extreme. For log-rolling is agreement among equals who are not compelled by duress or coercion to agree. But dictatorship is agreement among subordinates who are compelled by chief or boss to agree. Hence log-rolling may be said to be the democratic process of agreeing upon the rationing of economic burdens and benefits, but dictatorship is the autocratic process.

Yet even the dictator is not wholly autocratic. He must have with him at least an effective minority who are held to willing obedience by his personality, principles, and organization. As such, he is not so much a person as he is the institution of dictatorship.

If log-rolling is the democratic process and dictatorship is the autocratic process of rationing burdens and benefits, then the inefficiency of the former and the efficiency of the latter are evident. Human effort is wasted, delayed, and weakened in the log-rolling process of reaching, among equals, agreement upon the rules to be followed in rationing the burdens and benefits of the production and distribution of wealth. But in the autocratic process human effort is conserved, quickened, and strengthened by subordination to one acknowledged superior. In the log-rolling process many independent wills must agree. In the autocratic process the wills are not independent. It is on account of this predicament between the extremes of log-rolling and dictatorship that two intermediate processes of concerted action have been tried—coöperation and collective bargaining. The meanings of these terms have not been clear— indeed, it required three-fourths of the Nineteenth Century and the Russian Revolution of the Twentieth Century to work out the experiments which have now begun to clarify their meanings.

Prior to the decade of the 1850's, especially during the '30's and '40's, the abuses of the new capitalism, based on the individualism of Smith, Bentham, and Ricardo, were so flagrant that the opposing philosophy, associationism, gained wide-spread acceptance. It took several forms. At one extreme was Anarchism, by which was meant voluntary coöperation. At the other extreme was Communism, by which was meant compulsory coöperation. The essential doctrine of all was the substitution of coöperation for competition. Labor organizations took up the idea piecemeal, and experimented with it down to near the end of the Nineteenth Century. They tried coöperative marketing, to displace the merchant-capitalist, by setting up their own wholesale warehouses. They tried coöperative production, to displace the employer-capitalist, by organizing their own factories. They tried even coöperative banking, to displace the financial capitalist. They tried consumers' coöperation, to displace the retail merchant.

Some of these experiments survive, though in attenuated form, to the present day. Building and loan associations and credit unions are survivals of the coöperative banking of the '50's. The last grand attempts towards coöperative enterprise were made by the Knights of Labor and the Farmers' Grange, during the '70's and '80's. But all of these labor and farmer coöperatives broke down. The majority of labor coöperatives were unsuccessful, because it turned out that laborers were incompetent to elect the boss whom they must obey in the shop. The elections fell into the hands of politicians within the coöperative, and the issue became the log-rolling one as to who should control the manager and make the rules which he would enforce on the members.

Neither could the coöperatives elect the business man who could master the intricacies of the markets. The successful business man cannot be elected repeatedly by popular vote. He elects himself out of the struggles of competition and the rivalries for promotion.

Even if the coöperatives were successful, they still were unsuccessful. Success meant that their business expanded and they had to take on new workers. But those on the inside would not take in the new workers as coöperators—they took them in as hired hands. Hence the successful coöperatives became business corporations, and labor, as a class, remained where it had been. The coöperatives were unsuccessful if they failed, and unsuccessful if they succeeded.

But the trade union movement, which began in the decade of the '50's, abandoned all attempts, by coöperation, to displace the capitalists. The unionists fell back to where they could do something now by concerted action, namely, get more wages and shorter hours out of the capitalist system. They changed their philosophy from producing power to bargaining power. They left the employer in charge of the shop, and endeavored only to fix the price, shorten the hours of labor, and establish the working rules.

But even this was not collective bargaining. It was labor dictatorship. We can best show the double meaning by citing the labor organizations of San Francisco: [104] For several years these labor organizations controlled the building trades. They fixed their wages, hours, and rules, then took their schedules around to the employers individually and required them to sign individually on the dotted line. They called it "collective bargaining," but it was labor dictatorship.

That was a game which the employers eventually could play better than the trade unions. Suddenly the employers locked out the

[104] See Haber, Wm., *Industrial Relations in the Building Industry*, Chap. 14 on "The American Plan in San Francisco" (1930).

workers; and, when the unions tried to break the employers' association, they found that there were no independent employers with whom they could deal. The banks had affiliated with the employers, and an independent employer could not get credit. The merchants and material men had affiliated, and an independent employer could not sell his product or buy materials. The employers called it "the American plan," but it was, in fact, employer dictatorship.

Neither of these collective dictatorships was collective bargaining. By collective bargaining both sides are organized equally. Neither employer nor employee acts individually. But the representatives of each draw up a joint agreement, fixing hours, wages, and working rules. Then each individual contract of labor between an individual employer and an individual worker is controlled by the joint agreement. This is what is meant by the Trade Agreement. It did not come to be understood until the beginning of the Twentieth Century. Collective Bargaining is the working rules of trade agreements.

This labor history repeats itself in the farmers' coöperative movement. Against this movement the commission-men on the produce exchanges organize on a nation-wide scale. They obtain the support of the national Chamber of Commerce, representing hundreds of chambers of commerce throughout the country. They obtain the support of the banks. The Chamber of Commerce, through its president, protests to the President of the United States and to the Chairman of the Federal Farm Board. The program of the Board, they know, will displace the middlemen altogether The government is lending financial support to displace them.

As long as a capable President and a capable chairman of the Farm Board are in charge, the farmers are able to resist this opposition of the entire capitalist forces of the nation. But when the President and the Chairman retire or get tired, the farmers must elect their own managers, or politicians see to it that less capable men are placed on the Farm Board, or Congress cuts the appropriations. When the farmers are left to conduct their own struggle, are they able to elect competent managers? This is politics.

The issue turns on the double meaning of "marketing." It means "production of wealth" and it means bargaining for its distribution.

The middleman is a producer. He manages the technical process of assembling products and physically distributing them. In economic language, he creates "place, form, and time utility." Somebody must perform this process. Can a coöperative perform it more efficiently than business men who have shown their capacity by surviving? Can business men be efficiently displaced by popular election? These are the grave problems of collective action and institutional economics.

The other meaning of marketing is bargaining and pricing. Collective bargaining would mean, in this case, that the commission-men would be recognized as an organization with whom the organized farmers would, through their representatives, make trade agreements as to prices, deliveries, payments, and other conditions. Instead of displacing the middlemen by coöperation, they would be dealt with by collective bargaining.

The one great advantage of the competitive system is that it shifts bankruptcy to individuals, whereas bankruptcy of a coöperative bankrupts the whole or a part of an entire social class. If an individual business concern fails, then its competitors absorb its customers, and business as a whole goes on. But if a coöperative fails, then all of its members fail, and, worst of all, they lose confidence in each other and even in their government.

Collective bargaining has its difficulties, as well as coöperation. But it does this much. It lets the business man keep the chances of bankruptcy. There is one field of agricultural concerted action where it seems to be successful. The liquid milk farmers do not take over the marketing process by coöperative marketing. They only make trade agreements, as to prices and practices, with the middlemen who continue to do the marketing. They do not displace Capitalism, nor do they arbitrarily set their prices by agricultural dictatorship. They bargain collectively, and resort to arbitration, if necessary. Arbitration is rationing by a judiciary in individual or collective disputes.

Thus arbitration is a subdivision of the fifth kind of Rationing Transaction, which we name Judicial Decision. When an arbitrator or judge decides a dispute between plaintiff and defendant, he transfers from one person to another person an amount of money or goods, present or expected. He does this, not by log-rolling, because he is superior over the litigants; nor by dictatorship, because he is himself bound by custom, precedent, or by statute in the form of a constitution, a by-law or a trade agreement; not by coöperation, because he acts with authority; not by collective bargaining, though he listens to the pleadings and arguments of the representatives of the parties; and not by individual bargaining because this would be bribery. He does it by the judicial procedure of rendering a mere opinion, after weighing all the facts and arguments. Hence the judicial decision, bound by all the procedure of notice to litigants, hearing their testimony and arguments, weighing the facts and arguments in the light of custom, precedent, and statute, is judicial rationing of wealth.

b. The Economic Consequences.—We have now seen five different forms of Rationing Transactions, all of them being different methods of laying down rules by concerted action. We proceed to note their economic consequences, in the production and distribution of wealth, as Quantity Rationing, Value Rationing, and Price Rationing.

Quantity rationing is the direct authoritative assignment of a quantity of labor or of products of labor to particular workers or particular consumers, without bargaining and without money, but through commands obeyed by subordinate managers. In the judicial rationing it is known as "specific performance." But this is also the character of all quantity rationing. It is commands issued to individuals ordering them to perform a specified service or to deliver a specified product, without bargaining as to quantities, and without the intervention of money. Quantity rationing is specific performance. Its large-scale organization is the Communism of Soviet Russia.

But Value rationing is the payment of money, which, on account of its general, though variable, purchasing power, is the indirect and inverse rationing of labor or products. If the value of the money rises, then a specified payment of money is a payment of a larger quantity of the total wealth; but if the value of money falls, then the specified payment is a smaller quantity of the total wealth. Hence we name it Value rationing. *Directly,* it is money rationing, *indirectly* and *inversely* it is quantity rationing.

Value rationing may be named specific *payment,* where quantity rationing was specific *performance.* Value rationing is commands issued to individuals ordering them to pay or accept, without bargaining, a specified sum of money. Its large-scale operation is Taxes; its small-scale operation is judicial awards. The large-scale operation is directed by the log-rolling transactions of legislatures or by dictatorship.[105]

Price rationing lies between quantity and value rationing, because value is a quantity of product *times* its price. It differs from quantity rationing in that the price per unit is fixed, but the quantity bought or sold by individuals at that price is optional. It differs from value rationing in that it relates to the value of a customary

---

[105] The Constitution of the German Republic is so constructed that the President may convert it temporarily—and, it turns out, even permanently—into a dictatorship, by dissolving the legislature, with its log-rolling, and appointing a dictator supposedly not influenced by log-rolling. By this provision it becomes, without violating the Constitution, a Fascist Dictatorship.

unit of a specified product, whereas value rationing leaves optional the choice of quantities of services or products purchaseable with the quantity of money rationed. All price-fixing is price rationing. In the case of the post office, the prices of different services are fixed by the log-rolling process of Congress at relatively high prices for correspondence, low prices for newspapers, no prices for agricultural crop reporting, and the "franking" privilege for officials. Consequently, large profits are made on correspondence which pay the losses on newspapers and crop reporting, while the deficit is rationed to taxpayers.[106]

The most comprehensive scheme of price rationing is that introduced by the Soviet Republic in cases where quantity rationing was ineffective. The government "trusts," by fixing low prices for the peasants' raw materials and high prices for the finished products sold to the peasants, accumulate large purchasing power for financing the great Five-Year-Plan of constructing railways, building factories, and electrification. Price rationing is price-fixing, and, in this case, is compulsory "saving" by rationing, instead of the capitalistic voluntary saving by selling bonds.

c. Justification.—Thus rationing, in one or another of its processes or results, is the peculiar characteristic of concerted action in laying down rules for the managerial and bargaining transactions of individuals in the production and distribution of wealth. In so far as it encroaches on individuals it deprives them of liberty by imposing duties. Upon opposite individuals, this has the correlative and equal effect of reducing their exposures and increasing their rights. Since the economic consequences occur without the consent of individuals but are an authoritative distribution of burdens and benefits, the rationing transactions may be said to indicate the Struggle for Power, whereas bargaining transactions are the Struggle for Wealth. In Soviet Russia, where rationing has been substituted for bargaining, it has been observed by Professor Hoover that

"Some part, at least, of the energy which men of ability in the Capitalistic world expend in amassing wealth is canalized in the struggle for power. Within the State Trusts and Commisariats, within the Party, the struggle for Power is sharper than within institutions of Capitalism. The orthodox Party member of today finds tomorrow that his orthodoxy has been successfully attacked by a fellow Party member who hates or fears him, and he is ruthlessly expelled from the Party. The institution of the 'chistka,' or 'cleaning' has been evolved, and is used in every institution in Russia to give full rein to suspicion, envy and sadism. . . .

[106] Below, p. 805, The Police Power of Taxation.

Probably the greater part of the laborers in Soviet Russia do not feel that they are deprived of freedom in any way. As long as a man does not attempt to rise out of the mass of laborers there is little curtailment of freedom of a sort which the ordinary worker would feel. . . . Although the struggle for power is more intense than in the Capitalistic World, the great mass of the people do not feel the bitter necessity of safeguarding or improving their individual economic status, either by saving or increasing their earning capacity through advancement to more responsible posts." [107]

This is an extreme case of the substitution of rationing for bargaining. But the similar struggle for power, distinguished from the struggle for wealth, characterizes, in greater or less degree, all of that concerted action within any concern whatever, designed to control its rationing transactions, to which we give the generic name Politics.

It is for this reason that rationing transactions require justification in order to elicit the amount of concerted action needed to impose them. And this justification carries with it crimination of those who do not conform to the rules imposed. It is this justification and crimination that is the language of politics.

We may classify justifications and their explicit or implied criminations according to the two main principles of habitual assumptions and security of expectations. It is from habitual assumptions, as we have seen, that the ideas of right and wrong are derived, while from the wish for security of expectations is derived the principle of stabilization. The two go together, for every procedure of stabilization is justified as right and its violation criminated as wrong. And it is only within the limits of habitual assumptions and security of expectations that the concerted action of politics can operate. We can state these limits in their historical development as various aspects of the principles of standardization or stabilization.

The most inclusive principle of stabilization is custom. What has been, is what people expect. Politics cannot arbitrarily override custom. Hence the justification by precedent. But when customs change or conflict with each other, the principle of stabilization centers first on standardization of weights and measures, in place of the arbitrary changes surreptitiously introduced by interested parties. This makes possible the next step, the rise of business debts and their enforcement, instead of leaving them to honor and caprice. This leads to modern political movements looking to-

[107] Hoover, Calvin B., "Some Economic and Social Consequences of Russian Communism," *Econ. Jour.*, XL, 422; *The Economic Life of Soviet Russia* (1931).

wards the stabilization of prices, of business, and of employment, reaching its extreme in Russia. Finally the stabilization of international relations, by diplomacy or a world court.

These, it must be admitted, are ideal types and are open to the criticisms which we have advanced. They may not be agreed upon by all. Hence we fall back on the actual extent to which any or all working rules are sanctioned by the final authority of the orderly administration of physical force, from which there is no further appeal except John Locke's "appeal to heaven." To the extent that private violence is eliminated, then the practices and valuations arrived at must be considered reasonable for that time, place, and civilization. However obnoxious and revolting they are to individuals or to later civilizations, they are "natural" and therefore reasonable, as Quesnay maintained [108] regarding "natural rights," for the time, place, and civilization where they are "obviously" natural and reasonable. They accomplish the main purpose of keeping the concern agoing, and if by revolution and conquest they are changed and the change substitutes another concern, then the concepts of reason and reasonableness are changed as the new order becomes habitual.

For who can say, with any claim to authority, that the misery and poverty of millions of people in a modern capitalistic nation are due to the recognition of either divine or natural rights or to reasonableness in transactions, valuations, and rationing, superior to the superstitions of the Andaman Islanders, the slavery of Greece or the Southern States, or dictatorship of Italy or Russia? They are simply the way in which the complex of institutions works at the time and place, and no individual is divine enough to set up his standards of nature and reason different from the standards which collective action has set for him and others Reasonable value is not intellectual or rational—it is the valuations of stupidity, passion, ignorance, and the dominant collective action that controls individual action It is fondly hoped both for America and the world that these practices may improve, but even so there may be disputes as to whether it is improvement or decadence.

In any case, the dominant institutions decide by collective action what is reasonable, regardless of what individuals think. It is the process of reaching these decisions which we name Politics.

2. Merchant Capitalism, Employer Capitalism, Banker Capitalism—the Industrial Stages

The preceding relativistic meanings of natural rights and reasonable values are the evolutionary meanings of History. Whether

[108] Above, p. 125, Quesnay.

INDUSTRIAL STAGES

1 EXTENT OF MARKET	2 KIND OF BARGAIN	3 CAPITAL OWNERSHIP	4 INDUSTRIAL CLASSES	5 KIND OF WORK	6 COMPETITIVE MENACE	7 PROTECTIVE ORGANIZATION	8 CASE
1. Itinerant	Wages	*Customer-Employer* Material, Household, Board and lodging | *Journeyman*	Farm family, Skilled helper	Skilled supervision	Family workers	None	Itinerant individuals 1648
2. Personal	Custom order	*Merchant-Master-Journeyman* Material, Hand tools, Home shop	Merchant-Master-Journeyman	"Bespoke"	"Bad ware"	Craft guild	Boston "Company of Shoemakers" 1648
3. Local	Retail	*Merchant-Master* Material, Finished stock, Short credits, Sales shop | *Journeyman* Hand tools, Home shop	Merchant-Master-Journeyman	"Shop"	"Market" work, "Advertisers" auctions	Retail merchants' association	Philadelphia "Society of the Master Cordwainers" 1789
4. Waterways	Wholesale order	*Merchant-Master* Material, Finished stock, Long credits, Store-room | *Journeyman*	Merchant-Master | Journeyman	"Order"	"Scabs", Interstate producers	Journeymen's society, Masters' society	Philadelphia "Federal Society of Journeymen Cordwainers" 1794
5. Highways	Wholesale speculative	*Merchant-Capitalist* Material, Finished stock, Bank credits, Warehouse "Manufactory" | *Contractor* Work shop | *Journeyman* Hand tools	Merchant-Capitalist | Contractor | Journeyman	Team work	Prison, Sweatshop, "Foreigner", "Speeding up"	Journeymen's society, Manufacturers' association[a], Employers' association	Philadelphia "United Beneficial Society of Journeymen Cordwainers" 1835

1	2	3			4			5	6	7	8
EXTENT OF MARKET	KIND OF BARGAIN	CAPITAL OWNERSHIP			INDUSTRIAL CLASSES			KIND OF WORK	COMPETITIVE MENACE	PROTECTIVE ORGANIZATION	CASE
6. Rail	Whole-sale spec-ula-tive	*Merchant-Capitalist*: Material, Finished stock, Bank credits, Warehouse "Manufactory"	*Contract Manufacturer* Work shop	*Journeyman* Footpower machines	Merchant-Capitalist, Jobber, Wholesaler	"Manufacturer"	Journeyman	Team work	Green hands, Chinese, Women, Children, Prisoners, Foreigners	Trade unions, Employers' association, Manufacturers' association[a]	"Knights of St. Crispin" 1868-1872
7. World	Factory order	*Manufacturer*: Material, Stock, Credits, Power machinery, Factory		*Laborer* None	*Manufacturer* Vertical Integration		Wage and salary earners	Piece work	Child labor, Long hours, Immigrants, Foreign products	Industrial union, Employers' association, Manufacturers' association[a]	"Boot and Shoe Workers' Union" 1895
8. World	Leases, Stocks, Bonds	Bankers, Investors		*Laborer* None	Investors	Management	Wage and salary earners	Standard-ization	Price and wage cutters	Holding companies, Institutes, Cartels, Patents, Good-will, Unions	Shoe machinery (1918) U.S. Steel (1920)

[a] The "Manufacturers' Association" is the association based on the merchant or price-fixing function.

they indicate progress or decadence is a matter of individual or group opinion. They are ethical, not in the sense of subjective ethics, but in the sense of institutional ethics that sets up ideal types for collective guidance and brings order out of conflict. They keep the collectivity agoing, and the fate of history decides whether they are wrong or right.

The historical stages which determine survival may be distinguished as Industrial and Economic. They are inseparable and we are compelled to overlap them as we go along, but the industrial stages are the changes in Technology named, by Marx and his followers, the materialistic interpretation of history. The economic stages are the changes in institutions which we designate broadly as the stages of Scarcity, Abundance, and Stabilization.

We shall not attempt to go back to the anthropological stages but shall limit ourselves to the evolution of capitalism out of feudalism. We have to do here with those "big ideas" which we name social philosophies.

Capitalism is not a single or static concept. It is an evolutionary concept of three historic stages, Merchant Capitalism, Employer Capitalism, Banker Capitalism. The last named is now dominant, owing to the prevalence of the credit system, while the first arose out of the extension of markets and the second out of technology.

Different industries move at different rates of speed towards the final consummation. A typical American industry, shoe-making,[109] whose product is transportable, will illustrate the evolution of these stages with their changes in technology and ownership. Similar investigations may be made and compared, for other industries. The accompanying chart is an outline of these industrial stages and the accompanying evolution of classes, ownership, and organization.

In the early agricultural period the shoemaker was an itinerant skilled worker, traveling with his hand tools to the home of his employer, the farmer, whose family performed the unskilled parts of the work. The customer was the owner of the capital. The laborer's wage was paid in board, lodging, and money.

Next, with the emergence of towns, his customers travel to the shoemaker. He sets up his shop, perhaps at his home, and combines

---

[109] See accompanying chart "Industrial Stages." See Commons, John R., "The American Shoemakers, A Sketch of Industrial Evolution," Quar. Jour. Econ., XXIV (1909), reprinted in Commons, John R., Labor and Administration (1913), Chap. XIV. The cases are reprinted in Documentary History of American Industrial Society, III. See also Bücher, K., Industrial Evolution (tr. 1901), who first developed this evolution of marketing stages out of the evolution of technology. I have personally watched a similar evolution, "recapitulated" in a period of twenty years, in the men's clothing industry of Chicago, after the year 1900. See also the monumental work of Sombart, W., Der Moderne Kapitalismus, 6 vols. (1928).

in himself the functions, afterwards separated, of owner, merchant, employer, and journeyman or skilled laborer. He owns his materials, tools, shop. He bargains for the quality and price *before* the work is done, for which reason we name this the custom-order stage of industry. He is his own employer and employee. He is self-employed. The unskilled work is done by apprentices or helpers, the former bound to him by contracts of service in which he has the rights of a parent and the duty to teach the trade and the rudiments of learning. He is schoolmaster and trademaster.

This is the craft-guild stage of industry, the stage of master and servant. In America there remain records of only two craft guilds, the "Corporation of Shoemakers" and the "Corporation of Coopers," Boston, 1648. The charter was granted on the petition of the shoemakers giving them authority jointly to set up standards of quality and workmanship and to suppress "bad ware" and bad workmen by prosecution before the county court. They were prohibited from enhancing the prices of boots, shoes, or wages, and from preventing itinerants of the previous stage from working on the leather belonging to customers. Similar reservations were made in Europe during the Fifteenth and Sixteenth Centuries. It was both a duty and a privilege to exclude bad ware and incompetent shoemakers. As a duty, it protected the public. As a privilege it excluded the competition of inefficient workers. Eventually, in Europe, the privilege outweighed the duty, and the guilds were ultimately suppressed or their privileges withdrawn. In Boston the charter ran for three years and was not renewed.

Next is the retail shop stage and the beginning of the separation of the merchant function from both the master and labor function, as well as the beginning of *merchants'* associations designed, now, to prevent the competition of auctions, or advertisers, or cut prices on the open market. The merchant-master assembles a stock of shoes made in dull times at low wages, and instead of a price-bargain made *before* the work is done, as in the custom-order stage, it is made *after* the work is done. Hence the beginning of speculative markets, and the merchant-function gains importance at the expense of both the employer-function and the employee-function.

But the separation is not as yet complete. With the extension of waterways the merchant-master seeks retailers at a distance. He carries samples and takes orders for goods to be afterwards made and delivered. This was the stage reached at about the time when the American Constitution was formed, 1787, and the enthusiasm and parades of "manufacturers" and mechanics in honor of that instrument indicate their demand for the abolition of colonial tariffs which obstructed the wholesale-order business. Great prosperity ensued with the extension of free markets and confirmed the popularity of the Constitution.

But soon a new problem appeared. The journeyman was now making shoes for three markets at three levels of competition. It was the same shoe with the same quality of material and workmanship and the same hand tools. But in the custom-order market the price could be set higher than in the retail market, while in the wholesale-order market there was the additional expense of transportation and solicitation of business. Seeing that there was no change in tools or workmanship, if the quality was to be kept the same, the master-workman could meet these different levels of competition only by paying lower wages on shoes for the retail market than for the custom-order market and still lower wages on shoes for the wholesale-order market. The issue arose of three prices paid for the same work to the same workmen at the same time.

It was these different levels of wages for the same work that provoked into existence the first trade union of journeymen cordwainers, 1794 to 1806. The journeymen organized in order to exclude "scabs" and thereby to force the master-workmen to pay the highest or custom-order wage for all markets. The masters then organized in defense as an *employers'* association to keep down wages for the retail and wholesale-order markets, but not for the custom-order market. When it came to trial the journeymen were convicted and punished for conspiracy under the common-law rule which was hostile to combinations of workmen whether intended to benefit themselves or injure others.[110]

We come next to the wholesale-speculative stage of the industry and the appearance of the Merchant-Capitalist and the Commercial Bank. This stage is indicated from documents preserved from Philadelphia as of the year 1835. The merchant-capitalist differed from the master-workman in that he was not a mechanic who worked his way up from apprentice to journeyman and then became a master, but he was solely a merchant, usually from the outside and unacquainted with the technology of manufacture. The latter was left to the master-workman who now became a small contractor in a small shop, working along with his journeymen and apprentices, and selling his output to the merchant-capitalist. The merchant-capitalist owned the raw material and a warehouse where he employed

---

[110] *The Trial of the Journeymen Boot & Shoemakers of Philadelphia* (1806). *Doc. Hist.* III, 61 ff; Commons, J. R., "The American Shoemakers, 1648–1895," *Quar. Jour. Econ.*, XXIV (1909); Nelles, Walter, "The First American Labor Case," *Yale Law Jour.*, XLI (1931), 165.

designers, pattern-makers, and cutters, then furnished the materials in this partly fabricated shape to the small contractors who competed with each other to perform solely the labor work of converting the materials into shoes. This is the sweat-shop stage of industry, and the former master-workman becomes the sweat-shop boss, for he makes his profit, not by improvements in the hand tools, nor by buying materials and selling shoes, but solely out of the sweat of the workers, himself included.

This occurs on account of the bargaining advantage of the merchant-capitalist. By the extension of markets he has the option of all the different methods of manufacture. He can have his shoes made in distant localities and can import from foreign markets. He can make contracts with governments for convict labor. He can employ journeymen, women and children in their homes. He can employ small contractors, the former master-workmen. He intensifies their competition. He deprives the retail merchant of his employer-function. The employer now becomes the sweat-shop boss, without capital. The merchant-capitalist calls into being the commercial bank, and his "capital" is no longer the "technological" capital of the classical economists but is mainly the "business" capital of short-time credits advanced to retailers and financed by banks. For this reason we name his emergence the wholesale speculative stage of industry.

It was during this stage of merchant-capitalism that the philosophy of Anarchism, especially in France and America, was taken over from Godwin's "political justice" and converted into economics. Proudhon in France, and the so-called Associationism in America, adopted prior to 1850, from Fourier, proposed voluntary coöperation of master-workmen and small farmers—who correspond in agriculture to the master-workman in industry—to take the place of the merchant-capitalist. They proposed coöperative warehouses and co-operative purchase of raw materials. They proposed coöperative marketing of the product. They proposed coöperative production in the small competing shops or farms of the sweat-shop contractors or small farmers. In countries other than France and America, like Ireland, Spain, Italy, and Russia, where the farmers were peasants paying rack-rent to great landlords, anarchism took the revolutionary form of breaking up the estates and turning the ownership over to the peasants in small holdings; but this had already been done in France by the Revolution of 1789, while in the northern part of America the small holdings of farmers had come down from colonial times. Hence in these countries the anarchist philosophy was applied to the abolition, not of landlordism, but of merchant-capitalism.

When it came to reducing the anarchist philosophy to practice, all of the experiments broke down.[111] But during this period, in 1842, the shoemakers in Massachusetts gained a decision of the court modifying the common-law doctrine of the Philadelphia case, and holding that a combination of workmen designed to benefit themselves, even though the purpose of the strike was to exclude non-unionists from the shop and thereby to raise wages, was not an unlawful conspiracy.[112] Prior to this decision it had already been held that an association of employers, organized to defend themselves against the aggression of a shoe-workers' union, was lawful.[113] Now, the similar aggressive combination of laborers became apparently lawful.

From these decisions was laid the foundations for a shift from the anarchist philosophy of association to the craft philosophy of unionism, the French translation of which is syndicalism.[114] Unionism or syndicalism, whether associations of employers and manufacturers, or associations of employees, is an extension of the philosophy of anarchism in that it applies to associations the doctrine of non-interference by the state which the earlier anarchists applied only to individuals. To the extent that, by the decisions of courts, the state refuses to interfere and prevents private persons from interfering with the rules and regulations of private associations, to that extent are the ideals of anarchism incorporated into the common law, and what was a common-law conspiracy becomes a lawful right of association. Thousands of decisions of disputes, however, are continually drawing the line between lawful and unlawful practices of associations and of those who interfere with their practices, so that the very non-interference, itself, which the anarchists proposed by the abolition of the state, is accomplished only when the state intervenes to prevent interference.[115]

The next stage, made possible by the extension of markets through the railway and telegraph, is the incoming of machinery. We have already indicated the incoming of this stage in the decade of the 1850's.[116] It applies to all industries, but shoemaking was typical. Prior to the decade of the 1860's the inventions in shoemaking were only improved devices for hand tools—aids to skill rather than

---

[111] See Commons, J. R., and associates, *History of Labour in the United States*, I, 496 ff.

[112] Commonwealth *v*. Hunt, 4 Metcalf 44–45 Mass. Reports III (1842).

[113] Commonwealth *ex. rel.* Chew *v*. Carlisle, Brightleys' Nisi Prius Cases (Pa.) 36 (1821).

[114] On Syndicalism in France see Estey, J. A., *Revolutionary Syndicalism, an Exposition and a Criticism* (1913).

[115] Cf. Witte, E. E., *The Government in Labor Disputes*, for complete history and analysis of this procedure.

[116] Above, pp. 115, 116, Patents.

substitutes for skill. Quite different were the pegging machine, 1857, and the McKay sole-sewing machine, 1862. The factory system came suddenly forth on the basis of widespread markets and high war prices. In the collapse that followed after 1867, the first great labor organization, the Knights of St. Crispin, numbering 50,-000, included members from custom shops, retail and wholesale-order shops, and the merchant-capitalists' sweat-shops, with the two issues, resistance to wage reductions and refusal to teach "green hands" how to operate the machines.[117] The small contractor now becomes the "manufacturer," but without a market or credit, for both of which he still depends on the middleman, whether merchant-capitalist, commission-man, jobber, or wholesaler. The laborer has lost his tools, the middleman controls markets and prices, the "manufacturer" changes the meaning of his name from literally a hand-worker to an employer, the laborers change from "servants" to "employees," the organizations begin to change from craft-unions of skilled workers to industrial unions of all classes of labor; the manufacturers split into two associations: an employers' association designed to keep down wages, and a manufacturers' association designed to keep up prices.

It was at this stage of power machinery that the philosophy of Communism emerged. Karl Marx was the first thorough student of the British factory system, the beginnings of employer capitalism, a system probably fifty years in advance of other countries in the textile and metal industries. He predicted that all other industries, including even agriculture, would follow, as has, indeed, been true in many industries. Within the past thirty years the present writer has watched the men's clothing industry in America move from merchant capitalism to employer capitalism, from sweat-shops to factories, and the contractor has become the foreman.

In this process it is the manufacturer who attempts to free himself from the merchant capitalist by building up his own market through to the ultimate consumer, if possible, and back to the ownership of the sources of raw material. This so-called "vertical integration of industry" had its beginnings in the shoe industry with the Douglas Company in the decade of the 1880's. By setting up their own retail stores, and building up a customers' good-will, they passed around the middleman's control of markets to the manufacturer's control.

The succeeding industrial stage in the shoe industry is peculiar in that the ownership of machinery is separated from the ownership

[117] Lescohier, Don D., "The Knights of St. Crispin," *Bulletin of U. of Wisconsin*, No. 355 (1910).

of the shoe factory. The United Shoe Machinery Company, by taking advantage of the patent laws, manufactures and owns nearly all of the shoe machinery and leases it to the shoe manufacturers. The Supreme Court in 1918, on petition of the government to dissolve the company, nevertheless, with three dissenting justices, approved this arrangement as not inconsistent with the anti-trust laws. Seven manufacturers of shoe machinery had consolidated, and the court found that their combined patents covered as much as 100 different operations performed by different machines on certain classes of shoes; that the company handled between 150 and 200 different kinds of machines; that the combination did not suppress competition, although there was a single ownership of practically all the patents; that investments had been made in the stocks of the company and vested interests thereby acquired; that the company had patented new machines in place of obsolete machines and expired patents; that the company maintained a force of repair men to keep the machines in order for the shoe manufacturers; that it taught thousands of employees how to operate the machines; that it had increased the efficiency of the industry; that the original restraint of trade was in the patents themselves granted for the exercise of invention, and not in the joint ownership of the patents; that the "tying clause" of the leases, which required the lessee manufacturer to use exclusively machines of the company and to lease unpatented machines from the company instead of its competitors, were not oppressive, because the lessees were "willing" and were benefited by opportunity to lease all machines from one company; that by the leasing system the manufacturers of not large means were able to obtain machinery which they were without capital to buy.[118]

While the latest stage of the shoe industry is peculiar in that the manufacture of shoe machines is controlled, but the manufacture of shoes is highly competitive, other industries have reached a stage of integration somewhat similar.[119] In general they started with the device of holding companies under charters enacted by competing states, the result of which was to place their practices under the jurisdiction of the Supreme Court of the United States.[120] The court, by the common-law method of making law by the decision of disputes, dissolved these companies in some cases,[121] but afterwards in others, like the Shoe Machinery case (1918) and the Steel Com-

[118] U. S. v. United Shoe Machinery Company of New Jersey, 247 U. S. 32 (1918).
[119] Cf. Meade, E. S., *Trust Finance* (1903, 1913), for many details.
[120] Above, p. 52, From Corporations to Going Concerns.
[121] Northern Securities Co. v. U. S., 193 U. S. 197 (1904); U. S. v. American Tobacco Co., 221 U. S. 106 (1911), and Standard Oil Co. of New Jersey v. U. S., 221 U. S. 1 (1911).

pany case (1920) merely approved or disapproved of their practices. It was this integration and consolidation of plants that
introduced the stage of Banker Capitalism.

During the Nineteenth Century of merchant and employer capitalism, the commercial banker, with his short-time credits, was the
typical banker. During the Twentieth Century, the banking syndicate or the investment banker, usually affiliated with commercial
banks, arose out of their former intermittent activity in special
flotations of securities of corporations and nations, into a dominant
position in the consolidation of industries, the sale of foreign and
domestic securities to the public and the control of boards of directors whose corporate securities they sold and became substantially
responsible for, if they would maintain the good-will of investors.
They saved enterprises approaching insolvency in times of depression by taking them over and reorganizing and financing them on the
upturn of prosperity. Millions of scattered investors now automatically enroll themselves under the leadership of bankers by
transferring their savings to investments recommended by trusted
bankers. When the bankers reach the limit of their ability, as in
1932, then the government itself organizes a huge reconstruction
finance corporation to relieve the bankers of liability. Meanwhile
central banks controlled by bankers rise to a new importance and
Banker Capitalism comes into control of industries and nations.

3. *Scarcity, Abundance, Stabilization—the Economic Stages*

(1) **Competition.**—Industrial stages, arising out of changes in
technology, reach their culmination in the rapid large-scale transportation of commodities and in the instantaneous world-wide trans-
mission of knowledge and negotiations. Taking an historical view
we distinguish three corresponding economic stages: a period of
Scarcity preceding the "industrial revolution," the latter beginning
in the Eighteenth Century and continuing today with augmented
speed through collective action; a period of Abundance with its
alternations of oversupply and undersupply for a hundred years or
more, accompanying this industrial revolution; and a period of
Stabilization, beginning with the concerted movements of capitalists
and laborers in the Nineteenth Century, and the equalization of
competitive conditions, the "live-and-let-live" policies of the
Twentieth Century in America.

The basic principle on which these historic periods are constructed
is the distinction between physical control and legal control. Physical control is technology. Legal control is the rights, duties, liber-

ties, and exposures assigned to individuals by the community under existing circumstances of efficiency, scarcity, custom, and the physical force of sovereignty.

In a period of scarcity—whether due to inefficiency, or to violence, to war, custom, or superstition—the legal control and transfer are quite different from that in a period of abundance or a period of stabilization. In a period of extreme scarcity or war the community usually resorts to rationing both the input and the output of man-power, and there is the minimum of individual liberty and the maximum of communistic, feudalistic, or governmental control through physical compulsion. In the next period of extreme abundance and pacifism there is the maximum of individual liberty, the minimum of control through government, and individual bargaining takes the place of rationing. In the period of stabilization there are new restraints on individual liberty, enforced mainly by governmental sanctions as in Russia or Italy, but mainly, heretofore in America, by economic sanctions through concerted action, whether secret, semi-open, open, or arbitrational, of associations, corporations, unions, and other collective movements of manufacturers, merchants, laborers, farmers, and bankers.

In the historical period of scarcity the legal control of goods was not separated from the physical control. An owner physically handed over a commodity or service to another person, and custom and the common law read into the physical transfer a transfer of legal control. But in the periods of abundance and stabilization, the legal control and transfer have been separated in the hands of business men and financiers while the physical control and physical transfer go on in the hands of the workers under the commands of business men and financiers, transmitted through management. The two controls are correlated throughout, but the degrees, methods, effects, and lags of correlation are very different in the three periods of scarcity, abundance, and stabilization.

We shall not endeavor to go back into the primitive periods of scarcity characterized by the rationing systems of communism, but shall begin with the emergence of the modern bargaining system out of feudalism, and its first appearance as Mercantilism, or Merchant-Capitalism. The custom and the common law in this early capitalistic period of scarcity differed materially in the two kinds of output, namely, commodities and services.

Commodities can be transferred without transferring the person of the producer, but services are transferred in person. The transfer of commodities, also, in this early period, was, like the transfer of services, a movement of the owner, along with the commodity, to a market. Owing to the weakness of government and the violence and perjury of the people, it was necessary to encourage powerful lords to set up markets and to protect them against the inroads of robbers and liars. For this reason a market usually originated with a special monopolistic franchise, named "a liberty," and granted to a powerful individual or ecclesiastical magnate, authorizing him to hold concourse of buyers and sellers, with the privilege of taking tolls in consideration. of the protection afforded. These markets, thus established, were governed, eventually, by rules laid down by the common-law courts in the decisions of disputes, but originally by rules of their own making. The courts, in their decisions, developed the principle of the "market overt," or the public, free and equal market, as we have seen in the Chicago Board of Trade case.[122] That case is the modern "market overt." Afterwards these principles were extended to retail shops, until eventually the exclusive privileges of the market overt were eliminated, but the principles of publicity, equality, and liberty were extended to all markets. These principles were not something innate and natural, but were actually constructed out of the good and bad practices of the times. The early physiocrat and classical economists thought of them as handed down by divine Providence or the natural order.

In the first place the grantee of a right to hold a "market overt" was required to provide the standard weights and measures and a weigh-master. He was authorized and required to set up a special court (*pie poudre courts*) for prompt decision of disputes and enforcement of contracts. Every person was declared to have, of common right, "a liberty of carrying his goods to a public fair for sale," and therefore the owner of the soil or fair, or the local municipal authorities, could not distrain the goods themselves for non-payment of rents or tolls, but must "bring a suit themselves for rent." Any disturbance causing physical obstruction of the market place, whereby persons were excluded from a part thereof, was prohibited.[123]

These were the duties of the lord, or protector, of the market respecting the physical transfer of goods. But further than this it was necessary to provide rules respecting the transfers of legal control between buyer and seller on the market. These rules also were afterwards extended to all retail markets. Sir Edward Coke summarized the common law respecting the transfer of titles in markets overt, as it stood three hundred years ago when he compiled his Institutes. He said,

[122] Above, p. 711.
[123] Coke's *Institutes*, Second Part, I, 220–222 (1642).

"the common law did hold it for a point of great policies, and behovefull for the common-wealth, that faires and markets overt should be replenished, and well furnished with all manner of commodities, vendible in faires and markets, for the necessary sustentation and use of the people. And to that end the common law did ordaine (to encourage men thereunto) that all sales and contracts of anything vendible in faires or markets overt should not be good onely between the parties, but should bind those that right had thereunto." [124]

In other words, in order that buyers might be encouraged to come to the markets, it was necessary for the courts to set up the standards by which the buyers could obtain clear title to the goods which they purchased and thus to protect them against third parties who might claim that the goods were stolen. The market overt was a place where a clear title to commodities could be obtained, in an age of violence, theft, and perjury. Thus the sale of goods, as decided in the cases cited by Coke, must be in a place that is "overt and open, not in a back room warehouse, etc." The term "overt" in this case implies "apt and sufficient, as not to sell plate openly in a scrivener's shop or the like, but openly in a goldsmith's shop." The sale must not be in the night, but "between the rising of the sun and the going downe of the same." The sale at night was "good between the parties" but did "not binde a stranger that right hath." The sale must not be made by "coven between two of purpose to barre him that right hath," and "the contract must be wholly and originally made in the market overt," and not to have "the inception out of the market and consummation in the market." This, we see, is the rule approved in the Chicago Board of Trade case. But, if the seller acquires the goods again, the rightful owner is not barred, because the seller "was the wrong doer, and he shall not take advantage of his own wrong." Again, if the buyer knew that the seller had wrongful possession, "this shall not binde him that right hath."

These rules established the alienability, or what may, by analogy, be called the Negotiability of Commodities, and were suited to a Period of Scarcity and Insecurity when physical goods were actually brought to the market and there was no credit system, no manufacture and sale for future delivery, and no newspaper publicity of prices. The rules were evidently adopted by the courts, as Coke says, and as we saw in the Board of Trade case, to promote the public interest by encouraging buyers and sellers to come together and to bring their products to the market, with the assurance that

[124] *Ibid.*, 713 (1642).

purchasers in good faith for value received might acquire title against all the world. And this quality of alienability or negotiability, indeed, is the first rule of law needed to establish a free, equal, and open market. It was extended, in later times, to include incorporeal property as well as physical commodities, an extension to which the name "negotiability" is applied in the technical sense of the term.

Again the offenses of forestalling, regrating, and engrossing were prohibited at common law, for they consisted in the purchase or repurchase of commodities in larger quantities than the purchaser could use himself or could sell at retail, and so were considered to be attempts by rich persons to enhance prices and hence a denial of equality between buyers and sellers.[125]

But these offenses at common law practically prohibited all wholesale business except that of foreign importation, and the fact that such wholesale business was adjudged a criminal offense indicates on what small scale industry must have been conducted and how meager must have been the usual supplies of products that came to the market in this early period of scarcity. Some of these statutes against wholesale business were repealed as early as 1772 and the entire list of common-law offenses of forestalling, engrossing, and regrating was abolished by statute in 1844.[126] The preamble to that act repeated the preamble of 1772, which gave as a reason for repeal that it had been found by experience "that the restraints laid upon dealing in necessaries" by preventing a free trade in the said commodities, have a tendency "to discourage the growth and to enhance the prices of the same." What they actually prohibited was wholesale business and hence this act of 1844 completely opened up the wholesale markets of England, retaining only the offenses against spreading false rumors with intent to enhance or decry the price of any goods, and the offense of preventing by force or threats any goods being brought to any fair or market. The old rules were no longer needed and were indeed a denial of liberty and equality in an age of abundance, when it was necessary that goods should be sold and purchased at wholesale and rapidly transported from a distance.

After the discontinuance of the laws against forestalling, regrating, and engrossing, beginning 1772, the incoming of wholesale markets served clearly to separate the transfer of legal control from the transfer of physical control of goods. The seller no longer was required by law, in effect, to bring his goods in person to a market in small quantities, but the modern produce exchanges and wholesale markets could arise where, as in the Board of Trade case, the

---

[25] Coke's *Institutes*, 195–196; 4 Bla. Com. 158 (1765).
[126] 7 and 8 Vic. 24 (1844).

legal control of goods can be transferred by wire or 'phone upon mere samples and specifications, such transfer of legal control to take effect at any place or any point of time from "spot" to "futures."

Meanwhile the physical delivery, or transfer of physical control, goes on in the hands of employees, all the way from the farm or factory to the railway and the point of ultimate consumption. The legal transfer of legal power to control the disposition of goods, at any time or place for the purpose of buying and selling, is separated from the physical delivery of the goods in the hands of employees or consumers for the purpose of production and consumption. And the prices of commodities henceforth become, not the price of the commodity, but the price of enforceable promises of physical delivery of the commodity, specified as to time and place.

It was this distinction that the classical economists did not incorporate in their theories. Their "labor theories" of value were theories of the market overt, just then becoming obsolete.

The common law prohibited all other restraints of trade in addition to forestalling, engrossing, and regrating, as being prejudicial to the public welfare, in that they prevented individuals from freely coming upon the market or freely offering their products or services, or freely increasing the supplies of the same, for the benefit and sustenance of the people. It is the prohibition of these other restraints of trade, not peculiar to wholesaling, that has come down to modern times and has been extended wherever new methods of restraint have appeared, but has been greatly modified in the period of stabilization.

Thus the common law established during the period of scarcity, down to the middle of the Eighteenth Century, by the method of excluding what were deemed to be bad practices of business and by giving validity to what were deemed to be good practices, the fundamental principles of a free, equal, and public market, namely uniform weights and measures, alienability of commodities, free access of all persons and commodities to the market, and publicity, or open knowledge of transactions, as against secrecy. Although some of the common-law rules which were necessary during a period of scarcity and insecurity were abolished after the Eighteenth Century when governments were able to establish security and when inventions had ushered in the period of abundance, yet these four attributes of a free, equal, and open market have been more or less retained, namely, uniform standards of measurement, alienability, accessibility, and publicity. It is these that make up what we call intangible property.

This period of abundance, however, brought in exactly the opposite evil, destructive, unfair, or cutthroat competition. This situation had already led the courts, as early as the beginning of the Seventeenth Century, to begin to support and sustain the great list of "reasonable" restraints of trade coming afterwards under the general name of good-will, trade names, trade marks, and recently known as the "law of unfair competition." [127] But notwithstanding these reasonable restraints of trade, the Nineteenth and Twentieth Centuries experienced periodic and general oversupplies of commodities, occuring in irregular trends and cycles. These oversupplies led to destructive competition, price wars in manufactures and rate wars in transportation, the elimination of weak competitors, the consolidation or absorption of competitors into large combinations. At first these combinations to prevent rate wars and price wars were met by a renewal of ancient laws against monopolies, against conspiracies, and against other practices in restraint of trade. These were the anti-trust laws of the last decade of the Nineteenth Century. But these laws were found to be ineffective in operation in the four important departments of Transportation, Manufactures, Labor, and Banking.

In the field of transportation the policy of stabilization was frankly adopted by statute in the United States in the Interstate Commerce Law (1887), for it was realized that the practices of price-cutting and secret rebates were as injurious to the public as the practices of monopoly and extortion. But this policy of stabilization was not fully recognized, in the case of manufactures, until the enactment of the Federal Trade Commission Law and the Clayton Act (1914) which penalized price-cutting, almost as much as the old law had penalized price-boosting. And finally, the two decisions in the dissolution suit of the United Shoe Machinery Company (1918) and in the case of the United States Steel Company (1920) established, as the present policy of the courts of the country, the principle of stabilization. For it was judicially found, in the Steel case, that the Steel Company, although its practices were plainly concerted movements, this time of a holding company, similar to those which formerly had been held to be restraints of trade, nevertheless had not recently resorted to the destructive price wars that eliminated competition in dealing with the public. The court declared that the Company had not obtained freight rebates, had not reduced wages, had not lowered the quality of its product, had not created artificial scarcity, had not coerced or oppressed competitors, had not undersold competitors in one locality and maintained prices in

[127] Commons, John R., *Legal Foundations of Capitalism*, 263 ff.

other localities,[128] had not obtained customers by secret rebates or departures from published prices. Neither competitors nor customers, said the court, testified to any oppression or coercion on the part of the company, and, in fact, they testified to a general satisfaction with the well-known and published policy of stabilization of prices and deliveries, pursued by the company.

It is plain, therefore, that the policy of stabilization through publicity, for both transportation and manufactures, has been at least partially adopted as the policy which guides the common-law method of making law.

A similar practice of stabilization has been slowly developed in the history of labor organizations. The first extensive effort of this kind occurred in 1886 when the bituminous coal operators and coal miners throughout the competitive field of Pennsylvania, Ohio, Indiana, and Illinois agreed publicly on uniform wages and differentials of wages, such that the operators might have equal access to the markets without secretly or individually cutting wages. This stabilization of competitive conditions has become as important for the employer of labor as it has been for the customers of railways, and is perhaps in process of being as completely sanctioned as the similar practice of the Steel Company.

A more recent and equally important movement, as well as more remote from common law or statute law during the period of abundance, is the movement towards stabilization of the purchasing power of money and credit, the foremost economists in this field being Fisher in America, Wicksell and Cassell in Sweden, Hawtrey and Keynes in England, and the turning point in America being the Federal Reserve System established in 1914.

(2) **Discrimination.**—In these four fields, transportation, manufactures, labor, and banking, the principle of stabilization has proceeded as a remedy for a practice which is considered to be a denial of a free, equal, and public market, namely the practice which, in general, may be named Discrimination.

We have referred above to the rules of law which governed the market overt during the period of scarcity. That was the beginning of a free, equal, and public market where a concourse of buyers and sellers assembled under the protection of the lord of the market. But there was another class of sellers who did not bring their products to a central market, but who performed services for the

---

[128] This was afterwards disproved in the "Pittsburgh Plus" case, before the Federal Trade Commission, but not taken to the Federal Court. It forms the basis of Fetter's *The Masquerade of Monopoly* (1931), already referred to, above, p. 677, From Individuals to Institutions.

public indifferently, according as customers came to their places of business. These correspond to the modern manufacturers who sell their products, usually f.o.b. at the place of manufacture, but often at the place of delivery, as in the Pittsburgh Plus case.

Now, considering the great scarcity of producers of this type in that early period, and owing to the scarcity of mechanical skill and training, the early common law developed the rule that anyone who set himself up and offered to sell his services to the public indifferently, as contrasted with one who worked solely for himself or one who served a single patron or landlord, thereby assumed a threefold duty, namely, (1) to serve all comers, (2) at a reasonable price, and (3) under a liability for damages if he did not have or did not exercise skill. The list of occupations which were governed by these rules was large and included surgeons, tailors, blacksmiths, carpenters, victualers (grocery keepers), bakers, millers, innkeepers, ferrymen, wharfingers, besides all who could be classified as "common carriers." In fact, all of these occupations were "common occupations" in the same sense that a "common carrier" is generally one who offers his services to anybody who comes along. The law made no distinction as to whether a person held an actual monopoly or not. In fact, the term "monopoly" was applied, in those days, only to such of these occupations as were required to operate under a franchise, or a permit, granted by the sovereign, such as a ferryman, and were, therefore, legal monopolies based on special grants, or "liberties," rather than economic monopolies based on private property.

Bruce Wyman and E. A. Adler, in the citations referred to in the footnote,[129] have offered two seemingly opposing theories to account for the attitude of the common law, in those early days, respecting "common employments." Wyman based his explanation on the principle of scarcity, Adler upon the principle of publicity, or common employment. But the two explanations are simply the two variable functions of scarcity and custom. These "common employments" emerged with the break-up of feudalism, and consisted simply in the change from employment under the control of a single master to employment by any master who might come along. The blacksmith who worked for a feudal lord now worked for any or all of the lords indifferently. Since the courts represented the point of view of the ruling classes, it was but natural, in the sense of customary, that they should impose upon the unfranchised workers

---

[129] Wyman, B. and Beale, J. H., *Railroad Rate Regulation* (1906); Adler, E. A., "Business Jurisprudence," *Harv. Law Rev.*, XXVIII; "Labor, Capital, and Business at Common Law," *Harv. Law Rev.*, XXIX (1919), 24.

duties of service to any master who came along. A similar attitude
was revealed upon the abolition of slavery in the United States.
The ex-slaves, while they had become "freedmen" under the Thirteenth Amendment, were not free to refuse to work as they might
wish, and the Fourteenth Amendment was necessary in order to
grant to them equal freedom with their former masters.[130] So, likewise, the obligations of service were attached to all classes of work-
ingmen and merchants in the early stages of transition from serfdom
to liberty.

The principle of scarcity, too, was applicable, since, had there
been an abundance or oversupply of workers, their competition with
each other would have made it unnecessary to subject them to coercive rules of service. The two principles of custom and scarcity
did not become clearly separated until a later time, when certain
occupations like common carriers, or ferrymen, having exclusive
privileges of time or place, were retained under the older compulsory principle of common service, but the others were liberated
upon the principle of competitive abundance. Then, in more recent
times, the principle of stabilization, with its unions, associations,
corporations, syndicates, and similar concerted methods of restrain-
ing individual liberty in the interest of liberty for other members
of the group, reverts somewhat to the rationing principles of
scarcity as a modification of the bargaining principles of abundance.

In the United States the primitive rules applying to all common
occupations were occasionally applied but became obsolete at an
early period, except in the case of what were distinguished as public
service occupations or corporations. In these industries the law
has developed until regulations completely cover even the fixing of
rates, services, and capitalization by government, in addition to the
prohibition of discrimination. This is because, notwithstanding the
period of abundance which greatly increased the mechanical inventions and the use of mechanical power, yet these public service occupations were not only legal monopolies based on special grants
of power, but also economic monopolies, based on ordinary private
property, since they occupied strategic localities with only limited
opportunities for others to introduce competitive undertakings.

It was not so with manufacturing and commercial undertakings.
Here it was not necessary, in the public interest in a period of
abundance, that those engaged in these industries should be bound
by a duty to serve all comers, at a reasonable price. There always
remained an oversupply of producers and productive equipment and
no public purpose could be served by compelling a manufacturer or

[130] Commons, John R., *Legal Foundations of Capitalism*, 119.

merchant to serve all comers at reasonable prices when their customers could readily find alternative sellers or buyers. Hence these occupations were treated strictly as private businesses, and the law contented itself with maintaining only those four great attributes of a free, equal, and open competitive market, namely, standards of measurement, assignability, accessibility, and publicity.

Under the conditions of the early period of scarcity, it was impossible that the modern ethical or legal notion of "discrimination" should arise. This notion arises with the period of stabilization, and marks the importance of new customs and narrow margins of profit.

The public, or purchasers, did not, in the early period of self-employment, make their livings by buying regularly these commodities or services, but they patronized only occasionally, on market days, or when in need of a service which they could not furnish themselves. But modern business and livelihood are wholly dependent, at all times, on the services rendered by modern carriers, by modern manufacturers of raw materials or unfinished materials, by modern laborers assembled in great masses, or by modern banking and credit companies or syndicates.

Hence the modern business man, as purchaser, is injured, not so much by extortionate prices which he must pay, as by the fact that his competitor pays less than he does for a large and essential part of his purchases. Business is conducted on such narrow margins for profit and such large quantities that a competitor is put out of business completely if his competitor pays less than he does. But if his competitor pays as much as he does, even though the price paid by both is monopolistic and extortionate, he can pass along the price to the ultimate consumer. Hence it is that the equalization of competitive conditions, which can be accomplished only through stabilization, is deemed important by modern business men.

But, in the early times of general scarcity, it was not discrimination, as we understand it, but extortion alone that was an injury to the purchaser. Consequently, even when the word "discrimination" was used, it never signified a discriminatory *low* price—it always signified a discriminatory *high* price. In other words, the early common law, applying as it did to markets overt and to practically all occupations that served the public indifferently, had no rule against all discriminations as such—its rules were directed against extortion.

This was evidently the understanding of the Supreme Court of the United States as late as the year 1897. In that year the court had before it a suit in which a plaintiff living in Iowa sought damages from a railway company on the ground that the company showed partiality and favoritism to the said plaintiff's competitors living in Nebraska, by charging them lower freight rates, in proportion to the length of haul, than the rates charged to the plaintiff.[131] The Supreme Court held that it had not been shown that the plaintiff was charged a freight rate extortionate in itself. "He is only seeking to recover money which he alleges is due, not because of any unreasonable charge, but on account of the wrongful conduct of the defendant." The court then proceeded to inquire whether this alleged wrongful conduct was wrongful at common law, and the test employed was, not that of the social consequences of discrimination in charging one customer less than another customer, but merely that of the effect on the railway company's private earnings. Thus the court said:

> "Suppose that the officials of the defendant company had charged the plaintiff only a reasonable rate . . . and at the same time had, without any just occasion therefor, given to his neighbor across the street *free transportation,* thus being guilty of an act of favoritism and partiality—*an act which tended to diminish the receipts of the railroad company, and to that extent the dividend to the stockholders*—such partiality on their part would not, in the absence of a statute, have entitled the plaintiff to maintain an action for the recovery of the fare which he had paid, and *thus reduce still further the dividends of the stockholders.* So, but for the provision of the Interstate Commerce Act, the plaintiff could not recover on account of his shipments to Chicago, if only a reasonable rate was charged therefor, no matter though it appeared that through any misconduct or partiality on the part of the railway officials, shippers in Nebraska had been given a less rate."[132]

Such was the judicial concept of discrimination in 1897. It was merely a private affair, without social consequences.

Four years after this opinion, the same court, by the same justice (Brewer) declared, in sustaining an opinion of the Supreme Court of Nebraska, this time "under the common law," that not only must the charges be reasonable in themselves, but they must be "relatively reasonable"; no rate should be lower than another "without a just and reasonable ground for discrimination"; and discrimination was reasonable in so far only as the difference in rates corresponded to a difference in costs and conditions of rendering the service.[133]

---

[131] Parsons *v.* Chicago & North Western Railroad, 167 U. S. 447, 453, 455 (1897).

[132] *Op. cit.,* 455; italics not in the original.

[133] Western Union Telegraph Company *v.* Call Publishing Company, 44 Neb. 326, 337 (1895); 58 Neb. 192 (1899); 181 U. S. 92, 102 (1901).

In other words, the Supreme Court, between the years 1897 and 1901, changed its view of the common-law meaning of discrimination from what had evidently been the early meaning, which made no distinction between extortion and discrimination, to the more modern view which makes discrimination in itself illegal, regardless of whether there is extortion or not. According to the early view, the remedy for discrimination would have been only that of reducing the higher price to a level corresponding to the lower price. According to the later view the remedy for discrimination would be obtained just as well by raising the lower price (or prohibiting free transportation) to a level corresponding to the higher price. The evil sought to be corrected, under the later view, is the partiality or favoritism that gives a competitor free service or services at a *lower* price. The evil sought to be corrected under the earlier view was only that of charging an unreasonably *high* price, and the lower price charged to a competitor was not looked upon as discrimination in itself, but was admitted only as evidence tending to show that the higher price complained of was extortionate.

That the two very different meanings of discrimination should not have been distinguished was evidently owing to the slow process of inclusion and exclusion by which the common-law method enlarges the meanings of ancient terms to cover new evils not previously recognized as such. The Supreme Court, in 1901, evidently extended the common-law meaning of discrimination, in order to meet a real abuse that had come before it for determination, and the evil of discriminatory *low prices* had become, by this time, so flagrant and well known to the general public that there was no need of endeavoring to reconcile its opinion of 1901 with that of 1897.

The very earliest opinion which we can locate which consciously and knowingly made the extension of the meaning of discrimination so as to prohibit relatively *low* prices as well as relatively *high* prices charged to competitors was that of McDuffee v. Portland and Rochester Railroad Co., 52 N. H. 430 (1873), and the reasoning of the court will show the process of changing from the ancient *physical* meaning of discrimination to the modern *economic* meaning. The court there pointed out that, at common law, discrimination consisted in unconditionally refusing to "carry B, if he carries A" or practically imposing an "embargo upon the travel or traffic of some disfavored individual," or consisted in infringing the public right by making a highway "absolutely impassable." These common-law notions of discrimination, it will be noted, were physical in character, and the New Hampshire court characterized them as "directly" exercising unreasonable discrimination. The court then went on to extend the meaning of discrimination to economic discriminations which the court now named "indirect" discrimination, consisting in a "circuitous invasion" such as disagreeable terms, differences in price, no facilities or accommodations for one as against the other.[134]

The conclusion is that, not until the Supreme Court opinion of 1901 referred to above, could it be said that generally the courts had shifted the meaning of discrimination, in the case of railways, from mere evidence tending to show that a certain *high price* or other disadvantage was extortionate, that is, unreasonable "in itself," to the very different meaning that it was partiality towards some competitors and against other competitors, evidenced by a *relatively low price,* that constituted the evil of discrimination, regardless of whether the absolute level of both prices was high or low.

The general reason why the courts were slow in reaching this new meaning was on account of their earlier view, as shown in the Parsons case of 1897 above cited, that it was solely a private affair of the common carrier if it chose to reduce its own revenues by charging low prices to some customers while charging high prices to other customers, and that the social effects of such practice in suppressing competition and tending towards monopoly among its customers was not to be considered. This view led to the result that one who was discriminated against by being compelled to pay relatively high prices, compared with his competitors, had no remedy at common law unless he could show that the said high prices were extortionate or unreasonable *in themselves,* and not with reference to the question whether they were *relatively* high as compared with prices paid by a competitor. And this was so, even though some of the courts had declared that the system of low prices to favored competitors had an inevitable tendency to suppress competition and to concentrate the industry of the carrier's customers in the hands of favored individuals.[135] A federal court had even declared as late as 1889 that there was no injustice done to a lumber company when a railroad charged the competitors of that company a lower price, even lower than the cost of transportation, and even though this partiality might shut the plaintiff company wholly out of the market and drive it into bankruptcy, provided the plaintiff company were charged a price "reasonable in itself." [136]

[134] Further demonstration of this development of the meaning of discrimination will be found in Wyman, *Public Service Corporations,* 1280 ff.

[135] See John Hays and Co. *v.* The Pennsylvania Co., 12 Fed. 309 (1882).

[136] De Bary Baya Merchants' Line *v.* Jacksonville, T. & K. W. Railway Co., 40 Fed. 392 (1889).

Thus the Supreme Court lagged about fifteen years behind the popular and legislative change in the meaning of discrimination, and this may be figured on generally as its customary lag.

The foregoing account of the lag of the common law respecting the meaning of discrimination does not apply solely to what were known as common carriers. It applies also to all industries that may properly be designated "common occupations." This principle was partly adopted by the Supreme Court in the case of Munn *v.* Illinois (1876) and was well stated again, with a review of all the cases by the Supreme Court of New York in the case of People of the State of New York *v.* Budd.[137] Each of these cases had to do with a warehouse or grain elevator, which had never been classified, at common law, as a common carrier. A warehouse, it was admitted in both cases, had always been held to be a private business and had never operated under a license or legal monopoly which carried the public right of reasonable prices to be determined by judicial process. In fact, the several grain warehouses in Chicago and Buffalo, with which these cases had to do, were held to be actively in competition with each other, although they evidently were acting in concert. And the court held that it was not the question of monopoly or competition that was decisive, in the matter of prohibiting discrimination or extortion, but it was the question of whether the shippers of grain, that is, the customers of the warehouses, were placed at a disadvantage by the prices and the trade practices of the elevator companies.

It was ably and correctly contended, in the dissenting opinions in these two cases, that the public had no independent legal right to make use of the elevators, since they were not common carriers subject to the duty to render service to anyone who might come along. Yet the court held that there was an element of this kind of "publicity" in the elevator business, owing, partly to the nature and extent of the business, partly to their relation to the commerce of the state and country, and partly to the fact that even though they were competitors, yet, under the circumstances, they enjoyed special facilities for reaching understandings as to prices.[138]

Thus the incoming of the distinction between discrimination and extortion arises with the incoming of the period of stabilization. Discrimination is not an evil during a period of abundance because every person has an available alternative. It has become the serious

[137] 117 N. Y. 1 (1889).
[138] People of the State of New York *v.* Budd, 117 N. Y. 22, 24 (1889). A similar decision was made by the Federal Trade Commission in 1923, regarding the Pittsburgh Plus practice of the U. S. Steel Company, but not appealed to the courts. See Fetter, F. A., *The Masquerade of Monopoly.*

problem in a period of stabilization through concerted movements, live-and-let-live policies, and narrow margins of profit, since stabilization means the absence of alternatives, and this, in turn, would mean stability of discriminations and extortions as much as stability of fair and reasonable values and prices

Thus the process of making law by deciding disputes fits laggingly both the changing economic conditions and the changing ethical opinions of justice and injustice. It takes into account the most significant facts of the period of stabilization, the principles of futurity and narrow margins of profit. Modern business is conducted on borrowed capital in large amounts. Competitors are debtors. They must maintain the future solvency of their going business by keeping up their trade connections with material men, working men, and customers, all of which are properly summarized in the term "good-will." Good-will, though an intangible asset, is the most important asset of modern business. Competition which breaks into it is "predatory" competition. Hence the "live-and-let-live" policies, which look upon future security of the going concern as all-important, are bringing in the Custom of Stabilization and the decision of disputes conforming to that custom. The concept of good-will, as constructed by the courts, is grounded on the principle of scarcity, for its assumption is that opportunities are limited and margins are close, and therefore each competitor should endeavor to retain his present customers and his present proportion of the trade. This has become a part of modern "business ethics" which holds that cut prices are not good for customers, and it is converted more or less into "unwritten" law by the common-law method of making law by deciding disputes.

It will be noted that this historical analysis of Scarcity, Abundance, Stabilization, bears some analogy to Karl Marx's dialectics from his "thesis" of primitive tribal communism, to his "antithesis" of Eighteenth and Nineteenth Century individualism, and back to his "synthesis," a future world-wide communism. But his was a materialistic interpretation based on technology, which we have summarized in the preceding section on "industrial stages," whereas ours is also an economic evolution from primitive scarcity which explains communism and mercantilism, to abundance which explains individualism, to the many modern schemes of the regulation of alternating abundance and scarcity by subordinating individuals, partly or wholly, to collective action. Marx's communism was foreordained, but modern stabilization may be communism, fascism, banker capitalism, or any of the concerted movements that endeavor to bring order out of conflict and instability.

4. *Prices*

Doubtless the most far reaching and difficult of all stabilizations is banker stabilization. Banker control is world-wide and involves concerted action of the central banks of the world. It involves internationalism and cuts across the nationalistic tariff protective uprisings of masses of people. The first move for banker stabilization came, not from bankers or economists, but from politicians. In 1833, during the world-wide fall in prices, G. Poulett Scrope, member of the House of Commons from 1833 to 1868, addressed pamphlets to his constituents and then published in a book [139] his proposal to correct the fluctuations of the "legal standard of value" by a periodical publication of "an authentic price current," so that all commercial classes could "regulate their pecuniary engagements by reference to this Tabular Standard." This tabular standard afterwards came to be constructed on mathematical principles by Jevons and then to be known as index numbers of the average movement of prices. [140]

Scrope's idea had been preceded by others, but more out of curiosity than practical proposals for business contracts, [141] and he contemplated only voluntary agreements in long-term contracts. Not until Wicksell in 1898 and Fisher in 1911 was it proposed to stabilize the legal standard of money itself by Wicksell's bank control over discount rates and Fisher's control over changes in the weight of the dollar, so that not only long-term agreements but also short-term agreements of commercial banking should be made under collective control of a stabilized price level itself.

These proposals bring to the front the most important of all problems of public policy and reasonable value, for they are a world-wide aspect of the ethical question, arising out of conflicts of interest: whether individuals and classes should get rich by their own improvements in efficiency or by taking advantage of changes in the value of the unit that measures scarcity. In the all-controlling practices of the "paymasters" of a capitalistic civilization, they are the issue of efficiency profits versus scarcity profits.

The general level of wholesale prices in the United States fell more than 33 per cent from 1929 to 1932, and the level of farmers' prices fell about 55 per cent. But, taking 33 per cent as the average, the burden of all long-time debts was increased 50 per cent.

[139] Scrope, G. Poulett, *Principles of Political Economy Deduced from the Natural Laws of Social Welfare and Applied to the Present State of Britain* (1833).

[140] Jevons, W. Stanley, *A Serious Fall in the Value of Gold* (1863); *Investigations in Currency and Finance* (1884).

[141] See Comments by Jevons, *op. cit.*, and titles in Palgrave's *Dictionary of Political Economy* (1899).

This means that 50 per cent more commodities must be exported by foreign countries to the world market, in order to pay the gold debts of Europe to America, than were required in 1925 when the amount of the war debts was settled.

Likewise for our own people. It required in 1932 at least 50 per cent more commodities to be produced and sold in payment of interest and principal on public and private debts, contracted before 1929, than would have been required at the time when the debts were contracted.

This means financial exploitation of producers, here and abroad, to the extent of 50 per cent of their products, which they were now required to sell in order to pay debts and taxes in money, above the amounts that would have been required on the contracts when made three or more years before.

The first assumption that naturally occurs to anyone who considers the astonishing increase in efficiency of American industry and agriculture is that the "law" of supply and demand should be expected to bring about a corresponding fall in prices. If the efficiency of, say, the steel industry, or the wheat-growing industry, increases ten per cent in ten years, by which is meant that the same amount of labor and management produces ten per cent larger output in a given time, then we should naturally expect their prices to fall, on the average, about one per cent per year, or ten per cent in ten years.

These figures are taken arbitrarily, for illustration. The Federal Reserve Board estimated a much larger increase in efficiency of manufacturing industries from the year 1919 to the year 1927— an increase of 47 per cent in efficiency, averaging, therefore, five per cent per year. But, taking our figures for illustration, consider what would happen if *both* steel efficiency and wheat efficiency increased together at the same rate of ten per cent in ten years, and if the money prices of each declined ten per cent during that ten years.

We may enlarge the supposition. Suppose that steel stands for all manufacturing industries and that all of them increase their efficiency equally at the same rate; and that wheat stands for all agricultural industries, all of which also increase their efficiency equally at the same rate. All of the farmers, now, are selling all of their agricultural products to all the manufacturers, and the manufacturers are selling all of their manufactured products to all the farmers. Prices for everything on both sides have fallen equally 10 per cent.

But have exchange values fallen? This is the distinction between "nominal" prices and "real" prices. Nominal prices are the *amount of money* which a unit of the commodity will buy. Real prices are the *amount of other commodities* which that commodity unit will buy. But instead of the word "nominal" we use the word "institutional." The nominal price is the institutional price which we name simply price. The real price we name exchange-value. This is because money, by which nominal prices are measured, is only a selling and buying institution, yet it is the fundamental institution of a capitalistic civilization, through which we obtain ownership of the other commodities and services which we really want, in exchange for our own commodities.

Hence, instead of saying that we "buy money" with our commodities, we say that we are "selling goods for money." And instead of saying that we are "exchanging money" for commodities, we say that we are "buying goods with money." The real prices, or exchange-values, are not known until we first sell our commodity for the institution of money and then start out to buy any or all of the commodities we need. Hence we name the quantity of another commodity which we obtain for a *unit* of our own commodity, not the "price" of our commodity, but its exchange-value, as did the classical economists who eliminated money. And we name the quantity of money which we obtain for our unit of commodity, not its exchange-value, but its price. Exchange-value is the "real price." Price is the capitalistic price. Value is the quantity of commodity *times* its unit-price, in terms of money.

So it is with wages, profit, interest, and rent of land. Here, however, the "commodity," if we so call it, which we own, we do not sell. We sell only the *use* of it during a period of time. It is this use that is the true commodity which we sell. In the case of labor, debts, and investments, we call it a service—the service of working, the service of waiting, and the service of risking. Nominal, or rather institutional wages, are money wages, that is, the price obtained by selling labor-service or the use of labor-power, for the institution of money, during an hour, day, week, or piece. Nominal wages are the capitalistic price of labor.

But real wages, or the "real" price for the use of the laborer's labor-power, are the food, clothing, and other goods which the money wage will buy. We call them "real wages" but they are the same as what we here call the exchange-value of the service of working for others.

Likewise nominal, or institutional, interest is the amount of money which an owner of money receives for the *use* of his money as purchasing power during a period of time. It also is a payment for a service—the service of waiting. He who gets paid for this service of waiting is the creditor who buys mainly bonds with his monetary savings. On the money market this is named the "price of money" or the "value of money." It is the nominal, or money rate of interest, that is, the capitalistic or institutional price paid for the service of waiting. But the real rate of interest, or the "real price" paid for the service of waiting, is the quantity of goods which the creditor can buy with the money which he receives as nominal interest. This quantity of goods is the real price, that is, the exchange-value, of his service of waiting.

Also with profit. Nominal profit is the amount of the institution of money which a business establishment receives during a period of time after paying nominal interest, nominal wages, and all other prices. It is the capitalistic price received from the public for the service of assuming the risks of a business. But real profit is the quantity of all goods which this capitalistic profit will buy on the markets. The real profit is the same thing as the exchange-value of the service of assuming the risks of business.

So with rent and hire. Nominal or institutional rent, or hire, is the monetary price received, over a period of time, for the use of lands, buildings, horses, or any physical thing. But real rent is the quantity of goods which nominal rent will buy. Real rent is the same as the exchange-value of the *uses* of physical things; but nominal rent is the capitalistic price paid for the same uses of physical things.

In general, then, prices are the institutional values, or monetary incomes, or capitalistic incomes, received by all sellers of commodities, services, and uses; but exchange-values are the real values, the real incomes received by such sellers.

Yet while prices are institutional and exchange-values are "real," prices are very real in the capitalistic sense—they determine who shall get the results of efficiency. This is increasingly important when the general increase in technological efficiency has proceeded at the unusual rate since 1921.

The American Federation of Labor, at its convention in 1925, adopted a resolution looking towards coöperation with employers in increasing the efficiency of industry, provided labor should have its proper share of that increased efficiency in the two directions of higher wages as producers and lower prices as consumers.[142]

---

[142] *Report of Proceedings* of 45th Annual Convention of American Federation of Labor of 1925, 231: ". . . We urge upon wage earners everywhere: that we oppose all wage reductions and that we urge upon management the elimination of wastes in production in order that selling prices may be lower and wages higher. . . ."

Are these higher rates of wages (distinguished from annual income) demanded because they would prevent unemployment by enabling labor to purchase back the increased output, or simply because they mean higher standards of living? The first reason is unsound. Higher rates of wages would not have prevented the unemployment of 1930 to 1933. But the second reason is sound. Higher standards of living and shorter hours of labor are worthy of being demanded on their own account—in many industries even if there is no increase in efficiency.

But should labor obtain these higher standards by means of higher rates of wages as *producers* or by means of lower prices as *consumers?* The American Federation of Labor demanded both higher wages as producers and lower prices as consumers.

Here is the significance of the margin for profit. If employers' prices fall, on the average, in proportion to the increased efficiency, the margin for profit remains where it was and employers are in no better position to grant increased rates of wages or shorter hours than they would have been if there had been no increase in efficiency. Their answer to the demands of labor must be that they have already passed along to them, as consumers, the gains in efficiency, and have nothing left for them as producers. The ultimate conclusion is the sad predicament of advocating a system of rationing or "staggering" the limited amount of employment so as to put all labor on half-time, or "short rations." This compels labor as a social class to finance its own unemployed, instead of stabilizing full employment. This suggests the alternative conclusion that, on the average, the prices of commodities should be stable, and labor should get its higher standards of living as *producers* at higher wages, shorter hours, and steady employment through the year, rather than as *consumers* at lower prices and unemployment.

It is on account of the failure to keep quite clear these distinctions between the *margin* for profit, the *rate* of profit, and the *share* for profit, as well as the *rate* of wages per hour or day and the total *wage income* per year, that writers who discuss the subject slip from the one idea to the other without realizing what they have done. Foster and Catchings had an idea of the *margin* for profit which led them to suggest stability of the general price level, but they shifted to the *rate* of profit and then drew their conclusions from the inadequacy of the *share* that goes to consumers.[143] Industry, they say, does not, in prosperous times, disburse to consumers enough money to buy the goods produced, and this would apparently be corrected if prices should fall in proportion as

[143] Above, p. 526, The Margin for Profit.

efficiency increases. In this respect they followed the Nineteenth Century theories of Malthus, Rodbertus, the communists, and the trade unionists. But if the margin for profit is seen in its true light, then not only should the rise and fall of prices in business cycles be prevented as far as possible, but also the long trends of falling prices, such as that from 1815 to the gold discoveries of 1849, and again from the American Civil War to the new inventions for extraction of gold of 1897, or from 1920 to 1933. In order to prevent prices from falling excessively they must previously be prevented from rising excessively.

It is this precaution that reveals a double meaning of the word efficiency. It means speeding up the workers, and it means substituting machinery for labor. During the excessive inflation of prices in 1919, laborers could so easily get jobs from competing employers that they were careless about their work and even abandoned their trucks on the streets, in order to accept higher wages from competing employers. They "laid down on the job." In one instance known to the writer their efficiency was reduced two-thirds while their wage-rates were trebled. When the slump came in 1921 millions of these same workers were unemployed, and then, when business started up in 1922, labor had been "liquidated" and thereby speeded up by fear of losing jobs in 1921.

Hence the alleged increase in efficiency of 47 per cent, using the year 1919 as the basis of comparison, was due perhaps as largely to an increase in manual speed as it was to the introduction of machinery and better shop organization. The business cycle had demoralized the laborers in 1919, pauperized them in 1921, coerced them in 1922. It was done by what happened to the employer's margin for profit.

Therefore assuming, as we have done, an *equal* increase of true efficiency in all industries, amounting to one per cent per year for ten years, if prices of all commodities have fallen equally ten per cent, have the exchange-values, or real prices, fallen ten per cent? No. They remain exactly where they were. A bushel of wheat exchanges for exactly the same quantity of manufactured products as it did before, and a suit of clothes exchanges for just the same quantity of agricultural products as it did before. There has been a fall of ten per cent in money prices of both agriculture and manufactures, but no fall in exchange-values, or real values, between agricultural products and manufactured products.

Shall we say, then, that it makes no difference what the level of prices is, or whether the level changes? We might apparently say it would make no difference in our supposed case. But take an opposite supposition. Suppose, while efficiency has increased *equally* ten per cent for all commodities, yet the level of all prices is rising ten per cent, instead of falling. There would still be no change in the exchange-values or real values of manufactures and agriculture. The *prices* would be ten per cent higher, but a bushel of wheat would buy the same quantity of manufactures, and a suit of clothes would buy the same quantity of agricultural products. The difference would be that all prices would be ten per cent higher, by which is meant either that both wheat and clothing would sell for ten per cent more money, or that ten per cent less money would buy the same quantity of wheat or clothing.

If it made no difference in exchange-values, or real values, between manufacturers and agriculture when all prices fell ten per cent, it likewise made no difference in real values when prices rose ten per cent. But who got the increase of ten per cent in efficiency?

Take another supposition. Suppose that, when efficiency all around increased equally ten per cent, there was no change in the average level of prices. Wheat therefore sells for the same number of dollars as before, and the same number of dollars buys the same suit as before. Consequently, when the price level remains stable, the same thing happens to exchange-values or real values as when money prices rise ten per cent or when money prices fall ten per cent. But who now gets the ten per cent increase in efficiency?

When all prices *fell* ten per cent and all efficiencies increased equally ten per cent, to whom did the increased efficiency go? We must, apparently, distinguish between producers and consumers. This is the usual way of talking. Some are producers, others are consumers. But it does not fit the situation. In our supposed cases all farmers and farm laborers and all manufacturers and manufacturing laborers are *both* producers and consumers. Our distinction must therefore be, not between producers and consumers as though they were different persons, but between, let us say, the producing-selling function and the buying-consuming function of the same persons.

This distinction is important. Does the increase in efficiency go to the millions of participants in their producing-selling function or in their buying-consuming function? Let us look at the three different situations supposed above, respecting prices. Take the first case. If all prices fell ten per cent while all efficiencies were increasing ten per cent, would it be as producing-sellers or as consuming-buyers that the farmers and farm-laborers, the manufacturers and factory laborers, obtained the ten per cent gain in efficiency? Evidently, what happens would be that each side would gain, not by its own increased efficiency, but by the increased efficiency of the other side of the transaction. And each side would lose the gain that might have come from *its own* increased efficiency. They come out even, in this supposed case, because each side gains from the increased efficiency of the other side just as much as it loses—by the fall in prices—from the failure to gain the increase from its own efficiency. In other words, when prices are supposed to fall as much as efficiency increases, then each side gains in its buying-consuming function as much as it loses in its producing-selling function.

Take the opposite extreme, where, supposedly, prices increased equally ten per cent while efficiency all round increased also ten per cent.[144] The real or exchange-values, as we saw, remained the same, but prices all round rose ten per cent. Which function got the gain from the increased efficiency, and which function lost out? Evidently the producing-selling function got two gains. It got a gain of ten per cent on account of increased efficiency, and it got another gain of ten per cent on account of the rise in prices. Its total gain was twenty per cent. On the other hand, the consumer-buying function suffered a loss of ten per cent because prices were supposed to rise just that amount, and therefore a *given amount* of money available to buyers would purchase ten per cent less commodities than before. But, as sellers, they had obtained ten per cent *more money* with which to buy. Hence, again, we must split our producer-seller function into its two parts. The producer-seller function got two gains, a ten per cent gain from increased efficiency and a ten per cent gain from higher prices. This means that it got a ten per cent gain by means of its producer function and another ten per cent gain from its seller function. There was nothing whatever to offset or deduct from this ten per cent gain in efficiency as a producer. That was pure net efficiency profit or efficiency wages. But there was an exactly equal offset to its gain as a seller function, when it came to exercising its function as a buyer.

Here, we must make a further distinction between two kinds of consumers. There are ultimate consumers and there are business consumers. The ultimate consumer is the last buyer; the business consumer is an intermediate buyer. The association of manufacturers who bought steel for their production of machinery and farm implements called themselves "The Association of Rolled-Steel

[144] Mills, F. C., *Economic Tendencies in the United States* (1932), 38, 99, shows that the output per worker in manufacturing industries increased about 30 per cent from 1899 to 1914, when the prices of manufactured goods were increasing about 22 per cent. This controverts the usual idea that it is falling prices and not rising prices, at least over a period of time, that causes an increase of efficiency.

Consumers." But they were not consumers; they were producers. They had organized in order to obtain the privilege of paying lower prices for the semi-finished steel products which they needed, not for consumption, but for further production into finished products. Hence, to be exact, they should be called buyer-producers, instead of buyer-consumers. We shall consider them here as buyer-producers.

Thus producers can enlarge their profits in three directions: first, as *sellers* by raising the prices of their products; second, as *buyers* by reducing the prices paid to others for materials and labor; or, third, as *producers* by increasing their efficiency.

For the purpose of measuring these three methods of increasing profits and wages we need two systems of measurement. For the first and second methods of raising and reducing prices our unit of measurement is the dollar. For the third method, by the increasing efficiency as producers, our unit of measurement is the man-hour. The first and second methods depend on the relations of supply and demand, that is, upon the relative scarcities of commodities, and our measure of relative scarcities is the dollar. The third method depends upon increasing the quantity of products produced by the same quantity of labor, that is, upon increasing the efficiency of labor and management, and our measure of relative efficiencies is the man-hour.

We have previously considered these measurements. Here we see how it is that, in our supposition of an equal rise of prices all round, there is the exactly equal offset to the gain from the seller function. This offset came from the ten per cent increase in prices that had to be paid *as buyers*. Thus, while, as *producers,* each side gained ten per cent from increased efficiency, and while, as *sellers,* each side gained another ten per cent, yet as *buyers* each side lost what it gained as sellers, though retaining what it gained as producers.

These fine distinctions will be found to be important. A certain business man started out to show that the sciences of chemistry and electricity could be introduced into business and that thereby large profits could be made. His ideal was evidently efficiency profits, and he succeeded immensely. Suddenly he found himself stopping production and laying off his laborers, because he was waiting for an expected bankruptcy and unloading of inventories by the producers who supplied his materials, after which he might expect to buy his materials at lower prices. Why did he change from his first ideal of making a profit by increasing efficiency to the different ideal of making a profit by withholding production and beating down the prices of raw material? All business men were doing the

same thing at periods of falling prices in 1921 and 1931. All of
them were waiting for each other to be squeezed by falling prices,
and so they were in much the same position as the famous islanders
who eked out a precarious living by compelling each to take in the
others' washing. All of them were trying to make precarious profit
by going around the circle of taking it out of each other as *buyers*
at falling prices.

Or, when the opposite movement occurred and prices were rising,
then every business man and stock speculator thought he was very
smart if he sold at the peak of the market and "got out from
under" just before prices began to fall. "Getting out from under"
means letting the buyers hold the bag of falling prices. Why was
it, then, that in the period of rising prices both employers and wage-
earners "laid down on the job" and decreased their efficiency? This
occurred in the year 1919. It was because, as *sellers,* they were
trying to take their profits and wages out of each other, instead of
taking it out of themselves as efficient producers. This time it resolved itself into the precarious circle of taking it out of each other
by rising prices.

The third method of increasing profits and wages is the efficiency
method, where they do not try the circular process of taking it out
of each other by the general rising or falling of prices, but they take
it out of themselves by increasing their efficiency. Take the third
supposed situation, where prices remained equally stable, and where,
as before, real values or exchange-values were also stable. Now,
it is evident, neither side gained or lost anything as sellers or
buyers. Both prices and exchange-values remained the same. But
each side gained as producers—not as buyers or sellers—exactly the
amount of gain represented by its own ten per cent increase in
efficiency.

Hence, we have three possible price situations in our supposed
uniform increase of average efficiency, and we are called upon to
test the first natural assumption that all prices may be expected to
fall with increasing efficiency. The question now takes a different
turn. It is not, What should we *naturally* expect the law of supply
and demand to do to all prices when efficiency increases, but, Which
price situation should we expect will be the best for all concerned?
Is it better all around that the gains from efficiency made by producers should go to other persons as buyers? If so, then falling
prices will do it. Or, is it better that, as sellers, the producers
should get an additional gain not based on efficiency? If so, then
rising prices will do it. Or, finally, is it better that the gains from
efficiency should be retained by the producers themselves without

gaining or losing as sellers or as buyers?   If so, then a stable average of prices will do it.

We have, then, really three questions to answer, an economic, a political, and an administrative question.   The economic question is, What effect will the unregulated law of supply and demand have on prices when efficiency increases?   The political question is the ethical one, Who, in the conflict of interests, should get the gains of efficiency?   The administrative question is, Can the central banks and treasuries, if authorized by governments, stabilize the average movement of prices?

We shall not consider here the first and third questions.   We have already considered the third.   Of course it would not be worth while considering the other questions if we knew positively that the third could not be answered affirmatively.   We do know, however, that, since the war, governments throughout the world, and their central banks, have been working more or less on this question of the enormous fluctuations of the average of prices, trying to reduce these fluctuations.   We are not now considering whether they can reduce the fluctuations or not.   We are only considering what public policy they should take as their guide in administering the credit system of the world.   We are considering the problem of Reasonable Value.   The question is, Should they take the promotion of efficiency as their guide?   Is this a reasonable guide for public policy?

It must be remembered again that efficiency is not the same as production or over-production.   Efficiency is merely the *rate* of production, measured by man-hours.   To increase efficiency is not necessarily to increase the total output.   It may mean *a reduction of hours* with an increased output *per hour* and not an increase of total output thrown on the markets at reduced prices.

We may assume, with Adam Smith, that everybody seeks his own self-interest, regardless of the effects on others, in all his economic activities of buying, selling, producing, and consuming.   This consists in getting as much gain as possible and suffering as little loss as possible.   Everybody does this without regard to the effects on other people, unless he is restrained in some way that he cannot overcome.   If anybody claims that he is in business for the public benefit we may, like Smith, set it down as buncombe.   The question of public policy, then, is the question of Reasonable Value: Should his largest selfish gain and least loss to self be secured for him, by the banking system, as a producer, or as a seller, or as a buyer, or as an ultimate consumer?

There is really only one way in which a person who selfishly seeks his own largest gain can do so without getting something for

nothing by taking it out of other people, and that is by increasing
his efficiency. He can do this either by speeding up or by brain
work without speeding. If he gains *solely* by raising his prices paid
by other people, his gain comes solely from an equal loss to others
as buyers. He not only gets something for nothing, he gets something for less than nothing. The others, then, if they are also
producer-sellers, can recoup themselves only in one of two ways,
either raise their prices as sellers equal to their loss as buyers, or
increase their efficiency as producers equal to that same loss as
buyers. If they raise their prices as sellers they, in turn, get something for nothing by taking it out of other people and thereby come
out even. If they raise their efficiency but receive correspondingly
lower prices, then the others take the gains of their efficiency away
from them, and they do not come out even. If both sides raise
their prices, equally, but without increasing their efficiency, then
they endeavor to come out even on the gamble of getting something
for nothing out of each other. Finally if both sides increase their
efficiency but do not raise their prices, then they also come out
even, but each side gets its gain from its own efficiency, without
the intermediate step of taking it out of others for nothing in exchange.

The answer to the political and ethical question would then seem
to be, Every person seeking his purely selfish increase of profits
or wages should get his largest gain as a producer through increasing
his efficiency, not as a seller gambling on the rise of prices, and
not as a buyer gambling on the fall of prices.

If the former money cost of manufacturing a suit of clothes was
$33, and the money cost is reduced to $24, we cannot tell whether
the 28 per cent reduction in money cost was due to lower wages,
lower rates of interest, lower profits, lower prices of raw material,
or to an increase in efficiency. But if the man-hour cost is reduced
33 per cent, then we can say that there remains a difference to be
distributed as shorter hours or higher wages, or profit, or interest.

From the standpoint of public policy which would have been
better? The answer turns on the other question previously asked.
In view of the fact that both the producer-sellers and the consumer-
buyers are acting upon the purely selfish motive of getting as much
as possible for themselves without any sense of duty or responsibility to others, and therefore they would prefer the easier way of
taking it out of *other people* by means of charging higher prices or
paying lower prices and wages, instead of the harder way of taking
it out of themselves by increasing their own efficiency—Where, then,
should the inducement to business be placed?

Those who might answer this question, in the above case, by saying that the price of the suit of clothes should have fallen 28 per cent, would be taking the buyer-consumer standpoint that buyers should selfishly take away from producers the gains of efficiency. Would this be reasonable? Those who might answer that the price should not be reduced, would be taking the selfish producer-seller standpoint. Is this reasonable under all the circumstances? Neither side deserves any ethical consideration of justice, or righteousness, or pity, for each is seeking his own self-interest regardless of others. The consumers would take all they could out of the producers by lower prices. The producers would take it out of the consumers by higher prices, or out of the sellers of raw material and labor by lower prices and wages, if they could. The producers would not increase their efficiency if they did not have to, and they would not have to if they could go the easier way of taking it out of consumers by higher prices, or out of the preceding producers of their materials by lower prices, or out of their own laborers by lower wages.

Seeing, then, that neither side deserves any consideration of justice or ethics, or righteousness, or pity, because each comes into our court of political economy with the same dirty hands of selfishness, the social question must be shifted elsewhere. Which is better for the nation as a whole? Which is it that the nation as a whole wants, or should want? Should it want consumers to get all the benefits of progress in efficiency? Or should it want the producers to get all the benefit?

When the question is stated in this way, many will be inclined to answer, They should divide the benefit. But here certain other questions are raised. Whose efficiency shall be divided? How shall it be divided? When shall it be divided? How much of it shall be divided?

We do not need to guess, nor speculate upon the answers, nor let our theory of the "law" of supply and demand give us the answer. We have experience to go upon. The patent laws are an artificial interference by government with the natural operation of the "law" of supply and demand. They enable the inventor and the manufacturer, who operates the invention, to keep up the price of the output, by prohibiting anybody else from increasing the supply by means of the increased efficiency to be obtained through the use of the invention. The purpose of the patent laws, as agreed upon by the nation represented in Congress, is evidently to give to the inventor and manufacturer all of the gain that he can get from his particular patented increase in efficiency. Their efficiency, as producers, is not divided at all with the buyer-consumers. They get it all for themselves.

But there is a certain limiting factor imposed by the "law" of supply and demand. They cannot raise prices above the level charged by less efficient competitors who sell the similar product but who do not have the same patented instrument of efficiency. Thus the "law" of supply and demand continues to operate. It prevents their gain, as sellers, from coming to them by raising prices above those of less efficient competitors. They must get their gain solely as efficient producers. The law of supply and demand takes care of that. The "law" of supply and demand cannot be abolished —it can be used.

But they can reduce their prices if they want to, and if their efficiency enables them to, and thus can drive out their less efficient competitors. They thus determine for themselves how much of their increased efficiency shall be shared, by lower prices, with the buyers as consumers. They evidently use the "law" of supply and demand also for this purpose, by increasing the supply if they want to do so.

But the patent expires by law, after a certain number of years. Then anybody can use the patented device to increase his efficiency, and the "law" of supply and demand again operates to bring down prices and thus ultimately to turn over to the buyer-consumers all of the gains from the increased efficiency.

There are, of course, imperfections and abuses in the patent laws, but the above is their social philosophy and also the way they mostly work in practice. At first they give all the gains in efficiency to the producer. Then eventually they give all the gains to the buyers. The patent laws do this by controlling the "law" of supply and demand in three ways. First, by enabling the producer to restrict the supply of the efficiency device. Second, by permitting the producer to drive out his competitors by increasing his output and reducing his prices, thus sharing his increased efficiency with buyers as much or little as he wishes. Third, by depriving the producer, when the patent expires, of his previous control over the "law" of supply and demand, thus transferring to buyer-consumers all the gains of the increased efficiency.

Thus it comes about, in the case of patents, that the first thought —naturally occurring to everybody—that the "law" of supply and demand should be expected to bring a fall of prices with increasing efficiency, is true only if we add the collective purpose of the state in giving the gains of efficiency solely to producers at first and then gradually to consumers, and if we add also the power of the state to authorize the patentee to control the "law" of supply and demand for a limited period of time.

It is evident also, from experience, that his own government alone does not have the power to authorize the patentee thus to control the "law" of supply and demand; this is shown by the fact that practically all governments have united by treaties or otherwise to give the same patent in all countries to the same inventor or manufacturer. The "law" of supply and demand is world-wide and prompt, under modern systems of transportation and electricity; and there must be a world-wide control of supply and demand by these patent laws, if producers are to receive the gains of their increased efficiency.

There are, however, many kinds of improvements in efficiency which cannot be patented. Better lay-out of a factory, better organization of the labor-force, better purchase of materials, better inducements to employees, larger equipment of machinery—these cannot be patented. Here it is evident that not even the seventeen years of a patent are available, for producers to realize the gains from their increased efficiency. The gain must be gotten otherwise, without the help of patent laws, and must be gotten from day to day as we go along, and quickly, if possible, before competitors copy improvements.

But, even here, there are other ways, developed mainly by common-law decisions, by which these day-to-day efficiency gains may be protected and stretched out in time. The common law protects trade secrets. If an employee reveals a secret process to a competitor, the law will afford damages against that competitor to the full extent of all the profit which he made by stealing the secret—so careful is the law of the land to make certain that the "law" of supply and demand shall not operate to prevent an inventor of a process from having the full benefit of his increase in efficiency.

There is still another protection of efficiency—the common law and legislative protection given to the good-will and trade-marks of a business. If a manufacturer has acquired a reputation for giving good quality and good service, the law prohibits competitors from "stealing" his good reputation by using anything that looks like the name or sign of his reputation. This is really a protection also to efficiency, because an improvement in quality or service is as much an increase in efficiency as is an increase in quantity.

In these ways the public purpose of the nation, through legislatures and courts, shows itself in using all possible restraints and restrictions upon the free operation, under purely selfish motives, of the "law" of supply and demand, in order to protect efficiency by protecting the producer from being compelled to turn over to buyers, by way of lower prices, the gains which he creates by his own efficiency.

Now the proposition that there ought to be a world-wide stabilization of the average purchasing power of money, that is, of the average movement of prices, and that the governments of the world ought to authorize the Central Banks of the world to stabilize the value of money is in effect the same ethical proposition and public purpose as that which underlies the patent law and the protection of trade secrets, trade-marks, good-will, and business reputation. But it goes further and protects those who do not have these legal protections to their efficiency. One purpose, at least, of this stabilization is that the gains from increasing efficiency in all industries shall go, as much as possible, in the first instance, to producers and not to buyers; that the producers shall make their gains as efficient producers and not as mere sellers by higher prices received from buyers; and that, as either ultimate or intermediate consumers, they shall make their gains, not by lower prices paid as buyers, but in their other function as efficient producers.

The working out of the proposition is not as simple as the patent and similar laws and the court decisions; it is not nearly as simple as the supposed illustrations which we have above constructed in order to simplify the theory. Yet it is only an extension to *all* producers of that which public policy safeguards for individual producers. Its reasonableness depends on further conditions, such as class domination and antagonism, or international complications, which make it doubtful whether it *can* be done. If, for these and other reasons stabilization cannot be accomplished as an "ideal type," then we can still aim towards the highest practicable stabilization under all the circumstances. This is reasonable stabilization. But there must be a "goal" of some kind, as an ideal type; else there can be no concerted action enlisted to approach it as nearly as practicable.

This social ideal of shortening the hours and increasing profits and wages by efficiency instead of scarcity brings us to the question of an ideal type of index numbers that shall be used as a guide, and to the administrative machinery that shall enforce the guide. In general, the most serious problem of capitalistic civilization is unemployment. The paradox of doubling, trebling, and even quadrupling efficiency, while perpetrating great alternations of employment and unemployment, makes it probable that war or communism or fascism may be preferable to peace and liberty.

Consequently, with the great majority of people becoming a proletariat, the most important of all guides to stabilization is that
of maintaining full and steady employment. A rapidly rising price
level in 1919 and again in 1923 quickly restored full employment.
The rapidly falling price levels of 1920–21 and 1929–33 greatly
increased unemployment. This is because industry operates on
narrow margins of profit, and a slightly rising price level all along
the line has a multiplied effect in enlarging the margins of profit
and therefore increasing the demand, while a fall in the price margin
reduces the demand for labor.

But if the level of prices is allowed to rise beyond the level of
full employment, as in 1919, then it is mere inflation of prices and
wages because there can be no possible increase of employment by
production except by reduction in hours of work, when all are fully
employed. Full employment is the reasonable limit of inflation.
The matter was managed better in 1923. By selling securities and
raising the discount rates, under the conditions of industry and
banking at that time, the prices did not rise above the point of
restoration of full employment.

5. *The Police Power of Taxation*

(1) **Private Utility and Social Utility.**—The Police Power is
the American name for Social Utility in Action. It is a power of
the legislatures and courts, not the power of an executive—the
police-man. In federal legislation it is included in the power over
interstate and foreign commerce. It is the power to direct the
actions of individuals in one direction rather than in another direction. In this respect it does not differ from taxation. Each is
grounded on the fact that no individual is sufficient to himself, but
receives his income from others in exchange.

Two problems have always arisen from this social fact: the distribution of wealth, and keeping the concern agoing. Since the
time of Ricardo the distinction has been made between earned
and unearned income in the distribution of wealth. But a hundred
years have changed the meanings of these words. All are unearned
and all are earned, but in different degrees. A more specific and
less invidious terminology is needed. We distinguish them, elabo-
rating Ricardo's clue, as personal income, capital income, and site-
value income. And the going concern with which we have to do
sometimes goes, sometimes slows down, and sometimes stops. These
themselves greatly affect the distribution of wealth and the burden
of the two fixed charges, taxes and interest.

We have seen that while the *aggregate* of taxes paid by manufacturing corporations, during a period of years, has run only about
one or two per cent of the average costs of production,[145] yet the
burden of taxes on the average margin for profit has ranged from
33 per cent in 1919 to "infinity" in 1921; and doubtless again in
1930, 1931, and 1932, for which years the statistics are not yet
available. The burden of taxes on these corporations, which produce 90 per cent of the country's manufactured products, was 35
per cent more than the margin for profit in 1926, and it ranged
from 33 to 90 per cent of the margin in other years.

It is this margin for corporate profit, in the Twentieth Century
stage of the capitalist system, and not the cost of production of
Nineteenth Century individualistic economics, that determines
whether business shall go, boom, slow down, or stop. While taxes,
like interest—a fixed overhead charge—may take in the United
States 10 or 12 per cent of the total income of the people,[146] yet,
considering the average for manufacturing concerns, they range
from one-third to far in excess of the margin for profit.

The older economists were concerned mainly with questions of
distribution, that is, of the *shares* of the social output among individuals. But after corporations with huge issues of securities on
narrow and fluctuating margins for profit have taken the place of
individuals, the Twentieth Century economists become concerned
with the question, What makes this corporate capitalism go and
stop even more violently than the older individual capitalism? Of
all the answers given we narrow them down predominantly to prices,
taxes, and the margin for profit. There are other interests, like
laborers, but these can be laid off and carry no fixed charges.
While corporate capitalism is doubtless the most powerful stage of
capitalism, it is the most delicate and menacing, because it runs
mainly on a narrow margin of profit and loss. The individual
capitalist, like the farmer today, or the manufacturer in the time
of Smith and Ricardo, who made no distinction between profit,
interest, rent, and wages, might tighten his belt when profit, interest,
and rent disappear and continue to live on even reduced wages
for his whole family at work. But corporate capitalism goes bank-
rupt when interest, taxes, rent, and wages have exhausted the margin
for profit. For, the corporation becomes a debtor to laborers for
wages, to lenders and bankers for interest, to landlords for rent,
to the state for taxes; so that profit is only the margin left on

[145] Above, p. 526, The Margin for Profit.
[146] Concealed mainly in wages and salaries of public employees and interest on public
debts. Above, p. 526, Margin for Profit.

sales-income after these liabilities are met. The corporate capitalist mixes his private and corporate interest when he opposes highly progressive *personal* income and inheritance taxes which do not come out of the *corporate* margin for profit; but he is wise when he opposes progressive taxes on the higher margins of corporate profit where the big corporation, as disastrously seen in recent years, is as delicately balanced as the little corporation.

It is this delicacy, magnitude, and social menace of what has become banker capitalism, that requires what, in the terminology of Professor Seligman, is a "Social Theory of Fiscal Science." [147]

Seligman classifies what he names "groups" according to the nature of the *wants* of individuals, whereas we classify them as "going concerns" according to the working rules and sanctions which collective action employs in control of individual action. The similarities and differences may be readily observed from his classification, as follows:

SELIGMAN'S CLASSIFICATION OF GROUPS

How Conditioned	Nature of Want	Designation of Group
With one other	Sexual	—Marriage
Private { With several others	Social	—Club, fraternity, lodge, chapter
	Recreational	—Team, bank, gang, chorus
	Military	—Squad, troop, battery
	Vocational	—Union, guild, grange, craft
	Business	—Partnership, corporation, syndicate
	Factional	—Party, bloc, union
	Religious	—Sect, order, brotherhood, church
Public With all others	Protection Life Property Liberty	—Political organization, *i.e.*, state, federation, league
	Justice Common welfare	

With this system of groups, or going concerns, Seligman goes back to the classical concept of individual wants as the causal factors in economics, but notices, as did Pareto, that the wants themselves change and are immeasurable when shifted to the collective wants of one or any of these groups. This distinction between wants is based, not on "their original psychological character," but on the individual or collective "means of satisfying" the wants. These means are "separate," "reciprocal" and "collective," and the

[147] Seligman, E. R. A., *Pol. Sci. Quar.*, XLI (1926), 193 ff., 354 ff.

collective means of satisfying wants are further classified as "private and public wants, according as they are satisfied by private or public groups." The public wants and the means for satisfying them differ from the private, in that they are fundamental, universal, compulsory, and indissoluble, because membership in the public group is compulsory. This results in differences between public and private groups, in that with the public group there is no reciprocity, such as we have seen in a bargaining transaction contrasted with a rationing transaction, and that the advantages to individuals are indivisible and immeasurable. Consequently the prices charged, in the form of taxes, for the public services which satisfy collective wants are not based on the principle of cost or profit. They are based in varying degrees on the principles of special benefit, ability to pay; or even inversely to benefit or ability, like sales taxes.

Seligman's conclusion is that fiscal science is a part of social science in the wider sense; that fiscal science arises from common wants; that it distinguishes the private group from the public group; that the two groups are nevertheless similar in the process of requiring individuals to pay for satisfying collective wants; and that the long conflicting maxims of *ability to pay* versus *benefit received* must be abandoned as exclusive of each other, since each has its appropriate sphere of action.

We conclude that, for these reasons, it is Hume's public utility, or Pareto's social utility, or the equally immeasurable and even demagogic "public policy" or police power and taxing power, that determines by rationing and not bargaining or even managing, the boundaries in the process of distributing the social burdens and benefits to individuals and keeping the concern agoing by the production of wealth.

This taxing power in the process of its exercise takes into account the inducements and restraints upon individuals as well as the amount of revenue. It is economically a special case of rationing transactions, dominating both bargaining and managerial transactions. As such it is reached by the democratic system of log-rolling among special interests, or by the equally log-rolling activities of dictatorship or dominant interests. On this account it takes mainly into account the pressure of conflicting interests, and by no means follows the principles that may be set forth based on individualistic theories of private utility, except to the extent that those theories fall in line with the political principles of the conflicting interests that struggle to dominate the log-rolling.

This is seen in the fact that Pareto's "molecular" principle of social science may eventually be adopted in politics, as when England adopted in 1846 the free trade principles of Smith and Ricardo, with the rise to political power of the mercantile and manufacturing interests against the landed interests. But even this principle, after a hundred years, and after another political conflict, is abandoned for the protective principles of other economists, such as Carey and List.[148]

(2) **Sites, Costs, Expectations.**—The protective principle, in reality, goes much further than tariff taxation. All taxes induce, more or less, expansion in one direction by restraint in other directions. The mere *obtaining* of public revenue· is not their only purpose. But obtaining that revenue by shifting the burden on other people is the evidently observable purpose. Fiscal science is economic science in that it analyzes the means and effects of these collective efforts to make others pay the taxes, and this analysis has turned, in large part, on the historical changes in the meaning of the word "capital."

We have noticed the historical changes in this meaning from Ricardo's labor-cost of production in the past to Carey's cost of reproduction in the present, and to the present value of future net incomes expected from the ownership of the commercial debts, the stocks, bonds, and land values of banker capitalism.[149] In this shift of meaning, Ricardo's distinction between unearned rent and his earned wages, interest, or profit disappears. The disappearance takes place with Carey and Bastiat, because the "cost of reproduction" of the land includes all of the social as well as individual costs that would be necessary to produce alternative land equal to the value of existing land.[150] Ricardo's distinction of unearned rent also disappears—as stated by Fetter in 1901 at the turning-point of the last transition in the meaning of capital—because all future incomes, no matter how monopolistic, discriminatory, or unfair, are looked upon as future "rents," to be paid for the use of any and all kinds of property, so that capital becomes the present discounted value of those future rents.[151]

It will be seen, and has often been noted, that the changing meanings of Capital depend on changes in the meaning of Rent. Rent, in Fetter's popular usage of the term, has the same meaning as "hire," or payment made for the *use* of anything over a period

[148] List derived his theory from his experiences during his exile in America. List, Friedrich, *Das nationale System der politischen Oekonomie* (1841).

[149] Above, p. 443, Sidgwick.

[150] Above, p. 310, Value of Service.

[151] Fetter, Frank, "The Passing of the Old Rent Concept," *Quar. Jour. Econ.*, XV (1901), 416 ff.

of time. The rent of real estate is a payment per unit of time regardless of the many economic differences combined in the ownership of landed property. Interest is the rent, or hire, paid for the use of money. Wages are the hire paid for the use of labor. Rent and profit are the hire paid to an owner for the use of his horse. The entire Nineteenth and into the Twentieth Century of economic theory has been occupied with breaking up this feudal, legal, and popular meaning of rent into its economic differences; and the need of the distinctions becomes more urgent with the increase of urban land values and the relative decrease of agricultural land values.

Ricardo was the first to make the economic distinction of rent, provoked by the conflict of interests between capitalists and the feudalistic landlords over the protective tariff on wheat. In doing so he had to change the meaning of rent from the historic meaning of payment for the use of land to payment for the use of the "original and indestructible" qualities of the land. Thereby he made the rent of landlords an "unearned income," for which they rendered no equivalent service, whereas interest, profits, and wages were earned incomes.

Karl Marx, in extending Ricardo's meaning of labor from individual laborers to social labor-power, eliminated this Ricardian distinction, because he considered that rent, like interest and profits, were unearned incomes paid on account of private ownership, not on account of differences in productivity; and the distinction would disappear under common ownership, as it apparently has done in Soviet Russia. John Stuart Mill recognized, in part, Ricardo's distinction in his proposal of land nationalization, but not the Marxian capital socialization.[152] Henry George recognized it, also only in part, by his proposal of a single tax on land, because he included fertility, which Ricardo did not include.[153]

Neither Mill nor George made use of Ricardo's distinction between fertility and the indestructible qualities of the land. George, in his original work, though not in later works, did not even follow the single tax of Quesnay, who declared that only the *original* fertility of the soil was a divine gift to man, but that the maintained and enlarged fertility was advanced by the landlords and cultivators. George, at first, like Smith and Malthus, considered that *all* fertility of the soil produced wealth, by divine beneficence, in excess of that produced by labor and capital (Quesnay's *avances*) and

[152] Mill, J. S., *Dissertations and Discussions, Political, Philosophical, and Historical* (1875), V, 223 ff., "Papers on Land Tenure, 1870–1873."
[153] George, Henry, *Progress and Poverty, an Inquiry into the Cause of Industrial Depression and of Increase of Want with Increase of Wealth* (1879).

therefore should be single-taxed in order to relieve the productive capitalists and laborers of taxation. This, we know, as did Quesnay and Ricardo, as well as George in his later works, is not true. Fertility is exhaustible for the most part, and in so far must be reproduced, like any form of "capital" or Quesnay's *avances*.

But Ricardo's distinction is itself capable of a further distinction. His "original and indestructible" qualities of the land may be resolved into the *site* value, given to it by the needs of society, and the *foundation* value given to it by the producer and cultivator.[154] Site-value is merely scarcity-value, since it is derived only from access to markets, and is determined, therefore, mainly by social demand and the limited supply of sites where the demand is concentrated. But foundation-value is something that may be produced by the efforts of the individual owner according to his calculations of whether the income will reimburse his costs of production. In this respect foundation-value also is similar to Ricardo's destructible, improved, or maintained fertility, whose value was a labor-cost value. Cost-value, for him, was a measure of the amount of "capital," or labor incorporated, but scarcity-value was a "nominal value" because it either exceeded or fell short of cost-value. Since he was concerned, in his anti-tariff propaganda, not so much with urban land as with agricultural land, he did not distinguish foundation-value from site-value. But the distinction runs through urban land and agricultural land.

The capital-value of land, as Turgot suggested in his description of an "estate," [155] is a variable composed of five different factors: the market site for sale and purchase of products; the foundation for structures and fertility; the structures themselves in their depreciated or obsolete condition; the original fertility; and the improved, maintained, or depleted fertility. Each is more or less taken into account in real estate transactions, but the business of economic or fiscal science is to distinguish and give due weight to the divergent principles which account for the variabilities; then to apply them, if practicable amidst the conflict of interests and difficulties of assessment, to the concrete valuations of business and assessment of taxes.

Site-values range all the way from several million dollars per acre in the financial districts of great cities, to no value at all at Ricardo's remote margins of cultivation, inaccessible to markets.[156]

---

[154] Cf. the writer's earlier formation of the principle in *Pol. Sci. Quar.*, XXXVII (1922), 41 ff., "A Progressive Tax on Bare Land Values."

[155] Above, p. 487, Capital and Capitals.

[156] Cf. Commons, J. R., *The Distribution of Wealth* (1893), 136.

Site-value may be increased by good roads, railroads, telegraph and postal service, and it may be decreased by the same agencies if they serve to move population, industry, and merchandizing to other localities. It is therefore a peculiarly social value assigned to, or taken from, individual owners according to the technological changes in means of transportation whose installation is encouraged or restrained by public policy.

But foundation-value is a deduction from site-value, varying according to the cost required to make it suitable for structures and fertility. If the foundation is not suitable it must be improved by cutting down hills, blasting rocks, digging cellars, filling swamps, driving piles, building irrigation dams and ditches. These expenses may be either imposed on individual owners or on the taxpayers at large, depending on the dominant interests or habitual assumptions in control of public policy.

These apply to both urban and agricultural land. In agriculture the foundation is partly for structures but mainly for its capacity to take on fertility. If it is sandy soil, its capacity to take on fertility is low. If it is a high grade of silt loam, which, however, is "destructible," and has been worn out by destructive cultivation to Ricardo's state of indestructible foundation, it still has a capacity to be brought back to its original fertility. In both cases, it is the texture, the shape, the topography, the "lay" of the land, as well as the access to markets, that determine how much plant food and cultivation it will be worth while to put into the soil. The fertility, the plant food, and the results of preceding cultivation may be exhausted, and the land cannot usually and economically be made to take on more than its original fertility. But it can, by good cultivation, be made to take on that much or more. In some cases, like truck gardens, it is profitable to add more than the original fertility, and this excess is properly named "improved fertility"; while, if maintained at the level of its original fertility, it is kept, as the farmer says, "at par." Original fertility is "par" but improved or depleted fertility is above or below par.

American farmers, on their large acreage, have a means of determining what they mean by "par." Near their stables, from which they haul manure, the land is kept at par. More remotely, on account of the cost of hauling, they let their fertility fall below par. But whether it is worth while, economically, to keep it at par or above, depends on access to good roads and good markets.[157] If it is good for truck gardening and accessible to good markets, the farmer may even build it up beyond its original fertility by

---

[157] On good prices, see below, p. 834, Statics and Cycles.

abundant manures, artificial fertilizers, turning under green crops; in short, by intensive cultivation and good management.

In any case, farm land is quite like urban land. A good foundation for urban buildings, accessible to good markets for the kind of product produced and sold, furnishes, in the best locations, an opportunity to put up a skyscraper, in others to put up two- or three-story buildings, in others to put up homes accessible to factories and business blocks, and to stock the buildings with inventories of movable goods. If these improvements and inventories are inaccessible to markets, or if the owners have built and stored too many of them for the existing markets, then the improvements or inventories have been wasted, and they shrink in value below what they cost.

There is thus a rough correlation between the scarcity-value of the land sites and the cost-value of the structural and foundational improvements, as well as the inventories which it is profitable to put on the land. It is quite the same with fertility. There is a rough correlation between the site-value of the exhausted agricultural land and the cost-value of the fertility and other improvements which it is profitable to maintain at par or above. If the land is remote from markets, it is more profitable to let it run to pasture. If it is near markets, it can profitably be put to crops that rapidly exhaust it, and this exhaustion can profitably be counteracted by intensive cultivation and careful management.

Whether or not any given piece of land will follow this correlation depends on its ownership and management. Tenancy and bad management may deplete the soil, good management may keep it even above par. It is similar with urban land. One owner will build a skyscraper, the next will keep his land vacant, or occupied by a depreciated or obsolete structure. The rough correlation between site-value and the value of structural or foundational improvements, or improved or maintained fertility, is a correlation, not of what is always actually done, for there are variabilities, but of what is economical, that is, profitable, to do. The individual differences of landowners are great, and it is exactly these differences that are affected by the public policy that governs the system of taxation.

This rough correlation between site-value and structural-value on urban lands appears more clearly in the use made by Harry Gunnison Brown of the Carey-Bastiat concept of "cost of reproduction" under the equivalent name of opportunity-cost,[158] to measure not only the cost-value of improvements, but also the site-values of

---

[158] Above, p. 329, The Law of Substitution.

urban land. With this device of "opportunity cost" it is not necessary to go out to Ricardo's margin of agricultural cultivation in order to ascertain the site-values of urban lands. Yet, accepting, as does Brown, the Ricardian concept of rent as an "unearned" income (which Carey and Bastiat did not accept), the expectation of this unearned income is capitalized into a present site-value of the land, equally unearned from the social standpoint. Then if a person desires to construct a building that will bring to him, as its owner, a future net income of earned interest and profit equal to the future unearned rent of the site-value, the alternative cost of constructing that building will determine the upper or lower limit of the value of the site. At that point either the seller or the buyer of the site will be willing to sell or pay for it an equivalent of the alternative cost of constructing a structure which might be expected to yield a net income of profit and interest equivalent to the net income of rent, on the site-value.[159] Thus the two valuations, of site and improvements on the site, are kept somewhat in correlation by the alternative of buying the site or constructing an improvement that will yield an equivalent future net income.

This use of the Carey-Bastiat concept of reproduction cost explains how it is that the business community, as well as the courts, have eliminated Ricardo's site-value from separate valuations. It is indifferent to the business man or banker whether what he buys or mortgages is a claim to a future *unearned* income—in that it is solely a scarcity-value that has cost nobody anything to produce the means of acquiring it—or is a claim to a future *earned* income which it has cost the wages, interest, and profit of workers and management to produce. A dollar is a dollar, no matter what social discriminations or individual sacrifices lie concealed behind it. All that is asked by the seller or paid by the buyer, or loaned by the banker, upon the site as security, is the alternative opportunities of investing his dollars to obtain a future equivalent margin for profit.

The lack of a more precise correlation between site-values and construction-values is found partly, as we have noted, in the differences in individual owners. These individual differences, and each of the above five factors of which land consists, are affected by the system of taxation. They may be reduced to three variables to be considered in imposing taxes. One is the individual abilities which are the human resources of the nation; another is the opportunities to exert the abilities and to use the natural resources; a

---

[159] See Brown, Harry Gunnison, *The Economics of Taxation*, 5th ed. (1924), and preceding articles referred to by him.

third is the inducements to exercise the abilities and to conserve or enlarge the resources. These are inseparable but distinguishable. They cannot be measured exactly and therefore must be stated in terms of a "rule of reason," which Adam Smith named a "canon" of taxation.

(3) **Canons of Taxation.**—The differences in abilities are, of course, very great, but the main difference, from the standpoint of inducements, is that which Schumpeter has made the center of his theory of economic evolution,[160] the difference between the "static-hedonistic" laborer or peasant and the "dynamic" business man or capitalist. These differences underlie the essential distinction between wages, interest, and rent, on the one hand, and profit on the other. Profit is the inducement of the dynamic factor; wages, interest, and rent are the inducements of the static factors. Profit looks to the future, is speculative, takes risks, and, in doing so, animates the business faculty that attracts or commands laborers, investors, and landowners to do its bidding. The others must be induced by the business man through offers of wages, interest, rent; but business ability is self-induced by the prospect of profit. Profit is the constructive factor; the others are passive, awaiting the initiative of profit. And it may correctly be said, from the standpoint of social inducements,[161] that, not "land," or "labor," or "capital," but expected profit, produces wealth.

This is the justification of private property and inequality of compensation. If people would work voluntarily according to the socialist canon, "From each according to ability, to each according to needs," then private property and profit might be discontinued.[162] But people, as a rule, actually work on the acquisitive principle, *from* each inversely to bargaining ability, *to* each proportionate to bargaining ability. And this is the outstanding attribute of profit, the compensation to business ability. Others may be paid in proportion to their needs, or in proportion to their strategic position as owners of what the business man needs, but business ability is induced preëminently by prospects of a margin of profit according to ability to reduce prices paid *to* others and raise prices paid *by* others.

Yet business ability is limited by the opportunities to exercise it. These opportunities also have differential advantages as great as the differences in abilities, and these differential advantages are

[160] Schumpeter, J., *Theorie der wirtschaftlichen Entwicklung eine Untersuchung über Unternehmergewinn, Kapital, Kredit, Zins und den Konjunkturzyklus* (1912, 1926).
[161] Above, p. 348, Malthus and Ricardo; p. 526, The Margin for Profit.
[162] Cf. Lenin, Nikolai, *The State and Revolution* (1918), in *Imperialism* (1929), where the dictatorship of the proletariat is to continue until mankind acts voluntarily on this canon.

the very reasons for private property. Karl Marx even maintained, as we have said, in contrast to Ricardo, that it was private property and not differences in productivity, that caused the phenomenon of rent. Certainly if all property were held in common, then these differences in productivity would be merged into a single fund to be rationed according to the socialist canon, and Ricardo's differential productivity would become Marx's "average" productivity of social labor-power. Ricardo emphasized the differences in nature, Marx the differences in ownership, but the two are subordinate to differences in profits. Private property of all kinds, whether in site-value, foundation-value, structural improvements, original, maintained, or improved fertility, is justifiable exactly on the grounds that it is differential advantages that furnish the telling inducements to the dynamic factor to make all the profit possible, since only by differences in compensation will business ability come forth and give employment to the static participants. Luck, chance, gifts of nature, whether they exist in one's own faculties or in nature's or society's resources, are all alike in that the differential gains to be obtained from them are the big inducements to the business man to seek out the best instruments and use them to the best advantage to augment his own margin for profit.

This has its bearing on taxation. Taxation is the inverse of private property since taxes are deductions from profits, wages, interest, or rent. Under the régime of private property and liberty the profit-maker can withhold the exercise of his faculties and can withhold the utilization of his natural resources and capital equipment, by himself or by his employees under his commands, if the margin for profit is not deemed large enough. And, since taxation deducts greatly from the margin for profit, he *withholds* the use of both his faculties and his natural resources *directly* according to the burden of taxes and *inversely* to the expected profit; which is but saying that he makes the largest use of his faculties and natural resources *directly* in proportion to expected profit and *inversely* in proportion to taxes.

"Ability to pay" is usually invoked to justify taxation of personal incomes and inheritances, that is, taxes on the *preceding* acquisition of income by the individual. This is correct enough. It is also invoked to justify the general property tax, that is, taxes on the *prospective* acquisition of income.[163] In the former case, ability to pay leads, correctly, to progressive taxation by increasing the rate as the income or inheritance increases.[164] In the latter

[163] Seligman, E. R. A., *Essays in Taxation* (1895, 1900), 54–59.
[164] Seligman, *Progressive Taxation in Theory and Practice* (1899, 1908), 138.

case it leads to a uniform rate on the value of the property on the idea that the value of property owned measures the future ability to pay.

This is the popular notion of equality. A dollar invested in site-value is exactly like a dollar invested in foundations, structures, inventories, original fertility, or in improved or maintained fertility. Each dollar measures just as much future ability to pay as any other dollar. Why should there be made a distinction in taxation between one man who invests $100,000 in a farm *without* improvements and another who invests $100,000 in a farm *with* improvements? Or, why should there be a tax-difference between a man who invests $100,000 in vacant site-value and another who invests $100,000 in the cost-value of buildings, foundations, machinery, and inventories? Each has similar expected ability to pay taxes. Ability to pay is proportional to the number of dollars invested, and there is no difference between the dollars.

The difference is in the method by which a person gets rich. A similar question over the method of getting rich arose at the opening of the period that led to the Commonwealth of England. In the Case of Monopolies, decided in 1602, and in similar cases of that period,[165] the issue was between the holders of special privileges granted to them by the monarch as patents, franchises, or corporate charters, and the merchants and manufacturers not holding and enjoying such privileges. The common-law lawyers, who were the spokesmen for the latter, contended that when a merchant or manufacturer, skilled in his trade, increased his own wealth he increased by just so much the "common-wealth." But when a patentee of the king increased his wealth by means of his exclusive privilege, he, "not being skilled in the trade," merely extracted that wealth from the commonwealth without making a corresponding addition to it. This Seventeenth Century distinction between wealth and commonwealth is equivalent to the Twentieth Century distinction between private utility and social utility.

Ricardo used the same distinction with reference to his definition of rent. He who gets an income solely from rent (as defined by Ricardo) extracts wealth from capitalists and laborers without making a corresponding return, unlike capitalists and laborers who delivered to others an amount of wealth equivalent to that which they received from the others.[166]

---

[165] Davenant v. Hurdis, Moore (K. B.) 576, 72 Eng. Rep. 769; Case of Monopolies, 11 Co. Rep. 84 b, 77 Eng. Rep. 1260-6 (1602); Bates' Case, Lane 22, 145 Eng. Rep. 267, 11 Hargrave's State Trials, 29, 2 Howell's State Trials, 371 (1606); Commons, John R., *Legal Foundations of Capitalism*, 266 ff.

[166] Above, p. 348, Malthus and Ricardo.

So it is with the modern shifting of site-values from agricultural to urban lands. If a person increases the supply of cleared land, of buildings, skyscrapers, timber, forests, orchards, drainage systems, road improvements, soil fertility, and other products of profit-seeking; even if he increases the supply of bare land by management, expenditure on foundations, and on roads which bring more of it accessible to markets; he increases the supply of wealth of the state in much the same proportion as he increases his own wealth. But to see one's own wealth increase solely by an increase in the site-value of land, uncleared, unimproved, regardless of fertility, timber, structures, and without making it more accessible, is to see one's wealth increase by mere opportunity to extract it from the commonwealth without contributing a proportionate increase to that commonwealth. A similar increase in the wealth of each is a similar increase in ability to pay; but one is an increase only in private wealth (assets), the other is an increase in both private and public wealth.

But the popular notion of ability to pay is even more perverse than the general property tax. Taxes can be paid only out of income. Ability to pay is proportionate to income. Bare land does not yield an income. Hence ability to pay is diminished by holding land idle. The Federal income tax attempts to correct this perversity. An *increase* in the value of land or of stocks or bonds is interpreted to be income when the land or securities, after a period of time, are sold at a price higher than the price paid, and this increase is then taxed as income. But if there is no annual rent from the land there is no income to be taxed. And if there is a *loss* in capital value, the loser is permitted to deduct it from his other income and may escape the *income* tax altogether.

Similarly, the man who is "land poor" is less able to pay taxes than the man who improves his land by fertility or buildings and foundations. Indeed, it is possible that, on the average for the entire country, when computed by compound interest, less profit is made by those who merely hold land for a speculative rise in site-values, without improving it, than by those who engage in other business or make improvements. This probable fact is seized upon by economists, beginning with Carey, to show that taxes on site-values of land should not be higher than taxes on buildings, inventories, fertility, and improved foundations. But it takes the point of view of private profit instead of social utility, as though it were beneficial to society merely to withhold what society needs but does not own.

Therefore, if "ability to pay" is the only canon of taxation, it is concluded that the tax on an owner of vacant land should be less than the tax on an owner of productive land, even though the value of his unimproved vacant land is as high or higher than the value of his neighbor's land including improvements. This purpose is often accomplished when local assessors relatively undervalue the unimproved land because not productive, while taxing it at the uniform rate.

But if there is another canon of taxation that may properly be applied, namely, the effects on wealth production, guided by the public purpose of favoring wealth production, then the man who gets his wealth by mere rise in site-values should pay proportionately higher taxes than the one who gets his wealth by industry or agriculture. In the one case he extracts wealth from the commonwealth without adding to it. In the other case he contributes directly to an increase in both private wealth and commonwealth. Hence, looking at it from the commonwealth, or social utility, standpoint, there are two kinds of ability to pay: that ability which varies directly with one's additions to the commonwealth, and that which varies inversely to one's additions to the commonwealth. The first we shall name Ability to Serve, the second, Ability to Pay.[167]

But since the two kinds of ability exist together in the same individual, although in different proportions for different individuals and opportunities, the differences being thus differences in degree that cannot be measured, the canon of taxation might read: Taxes should be proportioned *directly* according to a person's ability to pay, and *inversely* according to his ability to serve the commonwealth.

This provisional canon, or rule of reason, rests on a corresponding concept of taxation. Shall we look at a tax, or taxation in general, from the standpoint of what has happened in the past, or from the standpoint of what will happen in the future as an effect of the tax? If we look at it from the standpoint of what has previously happened, then we shall emphasize equality, ability to pay, the original or free gifts of nature, the accidents of good luck—in short, the dollars obtained in the past—as the proper measure of taxes; and we shall quite properly look upon income taxes, inheritance taxes, or the uniform property tax on accumulations of the past, as the appropriate method of taxation. But if we look at a tax from the police-power standpoint of what may be expected as the economic results of the tax, then we shall inquire: What will be the best inducements to individuals to increase the commonwealth by increasing their own wealth? This is what we

[167] Similar to Horace Taylor's *Making Goods and Making Money*, above, p. 677.

name the police power of taxation. The police power looks to
the future; the taxing power looks to the past and to the accumulations from the past.

Indeed, it is well recognized that taxes and tax exemptions operate like the police power, and are often consciously employed
for the regulation of industry, morals, or welfare, rather than the
acquisition of public revenue. Professor Seligman has shown that
the American distinction between the taxing power and the police
power is, to a great extent, a legal fiction growing out of our
system of government, and is unnecessary from the economic and
fiscal standpoint.[168] Furthermore, we may add, under the decisions
of our courts, taxation is a somewhat privileged exercise of the
police power, since, considering that it is the principal means of
collecting revenue on which the very life of the state depends, the
courts do not always scrutinize captiously the incidental regulative
effects of taxes. This is seen in their permissive attitude towards
a protective tariff which evidently is not a tax for revenue but a
tax for the transfer of values from one class to another class. This
is what the police power does in its guise of control over foreign
commerce by the protective tariff.

For the police power is none other than the sovereign power to
restrain or suppress what is deemed, by the dominant interests, to
be disadvantageous, and to promote and foster what they deem advantageous for the commonwealth. Taxation then, is the most pervasive and privileged exercise of the police power; with the enormous
increase in taxes resulting from the war, along with its large effect
on the margins for profit, it is becoming the most effective exercise
of the police power. Even when not consciously intended to be
regulative, taxes nevertheless regulate, for they, like the protective
tariff, determine the directions in which people may become wealthy
by determining directions in which they may not become wealthy.
They say to the business man: Here is profit, there is loss. It
is impossible to avoid these effects of taxes, therefore impossible
to escape the police power of taxation, therefore impossible to look
upon taxes of any kind whatever as merely a means of obtaining
revenue according to any principle of equality, or ability to pay,
or accumulation of wealth, or any standard that looks solely to the
acquisitions of the past. Taxation is, in fact, a process of obtaining public revenue by proportioning inducements to obtain profits.
It always has these effects, and, in fact, all legislators and assessors
actually do consider the expected effects. However, it is but doing
openly, what taxing authorities are already doing privately or

[168] Seligman, E. R. A., *Essays in Taxation*, 273, 296.

blindly, even corruptly, if the science of finance attempts to guide the practice by setting up a canon of social utility, namely, the apportionment of taxes *directly* to ability to pay and *inversely* to ability to render a public benefit.

Of course, it can always be objected that such a maxim opens the door to the prejudices, passions, and struggles for power of individuals and classes, in politics, legislatures, and the administration of the taxing power. Everybody identifies more or less his private interests with public interest, and many there are who protest that openly to concede an opportunity for individual and class opinion to dictate the apportionment of taxes is to wreck the constitution by substituting class legislation for due process of law.

Well, it is already being done, and, with the increasing burden of taxation, will more vigorously be done. It is being done consciously, unconsciously, blindly, ignorantly, by greed and camouflage, by demagogic plutocracy or demagogic democracy. It is better to recognize this openly than to deceive ourselves. We can then base our case, as in fact always is done regarding any particular tax measure, on whether or not its economic effect will be what it is asserted to be, a public benefit. We can explicitly set up the standard of commonwealth along with that of private wealth. Respecting the particular measure in hand, namely, the general property tax, including the land tax, we can then pass from the dogma of natural rights and the ancient notions of the productivity of nature's resources, to the institutional doctrine of proportioning the inducements to individuals to acquire wealth by increasing the commonwealth.

If we look at what has happened in the past, then we might say that original fertility was a gift of nature and not a product of management, and the owner of it should therefore be taxed upon its value, as proposed by Quesnay, and by Henry George in his first book. But if we look at it from the standpoint of what will happen in the future, then we shall inquire: What will be a fair inducement to farmers to clear the land from trees and rocks and thus improve its foundation value, as well as to maintain this original fertility, and to improve it? Accessibility to markets and apportionment of taxes are two inducements which the state furnishes to the farmers to increase the wealth of the state by making a profit for themselves.

For the farmer is a business man. It is not his manual labor that produces wealth—it is his expected profits. As a mere laborer the farmer gets paid for the work which he has done in the immediate or remote past. As a business man he hires laborers and goes to work himself in expectation of the profits he will make in the future. Profits look to the future, wages to the past, and it is expected profits that produce wealth. The increase in profits is measured, partly by the increase in value of the foundations which he prepares for the soil, partly in the maintenance and increase of the soil fertility itself, partly by increase in the site-value of land out of which the expected profits are to be produced. And, in proportion as population increases and he expects his land to have accessibility to markets, in that proportion does the farmer have a greater inducement to cultivate the soil more intensively, to borrow or invest more savings in it for future crops, to put on more structural and foundational improvements, and to improve the highways which make the land more accessible.

Hence, there is a psychological explanation of the rough correlation between site-value and the cost-value of improvements. The more accessible is the land to markets and therefore the more probable the profits, the greater is the resulting supply of buildings, factories, fences, roads, and other structural or foundational improvements which both the manufacturer and the farmer are induced to construct upon the land. Land accessible to markets will carry more improvements profitably than land less accessible. The same is true of fertility. The more accessible the land to markets, the more probably will the farmer clear the land, cultivate it intensively, improve the fertility and maintain the original fertility. He does it by changing from forestry to pasture, from pasture to plowing, from plowing to dairy farming, from poor cultivation to intensive cultivation, from exhausting the soil to putting on manures and fertilizers and turning under green crops. Hence it is that both the cost-value and the supply of both improvements and fertility increase along with an increase in the site-value, or decrease with a decrease of site-value of the land on which the improvements and the fertility are founded.

There is, indeed, no absolute difference between site-values and cost-values. The difference is one of degree. Each is a limiting factor of the total commonwealth. Site-value is necessary for agriculture and industry, and he who increases the supply of available bare land, by opening up roads for the uses of industry and agriculture, adds thereby to the commonwealth, though he may even reduce the site-values of other lands which now become relatively less accessible. Hence there can be no dogmatic statement of a single universal truth or natural right, but only a canon, or rule of reason, that distinguishes the two at points where the degree of difference is evidently great enough to be practical and important.

It is for this reason that the maxim of taxation should be stated in terms that permit distinctions of proportion to be observed. The canon might properly read: Apportion taxes inversely to the extent to which the employment of faculties and resources increases the commonwealth.

This maxim is but a statement of what Adam Smith states as his second canon of taxation.

"Every tax," he says, "ought to be so contrived as both to take out and to keep out of the pockets of the people as little as possible, over and above what it brings into the public treasury of the state. A tax may either take out or keep out of the pockets of the people a great deal more than it brings into the public treasury, in the four following ways. . . . Secondly, it may obstruct the industry of the people and discourage them from applying it to certain branches of business which might give maintenance and employment to great multitudes." [169]

The maxim also seems to harmonize with Hobson's acceptance of the principle of ability to pay as "the supreme canon of economy and equity," coupled, however, with the first of the two following "negative conditions": "(1) It must not remove or impair any instrument of, or incentive to, essential or useful processes of production. (2) It must not remove or impair any essential or useful element of consumption." [170] And it seems to carry out Seligman's repudiation of the general property tax and his substitution of "product" rather than "property" as the basis of taxation, supplemented however, as he allows, by a tax on unproductive real estate.[171]

It is the fact previously noted, namely, the rough correlation between the cost of both improvements and fertility on the one hand, and the site-value of land on the other, that furnishes a principle for the separate valuation of fertility and bare land. In the case of urban lands there is no difficulty. The soil there has no value, except that which was given hundreds of years ago and is now amortized, and therefore no longer important.[172] It is even carted away. The value is pure site-value. But in the case of agricultural land a simple rule must be found for separating the value of fertility from the site-value of the land. The Grimstad

[169] Adam Smith, *The Wealth of Nations* (Canan ed., 1904), II, 311.
[170] Hobson, J. A., *Taxation in the New State* (1920), 12.
[171] Seligman, *Essays in Taxation*, 58.
[172] In the Grimstad and Keller bills these original improvements were to be amortized at the rate of 3 per cent per year, the rate applied to structural improvement. At the end of thirty years they would therefore become only a part of the site-value.

bill, introduced in the Wisconsin legislature,[173] and the Keller bill, introduced in Congress,[174] carried the rule that the value of fertility should be determined as one-half the fair market value of the land for exclusively agricultural purposes, "if kept at par." "Fair market value" is the usual rule of taxation. The fair market value, or "par," or what condition it would have if kept at its original state of fertility, is also a concept familiar to farmers. "Run-down" land is discounted. In a certain transaction, for example, a farmer purchased an exhausted farm at $100 per acre, expecting, within ten years, to build it up to the value of $200 per acre, which was the value of the farm across the road having exactly the same type of soil foundation, and, of course, the same accessibility to markets. According to the provisions of the foregoing bills (which exclude the value of structures and fertility), the better farm would have a soil-fertility value of $100 per acre and a site-value of $100 per acre, while the run-down farm would have only its same site-value of $100 per acre and no fertility or improvement value. The proper equality of the two, observing the Ricardian principle of site-value, would be a tax basis of $100 per acre on each piece of land instead of $200 on the improved land and $100 on the exhausted land.

The soil surveys of the state of Wisconsin show that depleted land, that is, land which has been exhausted to the point of unprofitable cultivation, has lost as much as 33 per cent of its chemically *total* plant food, but has lost, of course, 100 per cent of its economically *available* plant food. The question arises, should the value of that new fertility be calculated on the doctrine of *cost of reproduction* at current cost of fertilizers, hauling, and spreading? If so, its cost-value would be greater on land of low value remote from markets than on land of the same fertility more accessible to markets. It would even exceed the value of remote land worth $10 per acre in its exhausted condition, but would amount to a small part of the value of accessible land capable of similar fertility but worth $100 per acre as its mere site-value.

Such calculations of costs are not only impracticable; they are unsound in theory. The theory changes from cost to value.[175] Cost is a restraint. Value is an inducement. The real question is: How much value-inducement is needed to overcome the cost of keeping the available plant food always at par or even above par?

---

[173] 502A, April 1921. The theory here presented was worked out with the agricultural members of the Wisconsin legislature of 1921.

[174] H. R. 5733, Jan., 1924.

[175] Forty years ago I tried in vain to work this out on the classical theory of Costs. See my *Distribution of Wealth* (1893).

The inducement must exceed the cost of preparing the foundations, the cost of fertilizers and manures, the cost of hauling and spreading, the loss of profit by turning under green crops. This inducement of expected value is the whole question of what, under a system of private property and liberty, is the expectation of a reasonable margin of profit above cost, necessary to induce the maintenance and improvement of the fertility for the sake of future crops. When we consider the great uncertainties of farming, owing to weather, crop failures, freezing, frosts, floods, and drought; when we consider the inability of the farmer to control his market by stopping production abruptly as does the business man; it is reasonable to hold that where the urban man will not invest in buildings, factories, machinery, and materials beyond a point where he can expect to make a profit yield of ten to twenty per cent on the costs of new construction, the farmer should not be expected to build up or maintain fertility in excess of a total cost on which he can expect a profit yield of twenty per cent to thirty per cent. It is somewhere within these limits that the margin of error may be expected to fall. It may be deemed, therefore, taking all the facts into consideration, that the proportion 50 per cent for fertility at par and 50 per cent for site-value is about as near a reasonable estimate as can be made.

The determination is similar to that in the case of regulation of freight and passenger rates or of rates to be charged by other public service corporations. Much debate has been held on questions of "physical valuation," that is, cost-valuation, of these public utilities, as to whether the value should be placed at the "cost of reproduction new," or "in existing condition," or at "original cost," or at "accrued investment cost," [176] and whether or not the rate of profit allowed in calculating accruals shall include something above the rate of interest current at the time of accrual. These calculations have turned on questions of justice, which look to what the owners have a right to claim in the present in view of what they have done in the past. Similar debate has been had on the farmer's demand that the prices of farm products should be equal to the cost of production.

But when these questions of justice to investors or farmers are reduced to the practical fixing of rates or prices, the predominant factor that governs and even manipulates the calculations is that of economic inducement under all the circumstances. The question

---

[176] Cf. Bauer, John, "Basis of Valuation in the Control of Return on Public Utility Investments," *Amer. Econ. Rev.*, VI (1916), 568 ff.; Glaeser, Martin, *Outlines of Public Utility Economics* (1927).

then takes the form: What are the rates or prices that will enable management to make a profit and thereby to attract the necessary amount of investment and labor in order to give to the public the supply of service that it requires?

But questions of inducement necessarily go in a circle. The higher the price, the less will ordinarily be the supply of product that the public can take as consumers; and the lower the price, the less the supply that the management will furnish as producers. The only solution is the "rule of reason" provided in the common law: What would a jury of reasonable men think was reasonable under all the circumstances after hearing all the facts and arguments? It is on this basis of "reasonableness," which is merely the common law and good judgment, that railroad commissions and courts decide whether passenger rates shall be two cents, three cents, or four cents. Reasonableness is a matter of judgment as well as of justice, since it looks to the future effects of present acts, while justice, of itself, looks only to the past as justifying the claims of the present.

So it is in finding a reasonable proportion between the value of fertility and the site-value of land. The proportion cannot be found as precisely as that between the value of a building and the value of the site on which the building rests, because here there is no fertility to be valued. There will always be differences of opinion in the case of fertility, and a margin of error. But, in fixing the proportion at about 50 per cent for value of fertility to be exempt if kept at par, and 50 per cent for site-value of land to be taxed, the proportion is reasonable in view of the showing of soil surveys and in view of the profits needed if fertility is to be conserved.

There is also a consideration which might be looked upon as one of political expediency rather than reasonableness, but which is in reality one of providing equality of treatment of farm owners and urban owners. In the case of urban land the owner's physical capital, distinguished from his site-value of land, consists solely of structural and foundational improvements. In the case of the farmer his capital consists of similar improvements and also of fertility. Now, the assessed values of lands, lots, and improvements in Wisconsin in 1919, where improvements are valued separately from the land, show that, on the average, the value of structural improvements in cities was 60 per cent of the total real-estate values, and the site-value of bare land was 40 per cent. In the country the value of structural improvements was only 20 per cent, but the value of lands, *including fertility and site-value*, was 80 per cent of the total real-estate values.[177] This indicates that, on the average for the year 1919, the proportion of 50 per cent for site-value to be taxed, places the farmer on an equality with the urban land owner. At this ratio the cost of *improvements and fertility,* in the rural districts, becomes 60 per cent of the real-estate values while the site-value of land is 40 per cent, just as the cost of *improvements* alone in urban areas is 60 per cent, and the site-value is 40 per cent of the total real-estate values. In each case, 60 per cent of the real-estate values, on the average, would be exempt, and 40 per cent would be subject to the tax on site-values.[178]

It will be seen, of course, that this theory operates to the advantage of farmers, quite contrary to usual ideas of the single tax, which levies a tax on fertility as well as sites. In fact, the Wisconsin bill of 1921 obtained the votes of nearly all the farmers whereas, as is well known, the single tax is vigorously opposed by farmers and rightly opposed, as our analysis shows.

The farmers, it is well known, suffer a great inequality with urban lands in the general property tax. If the foregoing analysis is correct, the site-value tax is acceptable to farmers in that it places them on an equality with urban owners. It treats the farmer as a true capitalist conserving the natural resources of the state, just as the business man benefits the state by constructing buildings and factories. And, if the analysis is correct, it does not discriminate in favor of farmers against urban proprietors, notwithstanding the fact that much the larger yield of the tax, proportionate to acreage, would come from urban lands. This larger yield is owing merely to the fact that huge site-values in cities are condensed on

[177] Assessed value of land and improvements in Wisconsin (1919):

	RURAL	PER CENT
Exclusive of improvements	$1,289,332,819	79.08
Improvements	340,771,127	20.92
	$1,630,103,946	100.00

	URBAN	PER CENT
Exclusive of improvements	$460,256,606	40.13
Improvements	686,795,320	59.87
	$1,147,051,926	100.00

[178] Figures for the year 1930–31 for 16 states furnished to me by Mabel Walker of the Public Welfare Tax League show that for urban land the site-values were 45 per cent, and improvement values were 55 per cent of the total real-estate values; and that for rural lands the land values (including fertility) were 76 per cent and the improvement values were 24 per cent of the total real-estate values. The average allowance for value of exempt fertility, in such case, in order to equalize land sites in urban and rural communities, would be 40 per cent of rural land value instead of the 50 per cent for Wisconsin in 1919.

small areas and run as high as several million dollars per acre, whereas in the country, the site-values are spread out thin and run only from one or two dollars to $50 or $100 per acre. In either case it is an application to the general property tax of the canon: apportion taxes according to ability to pay and inversely to public benefit.

The canon rests on the fact that it is not *land* or *property* that is taxed under the general property tax, but *landowners* who are taxed, since taxes are paid out of income. In a legal sense a tax on land is a tax on property. Yet in an economic sense the tax, if certain, is not a tax, because it is discounted and the purchaser buys the land at the capitalized value of its expected income less the tax. In either view, however, a tax on land seems to be a tax on property and not a tax on the owner. The owner is, as it were, an agent, to collect the tax and to deliver it to the state.

This, however, is a confusion, either of physical with business concepts, or of capital with income. Land does not pay a tax—it is owners who pay in proportion to the value of their land; and taxes are usually paid out of income, not out of capital. If the land does not yield the necessary income, the owner must earn it or borrow it elsewhere. Hence a tax on land is a tax on the owner's "prospective acquisition" of income, whether he actually acquires the income or not, that is, whether he uses the land profitably or unprofitably. The tax is, indeed, assessed against the land. It is collectible against the land, and the legal remedy for non-payment runs against the land. Yet an owner pays the tax, out of his own or somebody else's income, exactly as he pays his income or inheritance tax.

Hence the principle of progressive taxation is applicable to large holdings of site-values whether the physical land be contiguous or separate. It is *owners* who pay the tax, and their ability to pay increases progressively either with an increase of actual income as contemplated in the income and inheritance taxes, or with an increase in prospective income implied in large holdings of site-values.

We are not here considering the administrative difficulties of untrained assessors in distinguishing site-value from fertility-value, but the difficulties are probably no greater than those already encountered and still prevailing in the administration of the American invention of Special Assessments. In this class of taxes the American people long ago [179] adopted the maxim, here contended for, of

[179] Beginning in New York in the Seventeenth Century. Seligman, E. R. A., *Essays in Taxation* (1901), 284.

taxation in proportion to ability to pay and inversely to ability to serve. It appears in the distinction between site-value and improvement-value.

Special assessments differ from general taxation, as the court says, "in that they are made upon the assumption that a portion of the community is to be specially and peculiarly benefited in the enhancement of the value of the property peculiarly situated as regards a contemplated expenditure of public funds."[180] Or, as stated by Professor Seligman, "a special assessment may be defined as a compulsory contribution, levied in proportion to the special benefits derived, to defray the cost of a specific improvement to property undertaken in the public interest."[181]

But in distinguishing the amount of these special benefits, exclusion was made of the value of improvements and structures, because it was evident that these improvement values were the products of somebody's labor, investment, and enterprise. But for the site-values whose values are increased by the public improvement, a state court as early as 1830, followed more or less by other courts, laid down the maxim that the owner should not pay more than the increase in value added to the property, nor, of course, more than his share of the cost of construction of the public improvement.[182]

Here the canon of taxation is derived from the constitutional prohibition against taking private property without due process of law, and it sets two upper limits to the use of the taxing power: the added value, and the cost of the public improvement. By setting these limits it may be said that the concept of social utility, although vague and unmeasurable in economic theory, was nevertheless reduced to a reasonable measurement. The total magnitude of social utility created by a highway or other public improvement is simply the actual cost of constructing it. And the upper limit to which the cost of that added social utility may be rationed to the benefited private owners is the estimated increase in the value of their property. To take more than this would be confiscation. To take less than the cost of construction, if that does not exceed the added value, would be a special privilege granted to individuals

[180] Ittner v. Robinson, 35 Neb. 133, 52 N. W. 846.
[181] Seligman, E. R. A., Essays in Taxation, 283. The authoritative work on the subject is Rosewater, Victor, Special Assessments: A Study in Municipal Finance (1893, 1898, Columbia University). For perversions and irregularities of special assessment administration see Briggs, H. R., Financial Survey of the State of Illinois (1933, published by Illinois Dept. of Works under investigations made by Bureau of Public Works, Wisconsin University). The subject is almost unexplored, notwithstanding the very heavy burden of special assessments in the United States.
[182] 3 Wend. (N. Y.) 452, 454 (1830). Cited by Rosewater, op. cit. (1893), 97, 98.

at the expense of the general body of taxpayers who pay the cost of the public improvement.

The result is that special assessments are governed by the canon of apportioning taxes directly to ability to pay and inversely to ability to serve. The ability to pay is increased by the increased value of the benefited site; the ability to serve is increased by the improvements which the owner or his predecessor has added to the commonwealth.

This special assessment canon of taxation, except in a few cases, was not adopted in the construction of the huge system of highways called for by the automobile. In this case the general taxpayers of the nation or state and the buyers of gasoline, not specifically benefited, pay the costs of the special benefits absorbed by privileged site owners. One reason for failure to adopt the special assessment principle can plainly be seen from our analysis. It operated, in the few cases where tried, with gross unfairness to farmers, and was quickly repealed on their protests. Its unfairness consisted in treating the farmers' fertility as land value, which, according to our Ricardian analysis, makes the farmers pay double their share of the special assessment compared with urban landowners. Thus the assessments were not extended to all the property benefited, including the values of urban lands, but only to the abutting landowners, mostly farmers.

This Ricardian distinction between site-value and the fertility-value was indeed never made in the American law of special assessments. This accounts for the fact that the principle has found wide acceptance in Municipal Finance, where there is no fertility to be valued, and has been adopted for agriculture almost solely for irrigation and drainage projects where evidently the fertility is actually created by the public improvement. Although structural improvements, in the special assessment laws, are rightly deemed not to absorb any of the value added by a public improvement to private property, and are therefore rightly exempted from the special assessment, yet the farmers' land-value is deemed to include the fertility maintained by the farmer as well as its site-value, whereas the urban land value is solely a site-value. Only site-value, and neither structural nor fertility-value (except in cases of irrigation and drainage), can be benefited by public improvements, because competition keeps down structural and fertility-values to the cost of reproduction, whereas site-values are determined solely by social demand for limited sites regardless of the cost of reproduction. If special assessments were made to run against only the benefited site-values and not the unbenefited fertility-values, evidently the farmers' share of the assessment for roads and highways would be less than it now is, compared with the share borne by the owners of urban site-values. This more accurate economic analysis of benefited and unbenefited property might be expected to remove a main objection to the acceptance of the special assessment canon of taxation. It would then carry out more precisely the canon of the American courts, in cases of special assessments, of proportioning taxes directly to ability to pay and inversely to service rendered to the commonwealth.

But trees do not grow into the sky—they would perish in a high wind; and a single truth, like a single tax, ends in its own destruction by conflict with other truths supported by other interests. There is a diminishing validity of truth as there is a diminishing utility of beef. Too much truth of the same kind is both distasteful and untrue. Truths must be proportionate to each other in order to get the optimum truth that will work in a world of conflict. Governments must have revenues in increasing amounts, not because they are corrupt and inefficient, which can be remedied, but because the social needs of education, ethics, morality, art, equality, liberty, protection of the weak, highways, health, recreation, grow faster in an improving civilization than do the private needs of food, luxury, ostentation. The power to tax is indeed the power to destroy; and this is the very reason for a canon of taxation which is not as exact as mathematics, but gives, like the court's rule of reason, proportionate weight to ability to pay and ability to serve the commonwealth.

Yet the principle may be applied, on investigation, to other sources of revenue needed by an improving civilization. If ability to pay is alone taken into account, as is rightly the case in the assessment of income taxes, it might seem that the same rate of progressive income taxes should be laid on personal incomes, capital incomes, and site-value incomes. But if ability to serve is taken into account, it would impose a lowest progressive rate on incomes imputed to personal abilities, a medium progressive rate on incomes imputed to capital improvements, and a highest progressive rate on incomes imputed to site-values of land.

Two of these distinctions are taken into account in the Federal income tax. These have been exhaustively investigated by a congressional committee on internal revenue taxation, under the direction of its chief of staff, L. H. Parker.[183] The committee

[183] *Preliminary Report on Earned Incomes, Report of Joint Committee on Internal Revenue and Taxation,* I, Part 3 (1928); *Report of Joint Committee to the Committee on Ways and Means of the House of Representatives* (1931).

discusses the subject from the standpoint both of equity between taxpayers and of inducements offered to productive factors to increase the commonwealth. The two are indeed inseparable.

The committee's investigator distinguishes earned income, investment income, and capital gain, as the terms are used in the Federal income tax. "Earned" income, or rather personal income, is "the gain derived from labor, such as salaries, wages, professional fees, and profits due to the personal endeavor of the taxpayer as distinguished from the profits arising from the employment of capital." "Investment income" is "the gain derived from capital, such as interest, dividends, rents and gains from the sale or conversion of assets held less than two years." "Capital gain" is defined as "the income from the sale or conversion of assets other than stock in trade held for a period of more than two years; for example, gains from the sale of stocks, bonds, patent rights, real property, etc., provided they have been held for the required period." [184] The last two we may disregard and may distinguish "investment" income as both capital income and site-value income.

The term "earned income" is equivalent to our "personal income." The arguments recited by the committee's investigator in favor of a lower rate, say $12\frac{1}{2}$ to 25 per cent lower on personal income than on investment income, turn on several reasons.

> "The productive agent of investment income, namely capital, is carefully guarded by the existing law from bearing any tax through allowances for depreciation, depletion, obsolescence and loss of useful value. Therefore the productive agent of earned income, namely the individual, should be protected through a similar allowance for the exhaustion of the individual's earning power." Quoting from the National Tax Association, the argument continues, "A doctor's skill, a lawyer's intellect, an executive's energy are not fixed and indestructible, capable of producing an income forever. Yet the income they produce is taxed on a parity with capital. Capital is permitted to replenish its loss by dipping into income through depreciation, obsolescence, depletion, but the human vitality, health and strength lost in earning salaries, fees and similar compensation cannot be deducted as depreciation, obsolescence, or depletion from the income of the earner." [185]

Thus the maxim derived from equity corresponds to the maxim derived from public benefit. The individual is a productive agent who increases the commonwealth by increasing his own wealth. But he is a living and dying individual, subject to illness, accident,

[184] Op. cit., Preliminary Report, 6 (1931).
[185] Ibid.

old age, unemployment. His income tax, therefore, both in equity and in offering larger inducements to his activity through his twenty to fifty years of productive life, under any comparison of reasonable equality or stimulus to production by earning larger incomes while he can, should probably be 25 per cent less than incomes derived from capital investments. The latter, though also productive (and not "unearned" as stated in the Federal law), yet go on producing incomes while the owner is sick, unproductive, senile, or dead.

This is what we mean by taxation inversely to ability to serve but progressively in proportion to ability to pay. Larger personal abilities have larger ability to pay, but personal abilities furnish to the nation a larger production of wealth than the capital investments which can be useful only when personal abilities are inventing, controlling, and operating them. Hence, they should be taxed at a lower but progressive rate.

But investments are of two kinds, not distinguished by the above-mentioned committee: investments in productive capital and investments in site-values of land. If our inventive and managerial ability can create the need and opportunity for a $20,000,000 plant, then it is important for the state or nation that we should offer inducements to that ability and inducements to that investment. But we should offer no inducements to the owners of the site-values, whose value is a social demand increased without the corresponding effort of personal abilities or the new construction made possible by new investments.

New construction nowadays, on account of inventions and technological changes in industry and agriculture, are far more important than ever before. They are subject more rapidly to depreciation and especially to obsolescence. It may be estimated that the new construction becomes exhausted by depreciation and effete by obsolescence, within an average period of 10 or 12 years, and therefore must be wholly reconstructed every 8 or 10 years, on the average. Recently it has been proposed that income taxes from capital investment should allow 10 per cent per year for depreciation and obsolescence. This is not an unjust reduction in view of the great increase of depreciation and obsolescence in modern capitalistic enterprise. Such a reduction in income tax offers an inducement to capital construction probably not in excess of enough to restore the rapid deterioration of value through the factors of depreciation, depletion, and obsolescence.

But investment, under the existing official definitions, includes the site-values of bare land. It is not possible to say whether site-values as a whole have increased more rapidly than other taxable values; but there has undoubtedly been a great shifting of their values from agricultural and small communities to the mercantile, manufacturing, and financial urban districts. This goes on without any productive effort of the owners, either their personal abilities or new construction financed by new investment, but solely by the increasing demand arising from an increasing population and the increasing centralization of industry and finance on favorable sites. This being so, the community can offer no inducement to owners of site-values of land to increase production. These pure ground-rent incomes are strictly unearned in the Ricardian sense; whereas the incomes of personal ability and capital investment in structural improvements, machinery, materials, and the upkeep of soil fertility are earned, in that they furnish an increase of the national wealth.

Without entering into the complexities of administrative details,[186] we may conclude that a reasonable classification of progressive income taxes, from the standpoint of inducements to increase the commonwealth by increasing one's own wealth, requires a classification of personal incomes at the lowest yet progressive rate; of investment incomes at a medium but progressive rate; and of site-value incomes at the highest rates, also progressive on large holdings.

(4) **Statics and Cycles.**—It is, no doubt, paradoxical that a policy of taxation should be based on inducements to increase the wealth of nations, as had been the policy of the classical economists in their revolt against mercantilism, when the need nowadays seems to be a general restriction of output owing to general overproduction. This is, indeed, the paradox of capitalistic civilization. But we conceive that two policies are confused: the stabilization of prices designed to restrain cyclical general overproduction, or to prevent depression; and the apportionment of taxes designed to increase production. They are two overlapping problems of modern collective action confronted by narrow but fluctuating margins of profit.

This dilemma requires a further classification of the effects of taxes, as to whether we are dealing with a static movement or a cyclical movement of prices, production, and employment. The foregoing analysis is concerned with a supposed static condition, derived from the classical tradition, where each factor is supposed to be fully employed in a state of equilibrium with the others, and the participants have an idealized freedom of choice. But such are not the actual historical conditions. In a period of rising prices and prosperity, each factor operates differently from its operation

[186] These are considered at length in the *Report of the Joint Committee*, above referred to.

in a period of stagnation or falling prosperity and prices. Expansion and restraint alternate, wave-like, and the static analysis is concealed by the cycles.

There are four discernible methods by which taxpayers avoid the burden of taxes: evasion, migration, shifting, and suppression. These vary with the cycles. By evasion the taxable property or income is concealed or undervalued. By migration the property or person moves from high-tax to low-tax areas. Evasion and migration compel the burden to be increased on other taxpayers in order to get the sum of money required by government. But these burdens, like the burdens of political or financial corruption, are not noticed in times of general prosperity.

Shifting moves the tax burden forward to buyers and consumers by higher prices, or backward to sellers and producers by lower prices and wages, while suppression reduces the quantity produced on which the tax is imposed. Shifting and suppression are not always distinguished, but they differ as do prices from quantities. They do not move together, for there may be shifting without suppression, or suppression without shifting. But even these effects of taxes are scarcely noticed in times of general prosperity.

Shifting and suppression are more subtle than evasion and migration. The latter can be seen. The older taxes on incorporeal or intangible property have been abandoned or reduced on account of evasion, or changed to income taxes. Taxes on physical property may be avoided by undervaluation. Income taxes may be avoided by emigration. These are matters largely of administration. But shifting and suppression require economic analysis.

In any case, the four methods of avoidance are highly variable according to variations of general prosperity and depression, and tax policies themselves are changed to meet these variabilities. In times of rising prices, as seen in our chart of the taxable margin,[187] it is easy enough to shift taxes, because everybody can simply "mark up" his prices by even more than the amount of his taxes. The tax is said to be "pyramided" or "snow-balled" and paid by the ultimate consumer. But the ultimate consumer does not at first complain. He is able to pay because he is fully employed, or quite able to mark up and get his prices as a producer, in a period of universal mark-up of prices. If the curve of gross sales rises, as shown in our charts, then evidently taxes have little or no effect in suppressing quantities produced. But in the opposite period of falling prices, of reduced volume of sales and employment, the tax burden eats up even more than the margin for profit, be-

[187] Above, p. 571.

cause the "mark-up" of prices is then only a useless gesture, and taxes can be avoided only by suppression of production and employment.

Hence a static analysis of the shifting and suppressive effects of taxes must be coördinated to the cycles of a general rise and fall of prices. At one period the shifting is easily done. It is not a burden, is not suppressive, "nobody pays the tax"—and public policy is indifferent in the midst of an optimistic harmony of interests. At another period shifting is nearly impossible. The burden is intolerable, production and employment are already suppressed, "everybody pays the tax"—and public policy is torn by the conflict of forcibly shifting the tax to other classes of people.

These generalizations require to be modified by special investigations of the different kinds of taxes. We may take two extreme cases as illustrative: a protective tariff, and site-value taxation. Protective tariff is designed to keep domestic prices above world prices in order to induce domestic expansion of the protected industries. The site-value tax is designed "to encourage business and improvements and to discourage land speculation by decreasing taxes on buildings and increasing taxes on unimproved land." [188] Each is protective—the tariff by discouraging the business of importing and encouraging the business of domestic manufacture; the site-value tax by discouraging the business of marking up site-values and encouraging the construction of manufacturing plants, office buildings, apartment houses, and residences. In each case encouragement of the one is effected by discouraging the alternative. One may be distinguished as positive protection because it raises profits by raising prices of the protected business; the other as negative protection because it raises profits by reducing the taxation overhead of the protected activities. In either case alternative activities are restrained or suppressed, and the suppression is most resented in periods of general depression when the margins for profit are already disappearing.

In the case of the tariff the protected business is expected to shift the tax to purchasers by higher prices, though ultimately to reduce prices by increased efficiency. The tax, agreeable to what was stated above, is actually shifted in periods of prosperity with their generally rising prices, without burdensome effect on the buyers because they also can raise their selling prices by also pyramiding costs. But in periods of depression and generally falling

[188] Williams, Percy R. (member Pittsburgh Board of Assessors), "Pittsburgh's Graded Tax in Full Operation," *National Municipal Review*, XIV (1925), 726. The "Pittsburgh Plan" here described conforms to the site-value tax.

prices, the protected industry cannot shift the tax by merely marking up the prices, because the customers themselves are not able to mark up their selling prices to cover the increased costs of production, and the supposedly protected industry is not protected.[189]

It is for such reasons that in periods of continued rising prices the free trade policy comes to the front and is usually able to reduce tariffs; but that in periods of generally falling prices the popular demand for still higher tariffs is overwhelming and all nations raise their tariff walls against the falling prices of imports from other nations. Groups of producers within the nation go further, if they can, and organize cartels to shut out price-cutters and restrict output. Most protective tariffs in American and foreign history have accompanied or immediately followed a period of falling prices. And recently, notwithstanding all expert opinion in different countries and even diplomatic agreements of international good-will, the high tariff is the popular protest of a whole people against falling prices. It has made parliaments and Congress reject the low-tariff recommendations of eminent economists and experts delegated to the League of Nations.

Thus the public policy of tariff taxation, although usually condemned by the static analysis as pyramiding the tariff costs upon the ultimate consumer, does not always do so. The policy rather follows the ups and downs of general world-wide movements of prices. In an upward trend of prices, such as that between 1897 and 1914, the consumers are heard complaining of the rising cost of living, and they are able to bring about a reduction of tariffs (Wilson tariff 1913). But in a period of falling prices it is the producers who are heard complaining, and they bring about higher and higher protective tariffs (1920, 1930). Whether and when the changing policies are effective or ineffective in shifting, or injurious or beneficial in suppression, requires investigation of the correlation with changes occurring in the ups and downs of the general movement of prices.

The same is true of the exemption of structural improvement and of materials in process by transferring taxes to site-values. The improvements are expected eventually to increase in supply and thereby to reduce the rates of interest and profit charges for the use of the improvements. But since these improvements are financed by new issues of long-term securities, the effects of the tax policy are concealed by the alternations of prosperity and depression. The new construction depends on long-time forecasts. In

---

[189] Based on investigations of agricultural and manufacturing tariffs for the Rawleigh Foundation, Freeport, Ill.

general it is increased in periods of depression when long-time interest rates are low, and reduced in periods of prosperity when long-time interest rates are high.   In any case, the increase in quantity of new construction is controlled more by the cycles and trends of prices than by the tax exemptions.[190]

Thus it happens that the effects of tax policies, whether they be evasion, migration, shifting, or suppression, are concealed, confused, or even reversed by the ups and downs of speculation that change economic science from statics to cycles.   Yet, even so, the cycles may greatly intensify the need of returning to Ricardo's distinction between site-value rents and the combined profits, interest, and wages, which was his distinction between landlordism and capitalism.   Recently a great capitalistic organization, the Liggett Company, operating 555 drug stores, addressed a letter to its 555 landlords, as follows:

> "The Company has done . . . everything in its power to reduce losses . . . every element of expense, except rents, has been pared to the bone.   Employees have suffered three severe cuts, yet have loyally responded with increased efforts in their work. . . . Further sacrifices cannot be asked of employees; further reductions in operating expenses are impossible. . . .   The only item of cost which has not been liquidated to somewhere near present-day values is . . . the cost of the space which it occupies with its stores."[191]

Here the conditions were similar to those of the period following the French Revolution, and of the extreme price movements when Ricardo developed his theory of conflicting interests.   But the capitalist now is the Liggett Company, and the landlord is the 555 owners of urban sites.   While, according to our preceding use of King's computations,[192] landlords received as rent in 1925 only about 9 per cent of the total pecuniary income of the people of the United States, yet in this case the fixed charges for rent were absorbing, in a period of depression, after all increases in efficiencies and reductions in wages and employment, more than 100 per cent of the remaining margin for profit, with its prospect of inevitable bankruptcy of a huge and efficient corporation.   It is not necessary, notwithstanding capitalistic business cycles, that Ricardo's meaning of capitalism should be confused with his meaning of landlordism.

---

[190] Cf. Haig, R. G., *The Exemption of Improvements for Taxation in Canada and the United States* (1915), on several of the difficulties in introducing and maintaining these exemptions.

[191] *New York Times*, Sept. 27, 1932.

[192] Above, p. 528, Share of Profit.

Landlordism, in the Ricardian meaning of site-values, extracts private wealth from commonwealth without rendering an equivalent service. But Capitalism, in Ricardo's meaning, increases the commonwealth by inducements to increase private wealth. A canon of taxation, in proportion progressively to ability to pay and inversely to ability to serve the commonwealth, is roughly equivalent to Ricardo's distinction between landlordism and capitalism.

But the shift in economic analysis from statics to cycles is a shift from Ricardo's static labor-cost of production as the measure of value, to the cycles of speculation on future pecuniary income as the measure of value. All capitalistic valuations are speculative, and speculation in land values is no more speculative than speculation in commodities, stocks, and bonds. For this reason, again, the Ricardian distinction between rent and profit becomes confused.

This confusion appears in King's argument [193] that not only the owners of land but also the owners of products get their profits, not according to the cost of production, but according to speculative increases in value above the cost of production. These increases in value are, all of them, "speculative or chance gains"; if one is "unearned" the other is "unearned." Therefore, to discriminate among them by taxing the land sites and exempting the improvements and products is unfair.

This argument is sound from the private standpoint of business enterprise. But it does not recognize differences called for when looked at from the social standpoint of effects of site speculation on industry and agriculture. All profit is, indeed, speculative gain on more or less narrow margins; all loss is speculative loss, depending partly on luck and chance. That is the very reason for profit in a capitalistic civilization. It is as true of gain from manufactures and agriculture as it is of gains from site-values of land. Indeed, on account of cycles and miscalculation, loss rather than profit may as likely attend speculation in land as it may attend speculation in industry or agriculture. If our criterion is merely that of the good or bad management, the good luck or bad luck, of the individual concern, then it follows, as King says, that "there is no logical reason whatever for distinguishing between gains in the value of land and increases in the value of securities or commodities held for profit or speculation. If one is unearned increment, the other must be also."

But if our canon may be also that of the economic effects of speculation on the wealth of the nation, then there is a difference

---

[193] King, W. I., "Earned and Unearned Income," *Annals American Academy of Political and Social Sciences* (1921), Vols. 93–95, 251.

between profit or loss attending the fluctuations of stocks, bonds, value of buildings, machinery, fertility, etc., in industry or agriculture, and profit or loss attending the fluctuations of site-values which society and not the individual creates or reduces according to the cycles. The problem is insoluble either by the individualistic natural-rights doctrine of the single-taxer or by the equally natural right to buy, sell, or use, of the individualistic opponent of the single tax—regardless of the effect of that speculative buying, selling, and using on the commonwealth. A person, in conformity with the common law, has a right to everything he has lawfully earned in the past, but it does not follow that the police power or taxing power may not be used, within reasonable limits, to determine the directions advantageous to the public in which he may make his speculative profit, by imposing burdens on making such profit in other directions disadvantageous to the public. In the case of industry and agriculture the individual makes profit or loss in the activity of increasing the supply of food, clothing, and shelter, which are contributions to the "commonwealth." In the case of site-values, he makes a profit or suffers a loss in a speculation which is not an increase in the commonwealth.

So it is with all speculation, whether in stocks, bonds, land values, or commodities. It may be necessary in the public interest to devise other methods, such as stabilization of prices, to prevent over-speculation on a rising market with its increase of debts, which wipe out the margins for profit on falling markets. These remedies are other uses of what is the police power, such as restraints on stock market speculation, in preventing, not speculation, which is advantageous, but over-speculation which is disadvantageous to the commonwealth.

Thus, while the static analysis has enabled us to break up the complex factors of taxation into their elements and to develop general rules regarding their variable effects, it is the analysis of booms and depressions that gives us the actual historical changes in both the public policy of taxation and the accompanying changeable effects on individual action.

6. *Accidents and Unemployment—Insurance and Prevention*

The penetrating criticism of the Wisconsin Unemployment Compensation Act by my colleague, Professor Morton,[194] goes to the fundamental principles developed in this book. It affords me occasion to explain in a more personal and practical way what must

[194] Morton, Walter A., "The Aims of Unemployment Insurance with Especial Reference to the Wisconsin Act," *Amer. Econ. Rev.*, XXIII (1933), 395–412.

have appeared heretofore to the reader of this book highly abstract and often conflicting and confusing. Moreover it offers an illustration of the very great difficulties in the way of putting into effect any project whatever designed to promote the general welfare in conflict with private interests.

Nearly all of the criticisms made by Professor Morton were brought forward by representatives of the Wisconsin Manufacturers' Association in successive hearings before the legislature during the past ten years. The plan was first proposed by me and the first bill [195] was introduced by State Senator Henry A. Huber, in 1921.[196] The employers' criticisms were highly practical and had to be met in a practical way. This was attempted in successive drafts of the bill until it finally emerged as enacted into law under the leadership of Assemblyman Harold M. Groves in 1932. As thus amended the Manufacturers' Association, while opposed to it, finally accepted it as preferable to other proposed bills, as did also the Wisconsin State Federation of Labor, and it was enacted into law.

The proponents of unemployment insurance were themselves divided into two camps, with two contradictory bills. One of them proposed a "State fund," administered by State officials and therefore leaning towards the theory of "social responsibility" advocated by Professor Morton. The other proposed "establishment funds" administered by each establishment, under collective supervision of organized employers, organized labor, and the State Industrial Commission, and therefore leaning towards the theory of "employer responsibility" advocated by Senator Huber and Assemblyman Groves.

Of course, in these hearings and debates, and in the public meetings held throughout the state, neither the language of the speakers nor their fundamental social philosophies were shaped up in abstract generalizations, as is now done by Professor Morton in addressing the economists. Yet the philosophical and theoretical issues were there, as Morton has extracted them from the propaganda of the proponents. What the debaters on both sides were dealing with was the most urgent of all economic evils, well recognized by them and the entire people, but now brought down to the practical problem of, Who could be made responsible, and Who was in a position to relieve or prevent it? It was, indeed, through the aid of these ten-year discussions and my participation in them that I finally reached the formulation of the more abstract theory of "institutional

[195] Drafted in coöperation with A. B. Forsberg, afterwards editor of *Selected Articles on Unemployment Insurance* (1926).

[196] Commons, John R., "Unemployment—Compensation and Prevention," *The Survey*, Oct. 1, 1921, 5–9; for comments on Huber Bill see article entitled "Taxing Unemployment" in *The Survey*, March 19, 1921, 880.

economics" which I now learned to define as collective action in control, liberation, and expansion of individual action.[197]

Morton's criticisms go to the foundations of my economic theory of responsibility, for the Wisconsin Act is based almost solely on a theory of the individual responsibility of each employer for unemployment, whereas Morton holds that the employer is not more responsible, as an individual, than others. The responsibility is a "social responsibility."

This, I take it, is the fundamental clash between "individualism" and "socialism." Morton's criticism of the individualistic position means that the burden of paying benefits to the unemployed should be rationed according to a "three-party plan"—employers, wage-earners, and the state—instead of a multitude of "one-party" plans, financed by the individual employers.

The act was so devised, as he points out, that each employer should be made responsible for only *his own* employees, and not for the unemployed of other employers. This removes the act from any "social insurance" or even "industrial insurance" philosophies, and makes the reserves, required by the act, each an individual establishment reserve, not merged with any contributions from other establishments. It carries the idea of individual responsibility of the employer for unemployment to the furthest limit possible.

This is inseparable from the theory of the act as a "preventive" measure designed to induce the employer to *prevent* unemployment, instead of only a *relief* measure designed to pay unemployment benefits to those who, through no fault of their own, are unemployed. But the premium rate, two per cent on the payroll, is so low that, according to Morton, as a *relief* measure the act is totally inadequate, and as a *preventive* measure it is wholly inefficient.

Here Morton's underlying social philosophy is that the whole capitalistic system of private property is responsible; that unemployment under that system is inevitable; and that therefore *relief* rather than *prevention* is the only goal for legislation while capitalism lasts.

> "Unemployment," he says, "is a result of the defective operation of our economic institutions. Only by recognizing that unemployment is a social and not an individual, corporate, or industrial responsibility can the method of assessment be broadened so as to afford adequate relief. Only the economic system as a whole can support the burden it creates." [198]

[197] First formulated in the article "Institutional Economics," *Amer. Econ. Rev.*, XXI (1931), 648–657.
[198] Morton, W. A., *op. cit.*

Morton goes on to contrast this philosophy of social responsibility with the philosophy of individual responsibility underlying the arguments of the proponents of the act. He says:

"Accordingly, in Wisconsin an appeal was made to the spirit of rugged individualism. The European systems were condemned because they taxed society for a scourge assumed to be unavoidable but made no attempt to prevent it. There was also a revival of Herbert Spencer's *Social Statics*. 'Why should one employer be penalized for the unemployment created by another?' was a common query. Employers were made to feel that the assessment was not an inevitable tax. It was not state interference with their business but an expression of faith in the competitive system. They were assured that they would not be forced to support the unemployed from someone's else plant or in another locality. Since the European plans were considered by many employers to embody the baneful 'dole' it was said that the Groves bill was fundamentally different. The former sought to alleviate unemployment; the Groves bill sought to prevent it." [199]

We should note, however, in this connection, that Herbert Spencer's philosophy is not only the laissez-faire *political* philosophy of Smith, Bentham, and Ricardo; it is also the philosophy underlying their opposition to *all forms of private collective action* as well as state action. Private collective action, the individualist economists claimed, was always monopolistic and opposed to the common welfare.

But it was not in this historical meaning of *laissez-faire*, as opposed to *all* collective action, that the proponents of the act made use of the individualistic philosophy. They appealed to individualism in exactly the opposite direction, namely, that both private and public collective action should be recognized as the means by which individual employers should be held responsible for unemployment. They appealed to the already existing Manufacturers' Association, the existing State Federation of Labor, and the Taxpayers organized as a State Legislature. It was *not* an appeal to individualism *without* collective action. It was an appeal to individualism *through* collective action. The way in which this appeal was expected to work out will be seen when we explain below the *administrative* features of the act instead of the strictly *legislative* features to which Morton restricts his attention.

I agree with Morton that our capitalistic institutions are built on the theory of *individual responsibility*. But they are also built on the

[199] *Ibid.*

theory of *individual initiative*. Without free initiative there can be no individual responsibility.

Further, the dominant psychology of the American people has always been, and now is, so stubbornly individualistic that social responsibility, in so far as it exists *effectively*, has come about only piecemeal.

By effective social responsibility I mean a willingness and ability to *pay taxes* and to insist on a competent *civil service* system adequate to maintain and administer the "social services." These needed social services are innumerable, examples of which are free education, health protection, child labor prevention, freedom of collective action of organizations, and many others, including now both a new kind of unemployment relief without the sting of charity, and a new idea of unemployment prevention by those who can be made responsible.

On past occasions when any one of these newly proposed social services has been put forward there has always been a bitter fight. In one case—the state protection of the freedom and citizenship of the slaves—the conflict ended in a revolutionary Civil War of four years. But this conflict, as it actually occurred, was not animated by any social philosophy of equality of Negroes with whites. Indeed, such a social philosophy was and is rejected by a majority of the American people. The conflict was directed towards overthrowing the political dominance of the slave-owners in controlling the legislative, executive, and judicial branches of the national government, and substituting a government based on the principles of capitalism. The individualistic principle of liberty of the slaves came incidentally, as a war measure, and subsequently as an ineffective administrative problem.

I have made extensive historical studies of these political struggles on behalf of both white and colored labor.[200] It is mainly upon such investigations and my own experience in collective action that I have often based my criticisms of the naïve theories of those who, for a hundred years, have acted on the assumption that their so-called "society," when once "it" has been shown a great social evil, would promptly accept the responsibility of alleviating or preventing the evil. I have seen, both in these historical studies and in my personal acquaintance, many of these public-spirited and self-sacrificing leaders and propagandists, from Robert Owen to the present-day generation, finally become disillusioned. They turn, according to character and circumstance, perhaps into able supporters of the

---

[200] Commons, John R., and associates, *A Documentary History of American Industrial Society* (10 vols., 1910); *History of Labour in the United States* (2 vols., 1918).

most conservative and reactionary capitalism; or perhaps into despondent pessimists holding that "nothing can be done"; or perhaps into a deistic or materialistic faith that an over-ruling Providence, or the great inherent forces of natural law, can be trusted to work out those reforms (whether individualistic, communistic, socialistic, single-tax, or otherwise), to which they had formerly devoted their lives. In studying these transformations I have, in a cold-blooded "scientific" way, traced their origins to an earlier creation in their own minds of an idealized society, an idealized workingman, an idealized capitalist, an idealized politician, remote from the actual because created in their own humanitarian image. They had overlooked the details of the *how* and the *why*. These are the practical problems of a greatly increased tax-burden, a civil service dominated by practical politicians and hungry job-seekers, and the negotiations behind the scene for control of the politicians organized as the political machine.[201]

In all such cases I have asked, What do you mean by "Society"? [202] Do you mean an abstract entity, as did the socialists and similar heterodox schools in the middle of the Nineteenth Century,[203] or do you mean "society in action" as you actually experience it in all forms of collective action? If you mean the latter, then you mean taxpayers' leagues, organized employers, organized labor, corporations, going concerns, political parties, and so on, as they actually behave in their various harmonies and conflicts of interest. Society in action is custom, politics, corporations, in short any form of collective action in greater or less effective control, at the time, of individual action.

But if, after years of conflict, the "social responsibility" is finally established, as for example, in the case of free education, first advocated "socialistically" as charged by its opponents a hundred years ago,[204] then eventually the American people, ignorant of the preceding historical struggle, may willingly impose huge taxes for its support. And, as they have actually done with education, they may establish a civil service system for the selection of teachers, separated, as far as possible, from party politics and personal favoritism. The argument against free and compulsory education was

---

[201] Cf. Commons, John R., "Horace Greeley and the Working Class Origins of the Republican Party," *Pol. Sci. Quar.*, XXIV (1909), 468–488; *Proportional Representation* (1896), 4, 28, 33, 37, 84, 142, 173, 198, on The Machine.

[202] Above, p. 612, Society.

[203] Above, p. 325, Division of Labor and Association of Labor.

[204] Cf. Commons, John R., and associates, *History of Labour in the United States*, I, 182–184, 322, 229–230; II, 228–229, 323–324. *Documentary History of American Industrial Society*, V, 27–29, 115–118, 107–114, 161.

the individualistic argument that it deprived the parent of control of his children; but it turned out to be enforcement of the parent's social responsibility for the education of his children. Even so, as is well known in this period of economic depression, all of the "social services" of the state and of private "social agencies" are suffering on account of the inability, in spite of willingness, to pay taxes, or maintain voluntary contributions, or keep "politics" out of the civil service.

It is, as always, the historical conflict between individual and social responsibility. But it is based, not on a philosophical or academic issue of "society versus the individual," regardless of economic, political, administrative, and individualistic obstacles, but upon the very practical problem of getting a new social responsibility effectively recognized and enforced in the midst of a population excessively individualistic, politically diverted, and administratively incompetent.

Thus I find, during my historical studies and some fifty years of participation in many varieties of collective action directed towards controlling individual action, that my method of reasoning goes back to Malthus, rather than to Smith, Bentham, Ricardo, Marx, Proudhon, Herbert Spencer, or any of the "logical" economists. These schools belong more to the Eighteenth Century Age of Reason, but Malthus definitely proclaimed the Age of Passion and Stupidity.[205] I call this Custom, however, instead of passion or stupidity, in order to avoid invidious reflections and to allow for a slow infiltration of reason provoked by uncomfortable experiences.

It is, nevertheless, this Malthusian kind of a passionate, stupid, individualistic, and even anarchistic, animal whom the logical economist "comes up against" in every type of collective action designed to promote the common welfare. Capitalism, like dictatorship and party politics, thrives on the stupidity of mankind. Is it not better, therefore, for peace of mind, so to recognize in advance the foundations of capitalism, than to turn out eventually disillusioned, hopeless, reactionary, revolutionary, or contented with "natural law" instead of a better organized collective action?

How then, shall the appeal be made to this Malthusian individual willingly and effectively to join, through legislation, administration, or any other kind of collective action, to impose a new form of social responsibility upon both himself and his fellow-individualists, by paying taxes, eliminating party politics, and selecting competent administrators?

The people of Wisconsin are markedly individualistic and re-

[205] Above, p. 244, Malthus.

ligious, notwithstanding the relatively small socialistic element centered in Milwaukee. To them two appeals were made, as stated by Morton, the appeal to their individualistic social philosophy and the appeal to their experience with accident prevention. Morton dismisses the latter appeal as a "doubtful analogy." He says,

"The bill was compared to the workmen's accident compensation act. Just as this legislation, by putting a penalty upon employers in proportion to their accidents, had induced them to employ safety measures which had resulted in a marked diminution of industrial accidents, so an unemployment penalty would provide an incentive to stabilize jobs. This analogy, though a doubtful parallel, underlies the Wisconsin act . . . penalizing the individual employer would induce him to avoid unemployment by efficient labor management." [206]

He goes on to give certain details of the act designed to create employer responsibility and establishment reserves instead of social responsibility and a common fund administered by the state.

I do not look upon this appeal to experience as a "doubtful parallel." Deductively it may be so. But practically it was the effective appeal that brought about the enactment of the law as it actually stands in all its details and imperfections. Morton's is the logical economist's way of reasoning, regardless of custom that grows out of past experience. The experience, in this case, was the joint participation of the leaders of organized but conflicting interests in administering the accident prevention laws. To the people of Wisconsin and to the organized employers and organized employees of the state, it was the best of reasoning. Though not necessarily logical, and perhaps even highly inconsistent at points, the reasoning was an expression of what their experience and practical knowledge led them to expect in the administration of the proposed unemployment law. The strenuously conflicting organized employers and organized workmen had, within themselves, the habitual assumptions derived from their experience of coöperation with the State Industrial Commission. They could tell in advance, not only how the Commission would call them in to aid in administering the act, but, more important, they practically could name in advance the leading employer who would be appointed by the Commission to represent the Wisconsin Manufacturers' Association, as well as the president of the State Federation of Labor who would represent labor, and the name of the individual deputy of the Industrial Commission, who would act as conciliator in administering the act.

[206] Morton, W. A., *op. cit.*

These three individuals had been working together for some ten or fifteen years in administering the accident prevention law. It was practically assumed that they would work together in administering the employment-reserve and unemployment-prevention law. This assumption turned out to be correct, though not stipulated in the act. Hence, their experience was, to them, not a "doubtful analogy"; it was the realistic reasoning of practical men in the midst of conflict and doubt. These assurances could not, in the nature of the case, be written into the words of the statute. But if they had not been the "unwritten law" of labor administration for twenty years in Wisconsin, the law could not have been enacted. At almost every point in drafting the new law, not merely a scientist's doubtful analogy, but a practical man's personal acquaintance, dictated the provisions of the new law.

Thus the unemployment statute itself, against which Morton's criticisms are directed, was partly an *enabling act*, with minimum standards, and it was to the expected *joint administration* of the act by the state Commission, the state Manufacturers' Association, and the State Federation of Labor that all parties looked forward. This is the way the practical man reasons. He does not reason abstractly regarding statutes. They are mere inexplicable words to him. He reasons upon the "unwritten law" of the way the statute will be interpreted and who will administer it. For him, administration is "legislation in action," [207] and it is *expected action*, not logic and words, upon which he bases his present conduct.

It turned out as was expected. The Industrial Commission appointed an "advisory committee" which, as was known in Wisconsin, would be the principal administrative authority, drafting all the rules and regulations, interpreting to employers and employees the long and detailed provisions of the law, and even propagandizing the employers of the state to come voluntarily under the law. The Commission itself would be, in effect, only the sanctioning authority, giving legality to the "recommendations" of the advisory committee.

Furthermore, it was known, after twenty years' experience in collective accident prevention, that the members of the advisory committee, representing "capital" and "labor," would not be chosen by the state Commission in bureaucratic or civil service examination fashion, but would be chosen by the organized interests themselves. The representatives would not be paid any salary by the state but would be paid by their own organizations. This provision, in the accident-prevention law, it was known, had eliminated party

207 Cf. Commons, John R., and Andrews, John B., *Principles of Labor Legislation* (Chapter on Administration, editions 1916, 1923, 1927).

"politics" from the state Commission in both the selection of "representatives" of employers and employees, and even in the selection of its own deputies, statisticians, and inspectors who were expected to work with the organized employers and organized employees. In fact, a new kind of civil service had been incorporated into the administration of the labor laws. It is a set of state officials effectively appointed by the joint action of conflicting organizations of "capital" and "labor," and therefore having the confidence of both sides. As such, the state officials act, not as compulsory "arbitrators" coming from a superior authority, the state, but as voluntary "conciliators," whose business it is to bring opposing interests together on a basis of "facts" known to be such on both sides, and thereby aiding them in drafting the "working rules" under which, as individuals, they must severally operate. Since these rules can be changed at any time, on the basis of further investigation and experience, it is a system of continuous conciliation, without dictatorship, of continually conflicting interests.

This outcome, when applied to unemployment reserves and unemployment prevention, may be seen in the two bulletins so far sanctioned and issued by the state Commission, but actually drafted by the advisory committee and their assistants. These bulletins give all of the interpretations of the law and the rules adopted up-to-date, and it is to these, rather than to the enabling statute, that the economist should look for the way in which the law actually operates. The latest bulletin, August 1, 1933,[208] gives the names of the members of the advisory committee and these show the truly "occupational representation" of conflicting interests in the rule-making body:

> "*Employer Representatives:* Fred H. Clausen, President of the Van Brunt Manufacturing Company, Horicon, Wisconsin; George F. Kull, Secretary of Wisconsin Manufacturers' Association, Madison, Wisconsin; Horace J. Mellum, Secretary of the Nash Motors Company, Kenosha, Wisconsin.
>
> "*Labor Representatives:* J. F. Friedrick, Member of Executive Board, Wisconsin State Federation of Labor, Milwaukee, Wisconsin; Fred E. Gastrow, President of the State Council of Carpenters, Madison, Wisconsin; Henry Ohl, Jr., President of the Wisconsin State Federation of Labor, Milwaukee, Wisconsin.
>
> "*Presiding Chairman:* Arthur J. Altmeyer, Secretary of the Wisconsin Industrial Commission, Madison, Wisconsin." [209]

[208] *Revised Handbook on the Wisconsin Unemployment Compensation Act and Approved Voluntary Plans for Unemployment Benefits or Guaranteed Employment,* Bulletin No. 2 on Unemployment Compensation (115 pp.), published by Industrial Commission of Wisconsin, August, 1933.

[209] *Ibid.,* 2.

It will be seen that, of the many forms of collective action discussed in this book, this one approaches the form known as Collective Bargaining, while the working rules agreed upon come under the name, Trade Agreement. While there are seven members of the advisory committee, it is significant that two of these seven, Mr. Clausen and Mr. Ohl, were the leading opponents in the legislative lobbies throughout the ten years of legislative hearings on successive bills. When finally the legislative act was drafted, in these conferences, it passed the legislature. What happened was that the employers' "lobby" and the employees' "lobby" were converted into the negotiators of a collective bargaining trade agreement, and the legislature decided the points where they could not agree. Although the employers opposed the law, they have, after its enactment, supported it in good faith.

But this collective bargaining goes further, and removes the mistaken implication of Morton's casual remark that "operation was postponed by Wisconsin legislature, 1933." Part of the operation was not postponed but the act is in operation as originally intended, with the necessary appropriation. The so-called postponement in 1933 was not made by the legislature. It was made, after much internal discussion, and with a second bill agreed to by bargaining within the joint advisory committee of opposing interests, and then sanctioned by the legislature without a dissenting vote.

The law of 1932 had provided three successive dates when different stages of the law should go into effect. The provisions for creating the joint administrative machinery, for adopting rules and regulations, for approval or disapproval of voluntary establishment schemes, and for acquainting the public with the provisions of the law, took effect on passage in 1932. This part of the law was not postponed and is now in operation.

The collection of premiums for building up the establishment funds was originally dated forward to go into effect July 1, 1933. This part of the law was postponed, not really by the legislature but on the joint recommendation of the employer and employee representatives. The recommendation was ratified by the legislature as mere matter of routine without a dissenting vote and without debate. The date of beginning payment of contributions was now set forward until such time, to be ascertained by the Commission's statisticians, as either employment in the state should increase 20 per cent or payrolls increase 50 per cent above the level of December 1932.

This postponement automatically postponed the third stage in the operation of the law, namely the payment of unemployment benefits, which had been set to begin one year after the beginning of collection of premiums for the unemployment reserves.

The reasons for this postponement are stated in the act. The original act read in part as follows: [210]

"The largest organization of employers in the state having declared it to be the intention of its members voluntarily to establish unemployment fund systems, it is the intent of the legislature to give employers a fair opportunity to bring about the purposes of this act without legal compulsion."

The postponement act amends by inserting:

"Therefore the opportunity to keep this act from taking general and compulsory effect shall extend until business recovery is well under way in Wisconsin." [211] That is, until the increase in employment or payrolls materializes as indicated in the act.

Furthermore, so strongly were the manufacturers in the state committed to the idea of voluntary individual initiative and responsibility that the original act provided that the compulsory features of the law should not go into effect at all if the employers of 175,000 employees should adopt approved voluntary plans. Under this provision, and on the recommendation of the Advisory Committee, the Commission went so far as to appoint on the state payroll, for "part-time services," the representative of the manufacturers, Mr. Clausen. This was done, as stated in the Handbook, in order "to explain the Act to Wisconsin employers and to promote the adoption of approved voluntary plans." Later, the Act of 1933, as recommended by the Advisory Committee, reduced the number of employees from 175,000 to 139,000. If the latter number of employees are covered by voluntary schemes before the date set for the beginning of compulsory contributions, then the legislative compulsion does not go into effect.

Evidently this postponement was sensible, and was in fact the original policy of the law, namely, that funds should be built up in periods of relative prosperity and paid out primarily in periods of depression. The difficulty was that the legislature of 1932 did not make a successful guess of returning prosperity when it picked on July 1933. But it is entirely within the spirit of the law that the date for collecting premiums should be set by a future "finding of fact," through the administrative machinery for collecting statistics. The statistics for September 1933 showed that employment had increased 35 per cent and payrolls 50 per cent above the basic date,

[210] *Ibid.*, 83.
[211] *Ibid.*, 83.

December 1932. At this rate of increase, the second stage of the law might begin at an early date, except for the further provision that it shall not begin before July 1934; and that the compulsory features should not go into effect if 139,000 employees are covered by voluntary schemes.

Thus the legislative law is partly an enabling act, setting up an administrative system of collective bargaining, along with certain minimum and maximum limits. The system cannot be understood as a mere statute administered by a bureaucratic commission with appeals to the courts. It is as nearly a voluntary system of collective bargaining as the nature of our constitutional government will permit, and it can be understood only in so far as the concerted action of voluntary private associations is understood. Already, before the enactment of the law, a few individual manufacturing firms, by a variety of devices permitted in the statute, had voluntarily gone beyond the minimum two per cent provisions of the act.

It is upon this minimum two per cent rate in the statute that Morton focusses his criticisms, especially of "inadequacy" for relief and "inefficiency" as an inducement to prevent unemployment. This criticism really goes to a fundamental theory of the relation of the state to the individual. If there is a theory underlying the law of what Morton distinguishes as "political economy" contrasted with a "problem in economics" (p. 411), it is a theory to the effect that very little can be accomplished towards public welfare by compulsory legislation compared with what can be accomplished by the willingness and initiative of private effort and private coöperation, if properly directed by the state in the competitive rivalry for profits. This involves a very opposite interpretation of the whole range of facts on which, as mere opaque facts, I agree with Morton and the original criticism of employers.

It will be seen, from this recital, how far removed from ideas of compulsory "social responsibility" and how near to ideas of *regulated* but *voluntary* individual responsibility, were both the representatives of manufacturers and the representatives of labor.

It may seem surprising, to one not acquainted with "labor psychology," that the labor lobbyists in 1932 should have abandoned in part their insistence on "relief" and should have gone over to an individualistic "prevention" measure. The labor lobbyists had been, in fact, supporting in the legislature of 1931 a compulsory "relief" measure in the form of a "state fund" to be administered by a state board, exactly the opposite of individual "establishment funds," and similar to the principle of social responsibility advocated by Morton. They thought the "state fund" might also provide preventive inducements. But when they realized that, as representatives of both organized labor and the socialist party, they were divided in their own minds by two conflicting "labor psychologies," the "socialistic psychology" of political parties and the "trade-union psychology" of voluntary collective bargaining, they abandoned their state fund bill and committed themselves to the Groves' establishment-fund and collective-bargaining bill.

Their idea of collective bargaining, as developed by Samuel Gompers fifty years ago, when he split off from the socialists, was "voluntary" organization of labor unions and trade agreements with voluntary organizations of employers, both removed entirely from political or judicial interference. And when they realized, as did Gompers, that a State Fund would mean the control of its administration by party politicians and unfriendly courts, but that the collective bargaining bill would give them an equal voice with employers, removed as far as possible from state interference and compulsory arbitration, in the regulation of all the employers' voluntary plans, they chose the latter. Their experience of twenty years in administering, along with employers, both the accident prevention law and the state employment offices, the latter especially in Milwaukee, was enough to convince them that their trade-union policy of obtaining equality with employers in collective bargaining was superior, under existing conditions, to their socialistic policy as a minor political party in the politics of the state.

A similar conflict within the employers' "psychology" is referred to by Professor Morton in his article. He states, quite correctly, that "the manufacturers favored the Groves bill (the old Huber bill) if it came to a choice between that and some alternative insurance plan," and he goes on, in a footnote:

> "In a recent speech to Wisconsin manufacturers the former president of the Manufacturers' Association Mr. Clausen now aiding the Wisconsin Industrial Commission in promoting the present law urged compliance with the provisions of the Wisconsin act for voluntary schemes. He warned them that unless this law went into effect they might at some future time be confronted with the Ohio plan which he stated he regarded as socialism."

The "Ohio plan" referred to was a bill introduced in the Ohio legislature on the recommendation of a special investigating committee, emphasizing relief rather than prevention. This bill was drafted along the "three-party" lines advocated by Morton, and was substantially based on the "socialistic" psychology, contrasted with the "trade-union" psychology.

Thus it was this "choice of alternatives" between the socialistic principle and the trade-union principle that· ultimately decided both the labor representatives and the employer representatives in choosing the Wisconsin trade-union principle of voluntary collective bargaining, sanctioned by the state government.

I do not know of any better way to understand the significance of this "choice of alternatives" in creating effective social responsibility than the historical method, which is the method of experience. Social responsibility is never accepted *effectively* by employers or any other class of individuals, until they are faced by an alternative which seems worse to them than the one they "willingly" accept. The historical method is a history of the choice of alternatives. In this case it is the historical "parallel" used as an appeal by the proponents of unemployment reserves and individual establishment responsibility, namely, the Workmen's Compensation and Accident Prevention law of 1911.

The unemployment prevention law of 1932, though more complicated, is evidently following quite precisely the accident prevention law of 1911. Since I participated in the agitation, enactment, and, for the first two years, in the administration of the accident compensation and safety laws, as well as having similar experience in a voluntary unemployment reserve and prevention trade agreement in the Chicago Clothing market, I may speak from personal experience of the way in which these collective movements actually operated.

The Wisconsin accident compensation law of 1911 had been preceded for several years by a bill successively introduced by the socialist representatives in the legislature. It provided for a state insurance fund, making "society" responsible for accidents, and compelling employers to contribute to that state fund.

Another theory on which it was thought "society" would pay the bills was the classical economic theory of cost of production, which I name Bargaining Power. According to this theory, if the tax on employers was uniform, bearing equally on the "marginal" employer whose costs were highest, then all employers would raise the prices of their products by the amount of the tax, and, of course, the tax would be shifted to the consumers by the normal operation of "economic law."

The legislature of New York had enacted a law, but it had been declared unconstitutional by the Supreme Court of that state as lacking "due process of law," because it confiscated the property of the employers without fault or negligence on their part.[212] The way

---

[212] Ives *v.* South Buffalo Railway Company, 124 N. Y. S. 920, 924 (1910).

in which this confiscation occurred was by means of an insurance fund which made each employer responsible for accidents in other employers' shops. They were already, by common law, responsible for accidents caused only by their own negligence. But the New York law made them also responsible for accidents caused by the negligence of the injured employee himself, or by the negligence of a fellow-employee, or by the natural hazards of the industry. The last named, according to both classical and common-law theory, were deemed to be "assumed" by the employee when he made his labor contract, and to be fully taken into account in the higher rate of wages he received as commutation of his expected risks.[213]   In other words, it was upon the classical economic and the common-law theory of individual responsibility, and its correlative, "no responsibility without fault," that the law of New York was declared unconstitutional.

Consequently, when a committee of the Wisconsin legislature, after 1909, took up the matter of drafting a bill for accident insurance, they determined to avoid unconstitutionality by proposing a "voluntary" bill, wherein only those employers who registered with the Commission their acceptance of the new law were deemed to be "under the law." Option was also given to withdraw their acceptance by giving due notice to the Commission. In order, however, to bring as much economic "coercion" upon the employers as it was thought constitutionally could be done, and thus to induce them "willingly" to come under the law, the legislature repealed certain of the above-mentioned common-law defenses of the employer in a suit for damages. This repeal affected adversely every employer who failed to elect to come under the law.

Thus an inducement to come "voluntarily" under the law was created by setting up two alternatives between which each individual employer could choose—the old employers' liability law of negligence in each individual suit for damages, but with some of his common-law defenses withdrawn, and the new workmen's compensation law for all accidents, without regard to negligence, or misdemeanor, or risks of the industry. He could choose voluntarily between *individual* responsibility under the existing common law and *social* responsibility under the new law.

The law was sustained by the State Supreme Court. But it could only be in a sense of humor that it was called a *law* when employers were given the option of choosing whether they would or would not obey the law. It was "constitutional" at the expense of social responsibility. The joke of "constitutionality" became evident during

[213] Above, p. 158, Adam Smith.

the first two years of administration of the accident compensation "law." The number of employers who "elected" voluntarily to come under the law covered, in the first two years, only about 10 per cent of the total number of eligible employees of the state.

This unwillingness of employers and the probable unconstitutionality of statutory compulsion turned out to be an advantage instead of a disadvantage. It compelled the state Commission to start a campaign to induce employers willingly to come under the law. The Industrial Commission law of 1911 had consolidated under one commission the enforcement of the accident compensation law and the drafting and enforcement of safety rules to prevent accidents. The commission turned its energies towards "accident prevention," rather than "accident compensation." The former "big stick" factory inspectors, attempting to enforce by criminal prosecutions the impracticable statutory safety laws, were converted into "safety experts" to advise employers how to reduce accidents. The employers, their foremen, and superintendents of factories throughout the state, were organized into local and district "safety conferences" and a state-wide conference. These conferences were enthusiastically attended; experts from private corporations outside the state were brought in; and there suddenly developed a remarkable "safety spirit." Employers showed that they could do much more voluntarily to prevent accidents than could the state by compulsion in preventing accidents. And, though the rate of accidents afterwards increased, during the rush of the World War, yet these conferences and efforts towards prevention remain today as vigorous as ever.

In the creation of this "safety spirit" the example of the greatest pioneer, the United States Steel Company, was used. This had, indeed, been the example employed in the drafting of the Industrial Commission law. That corporation had begun its safety organization as early as 1907.[214] The extensive investigations of the Commission seemed to show that only about one-third of the accidents could be prevented by safety devices, while two-thirds were caused by carelessness of employees and employers. The prevention of these two-thirds, and even the installation and use of the devices, could be brought about only by building up the "safety spirit" in the minds, not only of employers and employees, but equally in the minds of the general public.

Most important of all in promoting this creation of the "safety

[214] Cf. Eastman, Crystal, *Work-Accidents and the Law*, published by Russell Sage Foundation, 1910, as one of the volumes of the "Pittsburgh Survey." The investigations were made in 1907–08. (Charities Publication Committee.)

spirit" was the organization of small safety committees consisting of employers and employees with a deputy of the Commission as secretary, for the purpose of drafting rules and regulations to be afterwards given the force of law as "orders" issued by the state Commission. These orders took the place of the many complicated and detailed statutes enacted by successive legislatures and fought over by lobbies which usually consisted of legal representatives of the conflicting interests. The "orders" had these advantages: They were drafted by joint action of employers and employees and not by lawyers and legislatures ignorant of the technology of the industries. They could be changed, with further experience, by the same committees that had formulated them originally. Above all, they were workable and acceptable to both the employers and employees.

This brought them within the legal doctrine of reasonableness, and avoided the constitutional prohibition against taking the property of employers without due process of law; that is, in this case, without their consent. Several hundred pages of bulletins were issued from time to time, containing these orders having the effect of law, quite similar to the handbook on the Wisconsin Unemployment Compensation Act, above referred to.

This safety campaign of two years showed to the employers that they could make *more profit* by coming under the new law than by remaining under the old individual liability laws, provided that, at the same time, they entered into the safety spirit by preventing accidents. And furthermore, it was shown that, by preventing accidents, nobody, not even the consumers by higher prices, would bear any burden in paying the benefits to workmen stipulated in the accident compensation laws. In other words, appeal was made to a new kind of "efficiency," efficiency in preventing accidents, by which costs of production could be reduced, with the result that prices need not be increased.

Consequently, at the end of two years, the joint committee and the Industrial Commission recommended, and the legislature enacted a change in the compensation law to the effect that the *option* should be reversed. Instead of electing to come under the law they now were *assumed* to be under the law unless they filed notice of election *not* to come under. This reversal of the option brought 90 per cent of the workers under the law. Finally in 1931, after the constitutionality of a compulsory law had been sustained in other states and by the Supreme Court of the United States, the legislature substituted a compulsory law for the elective law.

Thus Wisconsin legislation required twenty years to pass from the old to the new system. During this time not only the administrative system of developing the safety spirit and the educational system of preventing accidents, but also the joint bargaining system between representatives of opposing organized interests, with the state government acting as a conciliator, became established.

Thus it was demonstrated that a statutory law does not automatically work out the effects intended by the legislature, as Morton seems to hold was expected when he analyzes only the wording of the statute. The statute, in order to be effectual, must be followed by positive collective action of organized interests designed to create the "safety spirit," or the "employment spirit." Without this "collective spirit" of willing coöperation, no law is effective. And it is surprising how little legislative compulsion is necessary—only one-half of one per cent of cost of production in the case of accident compensation—provided this voluntary collective spirit is positively created by organizing the conflicting interests concerned with its administration.

So it is already working out in the administration of the unemployment compensation and prevention law. Taking advantage of the wide-spread horror of unemployment, never before so seriously considered either by the public or by economists, the Wisconsin law attempts to bring home this distress positively to the employers who can, in the first instance, be made responsible for it. It endeavors, by administration, to create the "employment spirit."

The term "spirit," as used in these connections, was not permissible for the classical, hedonic, communistic, or other economists whose theories arose from analogies to mechanisms, organisms, or machines. Yet the actual term, "safety spirit," arose spontaneously among all of those who joined in a conscious collective effort to prevent accidents. Such a use of the term "spirit" is available only to those who investigate collective action. It is somewhat analogous to a religious revival. I have indeed often noted that collective economic pressure is even more influential than a religious revival in converting individuals from passion and stupidity into "reasonableness." It is the key to a scientific understanding of what is popularly known as "business ethics," "professional ethics," "trade union ethics," and similar forms of collective economics.

These methods are similar, in their purpose and effect, to other forms of social pressure, and may accordingly be placed in the same category as the *tabu*, the *index-expergatoribus*, public opinion, style, custom, boycott, the N. R. A. If these forms of moral and economic coercion are not fully effective in reaching the desired result, because of opposition, then the addition of a slight legal duress, with prosecutions only in a few flagrant cases, stimulates the spirit of voluntary social responsibility among the objectors as well as among thousands and millions of individuals who do not need to be coerced.

These arguments have a bearing on Morton's criticism, often brought forward by the employers themselves, that, as "a going concern," each establishment has already more powerful inducements to maintain continuous operation than the insignificant "cost" of unemployment compensation. They have especially heavy overhead charges and the necessity of maintaining the good-will of customers, which would be lost if they shut down. This is undoubtedly true, but see how it works. A large firm that I have known for thirty years has 10,000 employees in periods of full-time operation, but when a depression comes they lay off 8,000 workers and retain only a skeleton organization of about 2,000. The object of the Wisconsin law is to direct the attention to those 8,000 and not to the 2,000 who keep the establishment operating as a going concern.

Another exhibit which had much influence in the Wisconsin propaganda was that of a firm owned in New York, which brought in 5,000 workers from all parts of the country during the inflationary prosperity of 1919, and then, in the slump of 1921, laid off the entire 5,000 to be supported by the people of a small city and county where the plant was located. How was it possible to bring home to the New York bankers their responsibility to the people of Wisconsin other than by legislation that would hit the profits of the abstentee stockholders? Social responsibility has to be created positively by directing attention of those who are really responsible in the first instance, and these, in our modern huge "going concerns," are the unseen stockholders at a distance. They feel no responsibility for unemployment, and therefore they leave the responsibility to the local people who actually see the unemployed and must personally, by gifts or taxes, take care of them. And a very low rate of insurance is astonishingly magnified, if its effect bears directly, as we shall see, on the margin for profit.

From the point of view of economic and legal theory the Wisconsin accident and unemployment laws are the incorporation, into the theory of sovereignty, of the *voluntary* representation of organized interests. This is in vivid contrast to the older individualistic theories which represented a sovereign as a kind of overlord speaking for the consumers, and separated from, yet laying down laws, for the unorganized producers. This older theory, whether the "rule of the majority" or the rule of an organized minority, turns out to be dictatorship.

But *voluntary* representation of organized interests in collective bargaining, each electing its own leaders, requires recognition, on both sides, of the motives which animate the opposite side. In the present case it means recognition of the profit motive, in the now dominant collective action of corporations; and the *use* of that motive in such a way as to promote the welfare of the whole community.

This, as I have shown elsewhere,[215] was the doctrine of the common law in the first half of the Seventeenth Century looking towards a legal and economic doctrine of increasing the Commonwealth of England by increasing one's own wealth. It was indeed also the theory of Adam Smith, but Smith held that individual self-interest promoted the commonwealth, or wealth of nations, as a result of guidance by divine Providence and natural law.[216] The theory embodied in the Wisconsin law gives to approved voluntary agreements a sovereign power to promote the commonwealth by collective action in control of individual action. This joint collective action *is* the law; and its administration is the individual action of the employer in conformity with the working rules which have been developed by employer and employee with the coöperation of the state Commission.

From this collective standpoint, reasonableness is the upper practicable limit of idealism.[217] In ascertaining what is reasonable I therefore take as examples the *best* unions or *best* associations, provided they have been able to maintain themselves as going concerns. Then, by some form of collective action, political or private, I endeavor to bring others up, as near as possible, to their level.

This practice, it must be conceded, does not always conform to the *customary* meaning of "reasonable" in the decisions of the courts. The courts generally go on the assumption that whatever is "ordinary" is "reasonable." With them, "customary" is *not* the *best practicable*, it is something of a *mean* between the palpably inefficient or stupid and the exceptionally capable and efficient. After repeated observations I make the guess that only 10 to 25 per cent of employers or unionists are above this meaning of custom as "ordinary," while 75 to 90 per cent are below that level. By this is meant that about 10 to 25 per cent of employers or unionists can be expected voluntarily to do more for the welfare of others than the best that can be expected from any kind of compulsion, whether by the state or by private collective action.

This reasoning will appear in the definition of "safety" which,

---

[215] Commons, John R., *Legal Foundations of Capitalism* (1924), 225-232.
[216] Above, p. 158, Adam Smith.
[217] Above, p. 741, Ethical Ideal Types.

with the help of my students [218] and others, was incorporated in the Industrial Commission law of 1911. "Safety" was there defined so as to include the protection of "life, health, safety, comfort, decency, and moral well-being." And the statute goes on to impose a duty, or "social responsibility," on every individual employer to furnish such employment, such a place of employment, and such safety devices, safeguards, methods, and processes, as shall protect the life, health, safety, comfort, decency, and moral well-being of employees to the extent that the nature of the employment or place of employment "will *reasonably* permit." [219]

Here the statutory and common law of the state was changed by merely changing the meaning of reasonableness. Instead of "ordinary" safety, interpreted as a *mean* between the highest and lowest, "reasonable" safety now became the highest degree of accident prevention, which is actually in practice by the best firms. And, instead of many impractical statutes accruing over a period of thirty years, the meaning of safety was expanded so that investigation had to be made in the factories themselves to find what was the highest practicable limit already successfully in operation in the most "socially minded" class of establishments, for the protection of life, health, safety, comfort, decency, and moral well-being. Thereupon no question of unconstitutionality was raised against the orders of the Commission in these respects, because they were demonstrably "reasonable" as having been drafted by the advisory committees of employers, employees, and experts, having acquaintance with the best practicable methods and devices. And "reasonableness" becomes, not subjective and individualistic, but objective and collectively practicable. It may not be "idealistic," but it is reasonably ideal within the then stage of self-interest, passion, and stupidity. Moreover, it is capable of reaching a higher ideal if human nature improves.

In general, whatever is demonstrated thus to be "reasonable" in the sense of voluntary agreement of voluntarily organized, though conflicting, interests, may be expected sooner or later to be found to be "constitutional" by the Supreme Court. The Supreme Court, like European dictators, has very little respect for modern legislatures, but it does have an increasingly greater respect for voluntary collective action.

So I think it will turn out to be with unemployment prevention

[218] Especially Francis H. Bird, now professor of economics in the University of Cincinnati.
[219] *Wisconsin Statutes* (1931), Chapter 101, Secs. 101.01 to 101.06. Italics mine. See Commons, John R., and Andrews, John B., *Principles of Labor Legislation* (2d ed., 1920), 356 ff.; 422 ff.

and unemployment compensation. No statute is effective by its mere words. It must be interpreted, administered, and applied to each establishment, according to the circumstances and limits within which it fits and can be complied with. If there can be worked out a consensus of opinion as to the *best* of what is *practicable*, then that, by the judgment of those closest to the facts, is the upper limit of idealism. This limit is, in fact, none other than what is held to be reasonable in view of all the conflicting interests concerned, as well as under the changeable interpretations of the constitution of the United States by the Supreme Court.

Another feature of the accident compensation and safety laws was copied in the unemployment compensation and prevention law. The accident law provided three types of "insurance": Insurance with stock companies; "mutual" insurance by employers in the state; and so-called "self-insurance" by individual establishments which could show financial solvency and ability to pay the compensation.

The statistics collected by the state Commission during several years following the enactment of the accident compensation law seemed to show that the prevention of accidents correlated with the form of accident insurance permitted under the law. The best record of prevention came from the so-called "self-insurers." These were firms, possibly 200 in number, which "carried their own insurance," and thus were not "insurance" but were identical with "establishment funds," or "accident reserves." The next in order of degree of prevention were the firms united in mutual insurance companies, and the lowest were firms insured in nation-wide stock companies.

The unemployment reserve law, of 1932, copied the two forms of insurance, "self-insurance" or "establishment funds," and "mutual" insurance, but not stock company insurance. The object was to eliminate the private profit motive of stock companies, and to select the modes of insurance which had shown, in the case of accidents, the best records of prevention. By the mutual insurance provision, if employers voluntarily decided to merge their funds in a common fund, and thus become responsible for each others' unemployment, they were permitted to do so.

The central figure in the administration of accident compensation laws is the doctor. He determines the degree of injury and the ending of the incapacity to work, and therefore the amount and ending of the weekly compensation. So the central figure in unemployment compensation is the Public Employment Officer. The chief in charge is the person to whom reports of unemployment and re-employment are made and transmitted to the state Commission.

And he acts in unemployment compensation as the trial court determining the amount of compensation, the waiting period, and the beginning of compensation.

Here Wisconsin had already developed, under the state Commission, an efficient system of employment offices, some ten in number. Especially in the Milwaukee office the joint system of control by locally organized employers and organized labor had been worked out. This local joint administration of the employment office system was, of course, read into the expected administration of the unemployment law. Indeed, just as in the case of employing the doctor, the employers are expected to set up and participate in agencies for finding jobs with other employers for their own unemployed. The shorter the period of unemployment, the less is the amount of unemployment compensation. Employers become their own employment officers, even more effective, by appealing to their profit motive, than the state employment officers on salaries that go on without regard to profit and loss. And, to prevent abuse, the collective bargaining system of joint administration with labor unions had been found satisfactory for both employers and employees.

It was this example and this habit of concerted action that led to the acceptance of the Wisconsin Unemployment Compensation Law of 1932. That law is by no means a logical, deductive law derived either from orthodox economic theory or from legal constitutional theory in the United States. On this account and on account of the need for time in constructing the administrative machinery and in building up the "employment spirit" among employers, the statute first sets up the machinery and then postpones the collection of premiums, the creation of reserves, and finally the payment of benefits, as was done in the case of accident compensation prevention.

It was the foregoing historical method of investigation of collective action which led me to formulate, in 1921, as above stated, the principles of a law for the *prevention* of unemployment as distinguished from unemployment *insurance*. That the principle fitted automatically into the American business psychology, I discovered afterwards when I was asked, in 1924, to become chairman of the joint unemployment insurance scheme previously agreed upon by collective bargaining in the men's clothing industry of Chicago. I have no idea that the seventy or more business firms participating in that agreement had any knowledge or understanding of what I had proposed in 1921. But they automatically, in their traditional notions of competition, profit, and self-interest, had resisted the labor union's demand for contributions by *all* employers to a "market" fund, to be distributed to *all* the unemployed members of the union by a single central board. The employers reasoned that such a merging of funds would compel the prosperous and efficient firms, which therefore were able to give steady employment, to contribute benefits to the unemployed of their less prosperous and less efficient competitors.

This had, indeed, been the "insurance" idea of practically all European legislation on the subject, and it was decidedly the idea of the labor union in Chicago in its demand for a common fund. A compromise was reached wherein were set up some seventy separate "establishment funds" instead of a single "market fund." This required seventy different administrative boards for collection of premiums and payment of benefits, and I found myself "seventy chairmen" of seventy different boards.

Since the premium rate of $2\frac{1}{2}$ per cent was to be uniform throughout the market, the amounts contributed to the several funds differed widely, proportionate to the payrolls of each firm. Consequently the firms having the *largest unemployment* would be *least* able to pay unemployment benefits, and the firms having the *least unemployment* would be able to pay the *largest* benefits. Eventually a firm able to maintain steady employment (fixed at 47 weeks per year) and to set up a reserve equal to one year's future premiums, would make no further premium or benefit payments. Hence the correct name for the system is "unemployment reserves" and not "unemployment insurance." Reserves are set up by each establishment, whereas insurance would merge the reserves of all establishments in a common fund.

Evidently the "labor psychology" is not satisfied with such a deficient and discriminatory allotment of benefits. The laborers, especially in a union, feel themselves responsible for each other. Any who are unemployed not only excite the sympathy, but also the dread of the menace to the others who retain employment. The outstanding evidence of this labor psychology is the willingness of unionists to "share" the burden of unemployment by accepting part-time work in order that the short-time employment may be passed around to all.

But the "busines psychology" has seldom such sentiment of this kind, which would lead business firms to *share* with their competitors the reduced amount of output in dull seasons and business depressions. They, indeed, may resort to cartels with that purpose regarding output and prices, but, short of that remedy, the bankruptcy and elimination of rivals is a gain for the prosperous and efficient, by transferring to them both the customers and the employees of their defunct competitors. This may be named the "profit psychology," whereas the organized laborers' is more nearly a "solidarity psychology." The laborers cannot understand even why the prosperous and efficient employers should not *share* their prosperity and efficiency with all of the unemployed of the "marginal" and inefficient competitors. The rank and file of workers, as far as I have observed, want *relief*, and are not interested in *efficiency* or *prevention*. Their leaders are recently learning to emphasize prevention more than relief.

Here it is that the classical and orthodox theories miss the point regarding "labor" and "business" psychology. Those theories descend from a period of small manufacturers where it was easy for a journeyman to become a master-workman one day, hiring the journeymen, or a journeyman the next day, hired by the master-workman. Profits and wages were therefore not distinguished by Adam Smith in his general analysis. The same principles of competition applied to each, and brought profits to a substantial equality with wages.[220] Indeed, as already observed, the "profits" of the small contractor or manufacturer in the sweat-shop system are often below the wages of his journeymen.

But there is another distinction betwen the orthodox and the institutional theories. The modern employer is not an individual. "He" is an "institution"—the concerted action of entrepreneurs, bankers, stockholders, and investors tied together in a "firm" or "corporation," which we name a going concern if it "goes." Modern individualism is corporation-individualism. Here it is not the classical theories that apply, but it is the theories of "corporation finance," not yet incorporated in the standard individualistic theories.[221] The standard theories turn on "costs of production," and Morton correctly estimates that the 2 per cent payroll premium, stipulated in the Wisconsin law, is only about one-half of one per cent (0.5) of the total cost of production. Such an insignificant item, he argues, could have no effect whatever on employers as an inducement to prevent unemployment.

But "corporation finance" turns on the "margin for profit." Here the entrepreneurs (the stockholders), who assume the risks, are always "trading on the equity." The "equity" is the "margin for profit," or Morton's "net profit." The entrepreneur is the associated stockholders. They become jointly a debtor to all other partici-

[220] Above, p. 158, Adam Smith.
[221] These theories are being developed in purely empirical fashion in schools of commerce which have consistently been divorced from "departments" of economics. Compare such writers as Lyon and Gerstenberg on corporation finance.

pants, for interest, rent, and wages, and their margin for profit is
the difference between their *gross sales income* and their *gross current indebtedness,* the latter usually named gross operating and overhead expense.

Satisfactory investigations of the magnitude of the margin for
profit have not been made, but I have calculated, as above,[222] that
between the highest average margin in 1919 and the average *loss*
in such years as 1921 and 1924, for some 60,000 manufacturing
corporations, the medium margin for profit is about 2½ or 3 per
cent of the total sales income.

Supposing it to be 3 per cent, then the cost of production is 97
per cent of the sales income. If so, then one-half of one per cent of
the average *cost of production* would be about 15 per cent of the
average *margin for profit* (net profit). It might be much higher
or much lower for different corporations, or for the same corporation at different times.

Here is where *inducement* lies. The bankability of assets, the
security offered to lenders and bankers, the whole continuity of a
business establishment as a "going concern," turns on this very
narrow margin for profit, and 2 per cent on the payroll is magnified
many-fold when it is taken out of the margin for profit.

Otherwise, why should employers put up so vigorous a resistance,
as they did in Wisconsin, against an insignificant tax of 2 or 3 per
cent on their payrolls? The tax only begins to have significance
for them when they "get down to business," which they, of course,
quickly do, and realize that all of their economies, foresight, efficiency, bargaining, and other efforts to maintain solvency are focused
on this comparatively narrow margin for profit.

I have often wondered why it was that business men in their
arguments against unemployment insurance were apparently so inconsistent on this point of costs. At one time a mere one-half of
one per cent on total costs is argued to be so insignificant that it can
have no effect as an inducement to prevent accidents or unemployment. Then at another time, they argue that the imposition of that
additional cost will put them out of business in competition with
other establishments not burdened with that cost. They certainly
are not irrational, yet they are inconsistent.

Apparently their inconsistency turns on two theories of value, the
classical theory of cost of production and the business man's transactional theory of choice of alternatives in maintaining a margin
for profit. Morton contrasts these two theories and decides in favor
of the classical theory. He says:

[222] Above, p. 526, Margin for Profit.

"What method of comparison should be used to indicate the probable burden and effect of the unemployment levy? . . . Compared to costs, 2 per cent of the payroll is a small amount, about 0.6 per cent, on the average; compared to profits, its size varies, running as high under 'normal' conditions as 25 per cent. Those who estimate the probable effect of the tax by comparing it to profits believe that it will have a strong stabilizing influence. To those who compare it to costs, its effect appears negligible. This writer believes that comparison to profits leads to erroneous views; and he has, therefore, compared the tax to costs of pro duction and to risks."

He goes on to give the classical theory of costs and risks. Against this theory I set up the margin for profit theory which he rejects On the assumption that business men are rational and that their inconsistency is not really such, I proceeded to investigate the reasons for their apparent inconsistency. I found it in the theories which I have elaborated in this book; namely, the theories of Carey, Böhm-Bawerk, and Davenport, regarding the choice of alternatives; the corporation-finance theory of margin for profit; and the theory of strategic and routine transactions derived *volitionally* from the economists' *objective* theory of limiting and complementary factors.

By referring to the formula of a transaction the significance of the Carey and Davenport theories may be inferred.[223] We take it these are the Value theories of business men, as well as of the courts which take their economic theories from business men. When it comes to negotiating each transaction separately from all others, the uppermost immediate thought of business men is not the costs of production [224] but is the immediate alternatives which they are "up against" in the competitive struggle for profits. Hence their Value theories are not the "cost" theories of classical economists but are the "choice" theories of the immediately accessible alternatives open to them. They even will conduct business at a loss, rather than stop altogether, if the only available alternatives compel them to do so.

This choice of alternatives, along with operating business at a loss, is indeed emphasized by Morton in his use of the concept of a going concern. Rather than go out of business they will disregard costs and operate below costs. Costs are not primary; alternatives are primary. The business man usually speaks of these alternatives as the law of demand and supply and opposes this "law" to the classical "costs of production." They say, "We know that we do

[223] Above, p. 59, Formula of Bargaining Transactions.
[224] "Cost of production" is the price agreed upon by seller and buyer which I name "bargaining power" in the formula.

not conduct our business according to costs. We conduct it according to demand." But demand and supply, as we have seen, is simply scarcity of alternatives. And this is what the business man really means, converted into terms of economic theory, when he speaks of his transactions as controlled by demand or supply instead of costs of production. Carey and Bastiat were the first, while Böhm-Bawerk, Green, and Davenport were the next, to reduce this practice of business to a theory of value and cost. We have distinguished the two as dis-opportunity value and opportunity cost. It is an opportunistic theory arising from the abundance or scarcity of alternatives for business men in their two kinds of transactions as buyers and as sellers.[225]

But if costs do not control his transactions, is it expected profit and loss that control them? Profits and loss are the result of his "trading on the equity." The stockholders become debtors to all other participants, whether wage-earners, lenders, bankers, bondholders, preferred stockholders, material men. Their margin for profit is the difference between prices received for output and the debts incurred to other participants. It is this margin that we estimate to be, on the average, about 3 per cent of sales prices. And as an inducement to prevent accidents, one-half of one per cent on the total costs of production, is, on the average, 30 times as great if deducted from the margin for profit.

But here enters the third factor which we name strategic and routine transactions. The classical theory of costs is either a static theory or a theory of long-time trend of costs. By the former we mean that *all* the transactions are looked upon as *occurring at the same point of time*. By the latter we mean that the arithmetic results of all transactions are added together to get the *total costs over a period of time*.

But the transactional theory is the *transactions themselves*. Each transaction occupies a more or less brief point of time when the negotiations ending in the transaction are actually in process. It is a behavioristic theory of the way in which the business man conducts his multitude of variable transactions, at *successive points of time*, with the very different wage-earners, material men, lenders, and others. Each transaction, *at the time* when it is negotiated, is for him, at that time, the *strategic factor* to which he devotes his entire concentrated attention, in consideration of the actual alternatives open to him at that time and in that transaction. All the other future or past transactions are complementary, for the time being. They are the routine environment within which the then

<hr/>

[225] Above, p. 301, Ability and Opportunity.

strategic transaction is negotiated. Then, afterwards, another transaction, which was, at the time, a future but contributory transaction, becomes the strategic one, and the former strategic transactions now become, at the succeeding points of time, a routine matter, not immediately attended to.

Looking towards the past, a strategic transaction, when once consummated, becomes thereafter a matter of "routine" if it is continuously repeated, so that, instead of the terms "strategic" and "contributory," we have used the terms, "strategic and routine transactions."

The difference between the foregoing classical static or long-time method of looking at the margin for profit and the strategic and routine method may be seen in one of Morton's illustrations. He says,

> "Taxes, insurance, accounting costs, may each be a large part of net profit [margin for profit] but a small part of costs. To say that each of these items takes 25, 50, or 100 per cent of net profits gives an erroneous view both of their importance and of their incidence. From this type of reasoning, the notion now current arises that taxes are destroying all profits and consequently the incentive to produce. The same argument might be made regarding any single item of expense. Such items are a part of costs which the producer must try to shift."

This reasoning is undoubtedly correct from the static or long-time standpoint of the classical economists. It renders absurd the idea that *all* of the items of cost—taxes, insurance, wages, materials, etc.—can be added together in any computation of the margin for profit in a single transaction. This has already been noticed in our discussion of the margin for profit. What we named the profit and loss margin [226] is, indeed, a summation of all transactions, for periods of one year, but it necessarily omits from the exhibit each individual transaction which was a minor part of the total.

The same is true of our distinction between the "financial margin" as the margin for interest *after* taxes are paid; and the "taxable margin" as the margin for taxes *after* interest is paid; and so on for the other margins not there attended to, such as the wage margin for profit after all other expenses are considered routine.

Evidently these various margins are not cumulative in any one transaction. Each transaction has its own alternatives. The transaction which is uppermost, or strategic, consists in the particular negotiations regarding some one factor, in so far as it alone affects the margin for profit; *after* all routine or contributory transactions

[226] Above, p. 568, Profit and Loss Margin.

are eliminated from consideration at the time. If the whole series of transactions is summed up over a period of time—say a year as in our Profit and Loss Margin—it is as a statistical result for the period but is not the transactions themselves. The latter, if strategic, must be treated each as a single negotiation at the time when it actually occurs.

This is one of the well-known illusions of statistics. The individual is lost in the statistical summation.[227] But the individual transaction is the actual behavior. At one time when the individual is resisting taxation, he may say that while taxes are only 1 or 2 per cent of his costs of production, yet they are 40 or 50 per cent of his net profits *after* all other debts are paid. At another time when he is resisting unemployment or accident insurance, he may say, and does say, that while the rate is only 1 per cent of his costs of production yet it is, say, 30 per cent of his margin for profit. He makes the similar argument when he is negotiating the wage bargain, or the interest bargain, or the rent bargain. Each of those bargains is strategic for him *at the time* when he is negotiating it. Having once finished that negotiation, its repetition becomes a mere routine, or contributory, transaction, and therefore not, at that time, attended to.

From the standpoint of static economics which he instinctively rejects, his logic is absurd. But from the standpoint of the dynamic *time* factor involved in the succession of transactions, at the successive times when he is successively negotiating them, he is not absurd. He is just as rational as any finite being who cannot do everything at once, but must devote his finite ability to that one factor, which, at the time, is, for him, even though he may be mistaken, the then strategic or limiting factor. Here he is forced to consider, in that strategic transaction, the alternatives which he is "up against" for that single transaction, and he instinctively rejects an "academic" theory that practically treats him as an infinite being capable of making all his transactions at a single instant of time.[228]

This may seem inconsistent with the recent emphasis placed on "cost accounting." This cost accounting is something set up for the business man by statisticians and accountants as a guide to his transactions or a "talking point" in his negotiations. But he knows that, in his individual transactions, he cannot be bound by it. At that point of time he knows that he is bound by his alternative opportunities, his alternative dis-opportunities, and his then

[227] Above, p. 267, Averages.
[228] Above, p. 317, Inaccessible Options.

bargaining power. The relation between these three is pictured in our formula of a transaction.

It is in this way that we should treat the problem of "risk." Morton rightly connects, as did the classical economists, the risks of a business with the cost of production. But I make risk far more important than did the older theories. If the margin of profit averages only about 3 per cent on sales, and if costs of production are therefore 97 per cent of sales, then risk is 33 times as important in its effect on the margin for profit as it is on the costs of production. But these margins are highly variable in the multitude of variable transactions. Each transaction has its own risks and these must be commuted in the prices and quantities negotiated in that particular transaction.[229]

All of these various risks over a period of time are not cumulative in each transaction. They pile up on the strategic transaction at the time when it is negotiated, and the risk may be so great, in that one transaction, that all of the routine transactions are suspended, and the business stops until that one can be negotiated. If the risk is very great, as it sometimes is in borrowing and lending negotiations on account of expected falling prices, then a much higher margin for profit must be in sight than if the expected risk is slight.

Risk, then, becomes the whole problem of "confidence" or "lack of confidence," many-fold more important when compared with the margin for profit than when compared with the costs of production.

For this reason it certainly must be conceded, and, indeed, was taken into account in all the arguments and pleadings, that the 2 per cent premium on payrolls has a widely different pressure, at different times, in different transactions, and in different establishments, towards prevention of accidents or unemployment. In the extremes of great prosperity when the margins are high, and in periods of great depression when the margins are low, the effect is probably less than in "normal" periods. In such extreme periods other factors are relatively more strategic, and accident or unemployment prevention is less strategic. Nevertheless the pressure of the 2 per cent premium is always there, whether it be strategic or routine. Many accommodations and concessions were, however, made in the bill, and others will doubtless be made by the administrative bargaining, to take care of these variable risks.

It must be noted that the bill was, of course, limited to the state of Wisconsin. The taxpayers of that state were not in position to prevent unemployment because, as such, they were not in control

[229] Above, p. 429, Discount and Profit; p. 555, The Business Law of Supply and Demand.

of individual establishments. Arguments were made, as are now repeated by Morton, that the whole nation, and indeed the whole world, was responsible for unemployment, more than individual employers. Therefore the nation should bear the burden of relief.

The answer to this was made in the hearings that when enough states had adopted similar legislation, then they would have enough political influence to induce Congress, as had occurred in the assumption of several other social responsibilities,[230] to subsidize the states in proportion to the amount of benefits paid within each state. Especially in times of depression these national subsidies might be very large, an argument for which concrete evidence was brought in the Federal Relief Administration, and the National Industrial Recovery Acts (N. R. A.). It was also argued that the national government could accept responsibility for unemployment only in so far as its monetary and credit policies were responsible for unemployment. Its method of meeting this responsibility must be a national or world-wide stabilization of prices.[231]

A parallel argument was made respecting contributions of employees to the establishment funds, which Morton advocates. Here it was maintained, in reply, that the employees, like the taxpayers, were not in position to prevent unemployment. They could only contribute to relief. Hence nothing was definitely said in the Act about employee contributions. It might be assumed that the "open shop" employers would require their unorganized employees to contribute, since this was a part of their common-law rights in negotiating their labor contracts. And it might be assumed that, in organized "union" shops, the unions, as in the Chicago system, would require their members to contribute. Their contributions would extend the *relief* which wage-earners emphasize.

Thus Morton's requirement of a three-party contribution in order to enforce "social responsibility" was fully considered in the negotiations leading up to the act. But the social responsibility was left to future voluntary acts (in the legal sense of voluntary) of employees and the federal government, based on forecasting of what might be expected through voluntary collective action.

Finally we notice a confusion of the taxing power with the police power whose relationship we have previously considered in one of its aspects.[232] Morton continously argues that the insurance premium is a *tax* on the employer. If so, then it contradicts, as he contends, Adam Smith's maxim that taxes should be apportioned

[230] Such as education, vocational education, highways, etc.
[231] Above, p. 590, World Pay Community.
[232] Above, p. 805, The Police Power of Taxation.

according to "ability to pay." This maxim he finds is adopted in the European systems of unemployment insurance. There the premiums paid by employers are proportionate to the number of weeks in the year during which the laborers are employed. This is apparently proportionate to the prosperity and ability to pay of the employer. For example, an employer whose business is so prosperous and stabilized that he furnishes 52 weeks of employment pays twice as much tax as his competitor (with the same number of employees) who furnishes only 26 weeks of employment. As a *tax* the payments are in proportion to ability to pay, as evidenced by continuous operation of the plant.

But in the Wisconsin law the payments vary *inversely* to ability to pay. The employer who furnishes 52 weeks of employment pays no premiums or benefits whatever, but the one who furnishes only 26 weeks of employment pays 26 premiums on his payroll. This is of course a "regressive tax" increasing with a decreasing ability to pay.

But if we examine the matter closely this is characteristic of the way in which the "police power" works in the American System, distinguished from the taxing power, as such. The police power brings the heaviest pressure upon those who are *least socially minded*, while those who are *most* socially minded are not touched, because they voluntarily do for the common welfare what the others must be forced to do, or go out of business. In this case "socially minded" means ability and willingness to furnish steady employment throughout the years. The taxing power may, indeed, be used to have this police-power effect, as in customs taxes, luxury taxes, or as we have suggested, in placing a burden on those who get an unearned increment by exempting those who get rich by making others rich.

Hence if the Wisconsin Act is called a taxation measure, then it is the use of the term "taxing power," not to support government, but in order to induce those who have no social sense or personal ability, to accept social responsibility regarding unemployment, and to come up towards the level of those who feel bound by a social responsibility to relieve and prevent unemployment or else go out of business. Such a measure, in the constitutional use of the term in the United States, is a use of the police power and not the taxing power. It is not based on ability to pay in support of government; it is based on inducements to stabilize employment.[233]

[233] For further discussion of this subject see: Forsberg, A. B., *Selected Articles on Unemployment Insurance* (1926); Stewart, Bryce, *Unemployment Benefits in the United States* (Industrial Relations Counselors, 1930); my testimony in *Unemployment in the United*

7. *Personality and Collective Action* [234]

The theory of reasonable value may be summarized, in its pragmatic application, as a theory of social progress by means of personality controlled, liberated, and expanded by collective action. It is not individualism, it is institutionalized personality. Its tacit or habitual assumptions are the continuance of the capitalist system based on private property and profits. It is fitted to a Malthusian concept of human nature, starting from the passion, stupidity, and ignorance whereby mankind does the opposite of what reason and rationality would prescribe, and ending in an admiration for the individual who, by initiative, persistence, taking risks, and assuming obligations to others, rises to leadership.

Unregulated profit-seeking drags the conscientious down towards the level of the least conscientious; yet a considerable minority is always above that level, no matter how high it may have been raised by collective action. These indicate the possibility of progress.

The problem, then, is the limited one of investigating the working rules of collective action which bring reluctant individuals up to, not an impracticable ideal, but a reasonable idealism, because it is already demonstrated to be practicable by the progressive minority under existing conditions.

The various voluntary and political movements in the United States throughout the past hundred years do not eliminate the motive of self-interest. They reveal its limitations. Self-interest is always there. The accident compensation laws are estimated to return to wage-earners less than 30 per cent of their lost wages. They impose an onerous responsibility on wage-earners, and they add only about one-half of one per cent to the sales price to be shifted to consumers, or absorbed by greater efficiency of management. Trade unions lift a small proportion of wage-earners above the level of the mass, but they create a higher personality because relieved of fear. Farmers' coöperatives succeed only in small areas, small countries, and for small proportions of the agricultural classes, but they elevate their members to a higher sense of responsibility for each other. Monetary, economic, and price stabilization movements are disappointing in a world of war and economic conflict, but they lift individuals towards a higher sense of personal responsibility for prevention of conflicts.

The reasons for the limitation of collective action are historically

States, Hearings, Senate Committee on Education and Labor, S. Res. 219 (1929), 212–236; Douglas, Paul H., *Standards of Unemployment Insurance* (University of Chicago Press, 1933).

[234] Cf. Kallen, Horace M., *Individualism an American Way of Life* (1933).

evident: the resistance of conflicting social classes; the internal politics, factions, jealousies, and lack of leadership within the concern; the traditions and habits of the masses who prefer the evils that are customary to the uncertainties of experimentation; the reactions that therefore follow upon brief successes.

If the profit-motive, in the field of economics, can be enlisted in the program of social welfare, then a dynamic factor, more constructive than all others, is enlisted. It is an appeal to the business man to get rich by making others rich, and, if he does not respond, then to appeal to collective action.

This leads us to a comparison of the three grand experiments—Communism, Fascism, and Capitalism—which, since the recent World War, have made dramatic both the hitherto conflicting theories of economists and the different kinds of collective action on a nation-wide scale, which enlarge or suppress individuality.

CHAPTER XI

COMMUNISM, FASCISM, CAPITALISM [1]

Since the World War three systems of political economy have come to the front, the Communism of Russia, the Fascism of Italy and Germany, the Banker Capitalism of the United States. They may be compared from three standpoints: economic theory, social philosophy, and world history. The economic theories are demand and supply, cost of production, marginal productivity, satisfaction of wants. The social philosophies are human nature and the ultimate goal towards which they aim. The world history is the actual changes from the world war of the French Revolution, which lasted twenty-five years, to the world war of forty revolutions in the midst of which we now are. These three points of view are inseparable, and it is the- attempt to combine them that is coming to be known as Institutional Economics.

They begin with the individualism of Adam Smith and the French Revolution. Smith propounded the doctrines which that Revolution put into effect. They were an attack against corporations and guilds, against landlords, and against special privileges created by government. The French Revolution abolished corporations, divided the property of landlords and proclaimed the equality, liberty, and private property of all individuals uncontrolled by either the state or the guilds and corporations which held their franchises from the state.

Smith had substituted for mercantilism the economic law of supply and demand and the political law of property, equality, and liberty. The only control needed over individuals was the wants of consumers. Orthodox economists followed Smith for more than a hundred years, first as the classical economists, basing their theories on the labor-cost of production; then as the psychological economists, basing their theories on the wants of consumers. Both schools may be named the automatic equilibrium economists, basing their deductions on analogies taken over from the physical sciences, which.

[1] This chapter is partly anticipated in my article, "Marx Today, Capitalism and Socialism," *Atlantic Monthly*, August 1925; see my article "The Labor Movement" in the *Encyclopaedia of the Social Sciences*. Nazism is too recent to be included. It is German Fascism. For a competent analysis of Nazism by an economist on the ground at the time of the Revolution see Hoover, C. B., *Germany Enters the Third Reich* (1933).

in this case, becomes the equilibrium of supply and demand among individuals who are free, equal, molecular, and mobile. But it turns out that economic theory must be based on history as well as equilibrium.

Back of this automatic balancing was a philosophy of human nature. Adam Smith's philosophy was theological. Man was an intellectual being guided by divine reason. This divine reason was a benevolent Providence which would bring abundance to the whole world if only man, by the collective action of politics and corporations, would not restrain and coerce individuals. The French Revolution abolished corporations and landlords, and enthroned a goddess of reason.

But soon came disillusionment. Thomas Malthus foretold it in the midst of the Revolution. Man is not a rational being—he is a being of passion and stupidity, who does quite the opposite of what his reason tells him to do. He therefore cannot be left free but must be coerced by government.

After the battle of Waterloo the foretold disillusionment arrived. A world-wide depression of trade, for thirty years, with poverty and unemployment, ended again in the revolutions of 1848. Karl Marx now came forth with his Communist Manifesto. He revised Ricardo's labor theory of value and expanded its materialistic philosophy into class struggle. If labor alone created value, as Ricardo's theory seemed to hold, then labor should have the whole product, not however as individual laborers but as social labor-power by means of the dictatorship of the proletariat. The "laws" of supply and demand, of property, equality, and liberty, were abolished altogether, and in their place was substituted class war and the irrepressible conflict of capital and labor. This philosophy ended in the Russian Revolution, with Marx's faith in a class-less society thereafter.

Meanwhile Smith's individualism took a different turn—towards anarchism. It is this philosophy that ends eventually in the Fascist Revolution of Italy. The first anarchist, William Godwin, in 1793, would carry Smith and the French Revolution forward to the abolition, not only of corporations and landlords, but also to the abolition of the State itself, which was the source of all coercion over the individual. It was in answer to Godwin that Malthus propounded his philosophy of passion and stupidity.

Then, in the miserable decade of the 1840's, Godwin's successor, Proudhon, in his debates with Karl Marx, set up the absolute right of the individual to private property as against the state and against all collective property. Individuals might form voluntary associations, but in doing so the corporation would not acquire the individual's property, but the individual could leave at any time, without penalty for violation of contract, taking his property with him.

Proudhon's illusion of voluntary associations soon showed itself also to be impossible. The modern stock corporation began, in the 1850's, to take shape and to become a legal entity, based on enforceable contracts, owning the means of production, displacing the individual owner, and eventually employing propertyless laborers by the thousands in a single concern. So the next stage of revolutionary anarchism was revolutionary syndicalism, whose philosopher was Georges Sorel in France at the beginning of the Twentieth Century.

Sorel took over from Marx his doctrine of class war and the inevitable destruction of capitalism, but he changed it from taking possession of the state by dictatorship to taking possession of the factories by labor unions and the general strike. This was what happened in Italy after the World War. The laborers began to take possession of the factories, and the peasants of landed estates. The general strike paralyzed whole cities, as well as the railways and telegraphs. Syndicalism became organized anarchism and disorganized communism. It broke down by inability to get either raw materials from capitalists or credit from bankers, and, most of all, by the rise of organized strike-breakers, the Fascisti.

Here is something that Karl Marx had overlooked in his materialistic philosophy of history. He had correctly foretold the inevitable tendency of free competition and prolonged depressions to destroy the individual producer by consolidating the ownership of capital in the hands of a few and reducing the former independent individuals to wage-earners employed by them. But he had assumed that capitalism would then fall by its own incapacity, and that the mass of wage-earners would simply take possession by mere weight of numbers.

He had overlooked the possibility that the wage-earners themselves might split into two classes, the intellectuals and the manuals, the white-collars and the factory workers, the salary workers and the wage-workers, and that the real struggle for control of his decadent capitalism might be a struggle between these two classes, each of which depended upon his incompetent capitalists for their bread and butter. He counted too much also on the inevitable destruction of the small property-owners, mainly the farmers, his *petite bourgeoisie*, who afterwards showed great power of organized assistance.

This was what happened in Russia and Italy. It turned not on mere numbers. It turned on political leadership and ability to organize a fighting minority. The leadership was Lenin and Mussolini. The fighting organization was the Red Army and the Black Shirts. The method in both cases was the organization of violence —which is murder if it does not succeed and the State if it does succeed.

Lenin won out by his battle-cry, "All power to the Soviets," Mussolini by "All power to the Fascisti." The Soviets were what we know as central labor unions or federations of labor in the leading cities, representing the local trade unions of wage-earners. They became in Russia the armed workers returned from the wars. The intellectuals, as a class, were excluded from the Soviets.

The Fascisti were at first also returned soldiers, like the American Legion, also unemployed and looking for jobs. Then they were joined by professors and students from the high schools and universities; then by the white collar men from the offices; then by the small business men in the villages and cities; then by intellectuals from the various professions; then by sons of capitalists and landlords; then by ex-officers from the army. Ultimately all university professors were compelled to take the oath to support the Fascist régime. From the very beginning Mussolini was financed by funds contributed by manufacturers, bankers, and landlords. Eventually these became the unseen rulers of Fascism.

A similar line-up has been emerging in Germany. The Fascist party in that country is the office workers, the young men from the schools and universities, the small business men, the former owners of property who find their savings lost by inflation and themselves now unemployed and seeking jobs, like the manual workers. Hitler was also financed by bankers, manufacturers, and landlords, and he placed the unemployed military officers of the old régime at the head of his local units. We see, even in England, the beginning of a Fascist party. The Fascisti and the Soviets are indeed the two classes of salaried workers and wage-workers under modern capitalism, hating each other but both dependent on capitalists for their jobs.

When things settle down somewhat, we find, in Russia and Italy, the two dictators, Stalin and Mussolini, depending for their control over government on the loyalty to them of a fighting minority of one or the other of these two opposed classes. In Russia the manual laborers are supreme and have the better food, shelter, clothing, hospitals, and places at the theatres. The professors, engineers, scientists, technicians, experts, artists, actors, lawyers, office workers, and former capitalists are subordinate and have the worst places or no place at all, and are gradually starved, exiled, or killed.

In Italy it is the opposite. The loyalty of the Fascisti is maintained by preferences in the political jobs, by preferences at the public employment offices for private jobs, and all others who show their heads obstreporously are suppressed, killed, or sent to the island prisons. In neither Russia nor Italy is there trial by jury of peers nor an independent judiciary, nor a legislature. Every punishment is meted out by administrative process dependent on a hierarchy of officials, and judges appointed and removed at the will of the executive head of the government. There are, of course, no political parties—there is only one party, the Communist party or the Fascist party, each a mere fraction of the total population, but armed with clubs, revolvers, and other instruments of violence. Even the leaders of these parties are appointed and removed by the dictator.

Although Karl Marx was correct in his materialistic interpretation of history and in the ultimate elimination of free competition and individual liberty, yet he was incorrect in his interpretation of the class war. There is not one class or two classes, there are many classes, and whether the outcome shall be communism, or fascism, or capitalism, depends on personality, leadership, and ability to organize a militant minority.

Marx was even more nearly correct for the United States than he was for Russia or Italy. These countries were still mainly agricultural, and had by no means yet reached the capitalistic stage of industry and banking, with a few capitalists employing millions of wage-earners. In Russia the amazing Five-Year Plan attempts forcibly to convert a nation of peasants into a nation of wage-workers, and to accomplish in five or ten years what Marx supposed free competition would do in the indefinite future, perhaps a hundred years.

For America his prediction is more nearly correct. A hundred years ago nine-tenths of the American population were farmers and farmers' families. Today scarcely one-fifth are farmers, and the other four-fifths have moved over to the cities and villages where they become either the wage-earners and salaried workers employed mainly by corporations, or the small fascistic business men. It is even now estimated that, if agriculture would adopt the best machinery and chemistry already well known, then only 10 per cent of the population would be needed on the farms to feed and clothe the whole population, and the farmers, especially since the war, are rapidly squeezed down towards that 10 per cent. Agricultural machinery, chemistry, and concentration on the more fertile soils are doing for agriculture what mechanical power has done for industry and manufactures—converting the farms into capitalistic organizations operated by hired laborers or leased to peasants by a kind of annual piece-work system. The chain stores and chain banks are doing the same for the small business men and are converting them into white-collared wage-earners employed by huge corporations. A similar chain-farm system can already be seen in the foreclosures, since 1929, by insurance companies and the operation of scattered farms by a central organization. Already nine-tenths of the manufacturing of the nation is in the hands of corporations.[2] Automatically and by the force of free competition that former nine-tenths of the population who, a hundred years ago, were the small proprietors and the bulwark of American individualism, are becoming another nine-tenths who are wage-earners and salaried workers, the foundations of Communism or Fascism. Individualism becomes corporationism. Private property becomes corporate property. The remaining small proportion of farmers become revolutionists by defying the courts and sheriffs in their attempts to foreclose mortgages.

America clings to the traditions of colonial individualism, though its economic foundations are going. In the first fifty years of the republic there were scarcely any corporations except those which received special charters by act of legislature. All corporations were then looked upon as monopolies. The anti-monopoly movements of the time were anti-corporation movements. They were indeed legal monopolies because each was created by a special act of the legislature. In order to get a charter of incorporation the business men had to align themselves with the politicians. When the Whigs were in power only Whig lobbyists could get charters. When Democrats were in power only Democratic lobbyists could get charters. The political boss emerged as the go-between, controlling both parties on behalf of the capitalists.

Then, beginning with New York in 1848, in order, not to favor capitalism, but to get rid of political corruption, the legislature enacted general corporation laws whereby a charter was granted to any association by merely filing articles with the Secretary of State. Instead of abolishing corporations the legislatures made them universal. They were no longer monopolies—they were competitors. They established a new right of business men—the right of association. This new right is the beginning of modern capitalism. Capitalism begins, not with Adam Smith, but with going concerns.

The anti-monopoly legislation then took a different turn, culminating in the anti-trust laws of forty years ago. Every com-

[2] Above, p. 526, Margin for Profit.

bination, whether of corporations or individuals, in restraint of trade was illegal.

Then came a new discovery, thirty years ago, the holding company, invented by the corporation lawyers to evade the anti-trust laws, and enacted first by the legislature of New Jersey. It was not altogether new, for corporations could always own the stocks and bonds of other corporations. Its novelty consisted in creating corporations solely or mainly for the purpose of owning and voting the stocks of other corporations. Other states competed with New Jersey for this profitable business.

Almost unlimited powers were granted to the holding companies, and they had all the privileges in other states which they had in their own state. The only restraint upon them now became the Supreme Court of the United States. The court dissolved two of them twenty years ago—the Standard Oil and the Tobacco Company. But fifteen years ago, in the Shoe Machinery and Steel Dissolution suits, the Supreme Court sustained the holding companies under the new rule of reasonable restraint of trade—that is, the restraint that seems reasonable to the majority of the court. These holding companies became the culmination of banker capitalism, "now becoming more powerful than the government itself." [3]

With this development of Judicial Sovereignty, it is the corporation which legalizes Karl Marx's materialistic interpretation of history. But instead of bringing in the Communist or Fascist dictatorship by abolishing the judiciary, it is done by the supremacy of the judiciary over all state and federal legislatures and executives. It is the United States Supreme Court that now defines what is property, while those who naïvely read the Constitution literally assume that the definition of property is left to the states. Where Communism and Fascism abolished legislatures and courts by substituting decrees of the executive branch of government, the American system subordinates executives and legislatures to the decrees of the United States Supreme Court. The Federal Court becomes the American brand of dictatorship.

This is American Capitalism—not the Executive Sovereignty of Communism and Fascism since the revolutions of the World War; nor the legislative sovereignty of England since 1689; but the Judicial Sovereignty of the Supreme Court since 1900. Its executive instrument is not the decree of a dictator; it is the injunction of a court.

There are other contrasts of the American with the European systems. We cannot be quite certain of what is going on in Russia

[3] Bonbright, J. C., and Means, G. C., The Holding Company (1932), 339.

and Italy, because the opposition newspapers have been suppressed; private associations have been prohibited; the universities have been forbidden free investigation and teaching; and the official statistics are prevaricated. But we can make some broad comparisons.

The word "syndicalism" comes from the French, meaning simply "unionism." A union of employers or bankers is an employers' syndicate or a bankers' syndicate. A trade union is a labor syndicate. But history has changed the meaning of the word syndicate. In American it means the revolutionary syndicalism of Sorel, bent on overthrowing private property and government. In Italy it has come to mean patriotic syndicalism, organized by the government to support private property and the supremacy of the dictator.

There are, in Italy, four main classes of syndicates, the capitalist syndicates, the agricultural syndicates, the labor syndicates, and the professional syndicates. In order to carry on business or get a job each individual is compelled to become a member or at least pay dues to support his syndicate. They make rules and regulations fixing wages and even output, which are binding on non-members as well as members. They are organized on a local, a regional, and a national basis. Their officers and decrees must be approved by the dictator. The national syndicates now are known as National Fascist Federations. Recently they have been reorganized under the name of Corporations, which include, among others, the two opposing Federations of Employers and Employees, and we have a Corporate State, a window-dressing for dictatorship.

It is these compulsory corporations that have taken the place of parliament. They are both political and economic. It is as though the President of the United States should abolish all elections, all legislatures, and all political parties; should hold his position permanently by his control of the Fascist party which is not a party but is the police arm of the government; should then abolish the positions of Secretary of Commerce and Secretary of Labor and make himself the sole minister of corporations; should prohibit all strikes and lockouts by substituting compulsory arbitration; should bring these corporations together and in conference with them make all the laws governing industry, agriculture, and labor; but instead of statutes and a judiciary, should issue these laws as decrees of the executive head of the government, to be enforced by the administrative process of the Fascist party.

Such a transition is not inconceivable and indeed is already somewhat familiar in the American system of government. Under the Constitution a declaration of war converts the American government overnight into a dictatorship. The suspension of *habeas corpus* by the executive abrogates the judiciary. The creation of a War Industries Board, a Grain Corporation, a Shipping Board, a War Finance Corporation, is a Ministry of Corporations appointed by the Dictator. The corporations and federations appear before the Ministry as advisory bodies, representing, not individuals, but economic interests. Congress abdicates temporarily, but the reconstruction period after our Civil War shows how the President can control the elections; the Ku Klux Klan, the corporation dictatorships, and the manufacturers' and merchants' associations indicate how the local and state elections can be controlled. We already have the technique of Fascism, and Mussolini enlarges it only by instituting a permanent state of war for the sake of the unity of the Italian nation in its struggle against all other nations. The shift, in the minds of the dominant interests, is the shift from class struggle within a nation to world struggle between nations.

Russia, too, abolishes the class struggle within the nation. This is, curiously, the social philosophy of Communism. The dictatorship of the proletariat is held to be only a transitional period, to continue only as long as necessary to eliminate the profit-psychology from the minds of the people. It will be eliminated, they philosophize, when all have become wage-earners, and no one can hope to live on interest, rents, or profits. The Five-Year Plan is a magnificent venture, not only to bring Russia up to the technological level of America by the aid of foreign engineers, but also, at the same time, to change the psychology of the people from a profit, rent, and interest psychology to a wage psychology. When that is accomplished, then the dictatorship will disappear in a grand coöperative commonwealth of workers.

But by the force of circumstance and the resistance of Capitalism and Fascism in other countries the early philosophy of Marx and Lenin, which looked forward to an international class struggle of the proletariat, has been abandoned, and Russia asks now only for world-wide peace and opportunity to build her own national commonwealth. Communism becomes Nationalism.

In both Italy and Russia the former voluntary trade unions and coöperatives have been suppressed by the very simple device of appointing their officers and enforcing the appointments by the Fascist party or the Communist party. In Italy they become a part of the National Fascist Corporations. In Russia the unions are the workers' committees which give orders to the factory managers, while the coöperatives are simply the buying and selling agencies of the government.

It must not be supposed that, in Italy, the Fascist dictatorship is a dictatorship of big business. It may be, in harmony with Pareto's "demagogic plutocracy," because big bankers, manufacturers, and landlords furnish the funds. But it is apparently a dictatorship of small business, small property-owners, and salaried and professional workers. The parallel in America is the difference between the National Association of Manufacturers and such big corporations as the Standard Oil, the United States Steel, the General Electric, the General Motors, the Chase National Bank. There are about 60,000 manufacturing corporations in the United States, producing nine-tenths of the manufactured products, but it may be estimated that less than 200 of them are what we call big business. The other 59,000 are the relatively small manufacturers. A thirty million dollar corporation is now little business when its only competitor is a three hundred million dollar holding company. So in the fields of merchandizing and banking. There are relatively few great merchandizing and banking corporations, like Sears-Roebuck, the chain stores, or the Chase National Bank and its affiliates. The great majority are the small merchants, business men, and bankers in the thousands of towns, villages, and cities. And they do a relatively small part of the business.

In Italy it is these small business men who seem to have come into control of the Fascist corporations, for Mussolini gestures to big business that its big leaders, like our Rockefellers, Morgans, and Kuhn-Loebs, will go to the prison islands the same as our William Greens, Matthew Wolls, and Norman Thomases. We put Sinclair in jail for 90 days for contempt of court, and he comes out with greater prestige and greater confidence of his associates than when he went in, simply because he refused to testify against them. Fascism proposes to keep him there indefinitely.

The parallel also in America is between the farmers and the farm laborers. Fascism is the party which includes the farm owners. It is as though the Farmers' Union, the Farm Bureau Federations, and all the farmers' coöperatives of the United States should become the National Fascist Federation of Agriculture along with the National Fascist Federations of manufacturers and bankers. In short, Fascism is the dictatorship of business men, bankers, and farm owners.

As for the small business men and farmers in all countries, they are between the upper and nether millstone of modern technology and business depressions. On the one side big business is absorbing or controlling their markets. On the other side wage-earners are demanding higher wages and shorter hours. Big business can pay high wages, and it is only a matter of policy whether they cut wages or keep them high. They are, as it were, on a non-competitive level. But small business and farmers are compelled to cut wages, in periods of depression, or else see their property absorbed still more by big business through foreclosures or distress sales. The conflict is irrepressible. It may be seen in the efforts to form a progressive party, or a third party in America. Small business men, farmers, and organizations of wage-earners have supported these movements, but when it comes to the matter of wages and hours of labor or other labor legislation, the farmers resist and the party splits. Fascist Italy solves it by dictatorship of business men and landowners, by prohibition of strikes and lockouts, by compulsory fixation of wages and hours of labor, by decrees of the dictator.

But the fundamental contrast between the European and American systems is the contrast of poverty with abundance, of low standards of living with high standards of living. It is out of the latter that American Banker Capitalism emerges. It is this difference that makes unemployment a menace of revolution in Europe and only a menace of overproduction in America. A nation of wage-earners, like Germany or England, already on the verge of hunger even when fully employed, must support its workers in idleness by taxation when unemployed, else a civil war that ends in Communism or Fascism. Already European nations have been plunging towards this disaster. France, Switzerland, and the Scandinavian countries are least in danger. France still remains a peasant nation, and though the peasants may be poor they are not unemployed. Their farms feed them when industry collapses. In America, formerly, the wage-earners could take up free land, or return to their families on the farms when capitalistic industry collapsed. But now, with the incoming of capitalistic agriculture and the distress of the farmers themselves, the farms are less and less a refuge for the unemployed. The farmers dread too many farmers, just as the capitalists dread overproduction. With a nation becoming nine-tenths wage-earners and salaried workers, and farmers defying the sheriffs, unemployment and distress may become more of a menace than overproduction.

Italy's syndicalism meets the menace heroically. The dictator declares a flat reduction of 12 per cent in wages and salaries throughout the nation, in order that business may have a margin for profit and give employment to the unemployed. Russian dictatorship meets it in the other direction even more drastically. Owning all the manufacturing, marketing, and banking agencies, Russia pays low prices to peasants and coöperatives as sellers and charges high prices to the same peasants and workers as buyers, and, by means of the margin between the two, creates a fund of capital without borrowing, to employ the wage-earners in the construction of huge physical capital. Saving is compulsory saving, by keeping down prices of raw material and keeping up prices of retail goods. They have no unemployment, though they have poverty.

But capitalistic America without unemployment insurance or doles, has heretofore simply waited until starvation forced the laborers to accept lower wages before starting up industry again and employing the unemployed. The standards of living were doubtless lowered, but, by voluntary doles, they still remain above the poverty levels of Europe. Only within the past year has a National Recovery administration endeavored to keep up wages.

Building upon these higher standards of living, American capitalism has controverted the predictions of decadence uttered by Karl Marx. Partly by what may be named self-recovery and partly by forced recovery, capitalism is reaching a period of integration which apparently is strengthening the system more than ever before. Marx rightly predicted the concentration of capital, which we name big business. But he did not foresee the deconcentration of ownership made possible by corporations and high standards of living. The general incorporation laws have diffused the ownership of capital while promoting its concentration. Great corporations are discovering how important is this diffusion of ownership, both politically for its influence on the elections and economically for the augmentation of capital itself. They consciously distribute their stocks and bonds in the hands of thousands of investors, and they consciously endeavor to stabilize dividends where formerly "insiders" employed the new device of corporations to exploit investors just as they exploited the laborers. Recently the president of the United States Chamber of Commerce estimated that there are fifty-five million savings accounts, sixty-five million insurance policies and five million stockholders in corporate ownership. One corporation, the American Telegraph and Telephone Company, whose rates are regulated by commissions supposed to represent the consumers, reports more than 700,000 stockholders.

This extension of ownership may be named the extension of Investors' Good-Will, and it is this that has interested millions of Americans in the preservation of big Capitalism, while their own petty capitalism is being held up and effaced.

But capitalism has needed legislation for this purpose. Corporate charters are acts of the legislature, giving the sovereign privileges of unity, immortality, and limited liability. It is largely by state legislation, such as public utility laws, "blue sky" laws regulating the issue and sale of stocks and bonds, and similar laws that may be suggested, that well-meaning capitalists have been protected in the main safeguard of capitalism, the confidence of millions of investors. It must be said, however, that since 1929 investors' good-will has been shattered, and a federal blue sky law has already been enacted. This legislation is forced recovery coming to the aid of self-recovery.

Another use of forced recovery is labor legislation. It has only been during the past thirty years that labor legislation has begun to be effective and the Supreme Court of the United States has permitted it to be extended and enforced. The court has lagged behind in important cases, influenced by the social philosophy of business and farmers; but big business is really more sensitive because it does not have the votes. The unexpected outcome has been that labor legislation and public opinion are more easily enforced on big business than they are on little business. The United States Steel Corporation defeated the eight-hour strike and then announced the installation of the eight-hour day on the terrified petition of politicians. Little business is not as sensitive, because it has the votes and does not have the profits. The General Electric Company installs unemployment insurance without waiting to be coerced by legislation. Other corporations have preceded or are following the General Electric. Perhaps, after all, big business will capture the good-will of labor while in the process of squeezing little business and the farmer.

Another forced recovery of Capitalism is trade unionism. American trade unionists have been only 15 per cent of the wage-earners, while European trade unions have been 60 to 70 per cent of the wage-earners. Yet American unionism is more powerful than European unionism. It raises the wages of its members two or three times as high as the wages of unorganized laborers, and even higher than the earnings of small farmers, whereas in Europe there is much less difference betwen the wages of the organized and the unorganized. While little business and farmers, pressed by competition, are unable to pay these wages, big business is learning that the easiest way to keep out unionism is, as they say, to "beat them to it." They are learning to do as much or more for their employees than the unions can do for them. They organize their employment departments the same as they had previously organized their production, auditing, legal, and financial departments. They have their personnel experts in labor psychology and they even imitate the unions by company unions. Yet even these self-recoveries are shattered by the depression of 1929, and the first to go are the personnel experts.

More important, they are learning not to use the injunction, whereas small competitive business is struggling hard to retain the injunction to keep the unions out of their shops. The injunction is none other than a judicial decree, arising from the American system of judicial sovereignty, and is analogous to the executive decrees of Mussolini dissolving the trade unions and governing labor directly by dictatorship. Big capitalism does not need it, and it is the American parallel of Italian Fascism. Anti-injunction laws, if the courts would observe them, would keep the courts out of politics and place labor associations somewhat on an equality before the law with employers' associations.

Another strength of American capitalism is promotion within the ranks. Professor Selig Perlman (in conversation) has likened it to the Catholic Church. The lowest day laborer, from the poorest family, may become foreman, superintendent, general manager, then chief executive. Thousands of such cases are known in our big corporations. Under the old individualist system the individual became wealthy by building up his own business, which went to pieces in the hands of his sons and sons-in-law. Now he builds up a corporation that lives when he is gone, and his successors are not his relatives who remain mainly bondholders, but are the poor boys who have risen to high managerial salaries mostly by sheer ability.

Europe has not yet learned this trick of promotion. Class feeling keeps the manual worker in his inferior class, and the higher executives come in from the families of privileged and educated classes. But American chief executives are proud if they can point to their lowly origin as day laborers. I have occasionally come across a belligerent socialist or trade unionist converted into an ardent propagandist of capitalism by this uplift along the hierarchy of American corporationism. A salary of $100,000 a year to a competent executive is insignificant for a corporation with a billion dollars a year of sales and purchases depending on his daily decisions. But such salaries are too fabulous for the imagination of small business and democratic government. A chief executive of a billion dollar corporation, with half a million stockholders, although scarcely an owner of the stock himself, gives orders to the dummy board of directors and they listen and obey. He and they are placed there by the bankers.

By reason of these selections, promotions, and high salaries the corporation is far more versatile than the individual. It can employ expert specialists for each side of its work. It can employ lobbyists and politicians to control the legislatures and line up the voters. It can employ lawyers to draft laws and win decisions before the courts. It is in itself a manufacturers' association of stock and bond owners keeping up prices by its sales department and an employers' association keeping down labor costs by its labor department. And it has its public relations department, employing newspaper graduates to persuade the people. With such versatility in the selection of managerial ability, big capitalism is stabilizing itself against the little capitalists, the farmers, the wage-earners, and even the government. In these latter cases there is no merit system of promotion, no security of tenure for the efficient individual, no high salary for the ambitious.

The main strength of capitalism is the Banking System. Great corporations move their headquarters to New York, and either their Boards of Directors must be satisfactory to the bankers, or they must themselves control the banks. This connection has come about during the past thirty years, by the simple necessity of maintaining investors' good-will. The banks float the securities of the corporations and arrange commercial credits. They discovered that if they would maintain their own reputation with investors who bought the securities, they could not leave the corporations to the manipulation of insiders. So they must necessarily control the corporations which they finance. The bankers also work together in syndicates and they work as international syndicates, each selling to the investors of their own nation the securities of foreign governments and foreign industries. Thus American capitalism is Banker Capitalism, instead of the former Merchant Capitalism or Employer Capitalism. But even so in periods of inflation and depression they have exploited the millions of investors and lost their good-will. "Blue sky" laws protecting investors will be in fact another forced recovery of Capitalism. These laws are blindly opposed by those who do not understand the good-will of investors.

Then in the public interest and the need to economize the scattered gold reserves in order to furnish a flexible currency, the Congress unites the bulk of the banks in a great Federal Reserve System, like similar central banks of the world. The System makes its own rules and governs its members and borrowers, much like a trade union. The banking system the world over has become the head of the modern systems of national and international economic government, not only because the banks sought aggrandizement for themselves but because dire public necessity required unity of operation in place of the older competitive individualism. Great industrial corporations are represented on the boards of directors of the twelve reserve bank boards, and the alliance of banking and industry is complete.

Then the government appoints a Federal Reserve Board to supervise this stupendous bankers' government of its own creation, but with low salaries and insecurity of tenure in dealings with men of fabulous salaries and the shrewdest of ability which modern capitalism enlists in establishing its supremacy.

It is here, when we come to the banking system, that the postwar economists of the world are forming a new alignment, which may be distinguished as the Bargaining School and the Managerial School of economists.   Both arise from the same causes, periodic overproduction and unemployment.   But they reach different conclusions as to the future and the remedies.   The managerial school, when carried through to its conclusions, looks to a great Economic Planning Council which shall prevent overproduction and unemployment by rationing.   The bargaining school looks to a concerted international money and banking policy, something like the Bank for International Payments, and control of the world's gold and silver bank reserves, designed to prevent recurrence of overproduction and unemployment by stabilizing the general level of prices. The ultimate difference between the schools is that the bargaining school endeavors to retain, under new conditions, the older principles of equality and liberty in all bargaining transactions that determine prices, while the managerial schools rest on the still older principle of superior and inferior in all managerial and rationing transactions which determine output and efficiency.   The one looks towards equality of Bargaining Power, the other towards rationing of Producing Power.   The one looks towards Reasonable Capitalism, the other towards Communism or Fascism.

The managerial school is now predominant, owing to the amazing success of scientific management and the revolutionary adoption of power-driven machinery and mass production of the past thirty years.   The engineer comes to the front as the general manager of a nation, unmindful of the politician who is the expert in mass psychology.   These engineering triumphs are visible before everybody's eyes.   But the bargaining school is not as convincing because the price mechanism of the world is invisible, and there is no great international bank with years of success to be pointed to as an exhibit.   Yet it is probable that huge corporations do not grow so much by Marx's technological efficiency as by the booms and depressions of Banker Capitalism.

The older economists of the individualist school of Smith and Ricardo argued that there could be no such thing as *universal* over-

892   INSTITUTIONAL ECONOMICS

production. There might be *particular* overproduction in one industry or establishment, with a resulting fall in prices and wages
for that industry. But this would correct itself by the free movement of capital and labor from that industry to other industries
where there had been no fall in prices or wages. The result would
be a falling off of production in the overproduced industry and an
increase of production in the underproduced industry, so that an
automatic tendency towards equilibrium would be continually going
on between different industries, and they would equalize themselves
around the comparative costs of production. An increase in supply
of one product created an increased demand for all other products,
and there could consequently be no universal overproduction and no
universal unemployment in all industries at the same time.

But this reasoning was based on a theoretical elimination of
money, and an ignorance of the modern large concerted bargaining.
The bargaining school, on the contrary, shifts the argument from
the supply and demand of particular commodities to the supply and
demand of money and credit for all commodities. A universal rise
in prices for all concerns, however caused, multiplies the margin for
profit on sales in all industries. This induces all employers at the
same time to compete with each other for universal overproduction.
Then a universal fall in prices, owing to universal contraction of
bank credit or central bank monopolies of gold, or distress sales of
overindebtedness, reduces the margin for profit in all industries.
All industries, big and little, stop together and lay off their workers,
because there is no possibility of shifting from an overproduced to
an underproduced industry. All are overproduced at the same time.
Since 1927 the central banks of France and America have im-
pounded two-thirds of the world's monetary gold. Most of the
important countries have been compelled to abandon the gold standard on account of the fall in gold prices of commodities.

Modern capitalistic industry has proved that there is universal
overproduction and unemployment. Every industry and every nation complains about it at the same time. The evidence is a universal fall in prices. There is overproduction of coal, of oil, of
transportation, of manufactures, of merchandising, or agriculture,
all at the same time and in all capitalistic nations. This was impossible under the older molecular theories of individual demand
and supply.

The labor unions were the first to recognize it and to organize
against it, eighty years ago. Then the railroad companies, sixty
years ago; the manufacturing companies forty years ago. Now
agriculture, the last refuge of individualism, is falling in line with

its allotment schemes for shutting down the marginal farms and restricting production.

In view of this universal overproduction the managerial school of economists is passing through three stages of their philosophy. The first is the Scientific Management stage for individual establishments. The second is the Regularization stage for an entire industry. The third is a National Planning Council for all industries of an entire nation.

The word Rationalization is used in Europe to include both what are here called Regularization and National Planning. The originator was the great German business man and director in a hundred corporations, Walter Rathenau, twenty years ago; while Frederick Taylor, the engineer, forty years ago, originated scientific management in America. The World War compelled all countries to follow Rathenau for the time being, but Russia and Italy are following Taylor and Rathenau in time of peace.

The scientific management and the regularization stages of the managerial economists turn out to be diametrically opposite. In the scientific management stage the philosophy was an Increase of Output by eliminating waste in the factory and making labor and machinery more efficient. But in the regularization stage the purpose is, not elimination of the wastes of production in the factory, but elimination of the wastes of overproduction on the markets. The managerial philosophy now changes to Restriction of Output in order to balance production with consumption and meet the actual demand without losing control of prices. The automatic balancing of the Nineteenth Century economists becomes the regulated balancing of the managerial economists.

Both the first and second stages of the managerial economics are scientific, because based on measurement. But the unit of measurement is changed. In the first stage the unit is the man-hour. In the second stage the unit is the dollar. By increasing efficiency in the factory, the output per man-hour is increased. By restricting the output sold to the market, the dollar income is increased.

Both results are considered by the more naïve of the managerial school to be an increase in efficiency. Hence the word Efficiency acquires the double meaning of Increase of Output and Increase of Income. One is the scientific management stage of the engineer; the other is the regularization stage of the business man. The engineer's unit is the man-hour, the business unit is the dollar, and the managerial economists pass from the hour to the dollar.

At this regularization stage of the managerial school, when the dollar becomes the unit of measurement, the bargaining school also changes from individualism to collective stabilization of world prices. But within the managerial school three general methods of regularization can now be distinguished, which may be named Fair Trade Capitalism, Syndicate Capitalism, and Banker Capitalism. The three methods may slip into each other and there are borderline cases. But, in general, fair trade capitalism is the association of small competitors who agree to a Code of Ethics which is morally but not legally binding upon its members, and carries no legal penalties for violations.

Syndicate capitalism goes further and adopts the trade-union principle of imposing penalties upon its members for violations. Syndicate capitalism is lawful in Germany under the ambiguous name of Cartels,[4] but it has been unlawful in America. Consequently, in America, capitalism is becoming either fair trade capitalism or Banker Capitalism. The method of Banker Capitalism has come to be known as the follow-your-leader method, the leader being a dominant corporation.

According to the syndicate method an entire industry is brought into one organization, including all the big and little manufacturers, the efficient and the inefficient. Then the syndicate, by a study of the markets and the prices they wish to maintain, arbitrarily fixes the total output of the industry for the coming period of a year or so. With the total output thus fixed, the syndicate then rations to each establishment its quota of the total output in proportion to its capacity or to the amount it had already been selling. No establishment is permitted to exceed its quota. There have been several examples in America. The outstanding one has been in the anthracite coal industry; a new one recently claiming attention is in the crude petroleum industry, copied by exhortations to the agriculturists to do the same.

But these syndicates have hitherto been held by the United States Supreme Court to be unreasonable restraints of trade, and have been enjoined. So the American system of Banker Capitalism came into existence during the past thirty years, with the holding company and the follow-your-leader method.

According to the American philosophy of liberty, you cannot by law compel a person to produce, or sell, or compete if he does not wish to do so. He has a natural right to *withhold* production just as much as he has a natural right to *expand* production. Consistently enough, when the individual becomes a holding company

---

[4] Which in some cases are merely fair trade capitalism—*Konditionenkartellen.*

financed by bankers, the company has the same natural rights as
the individual. To deprive the company of this right to withhold
is to deprive it of liberty, which cannot be done under the Fourteenth Amendment to the Constitution. So the American method is
not a syndicate method of compulsion to withhold production—it is
a voluntary method of follow-your-leader, and comes about as follows:

It is not needful for American capitalism to combine all competitors in a single holding company. It is only needful to combine
the strongest companies and the strategic companies. These include
the companies that own the natural resources, the companies that
do the intermediate manufacturing and transportation, the companies that own trade-marks, good-will, and patents which furnish
access to the patronage of customers, and the great bankers who
finance the company. This is Integrated Capitalism, or Banker
Capitalism, because the integration can be financed only by bankers.
The United States Steel Company, created by a banker syndicate,
and sustained by bankers, in some of its branches of manufacture
controls less than half of the nation's output. But if a small competitor, in the stress of hard times and lack of orders, ventures to
cut prices in order to pull customers away, a mere announcement
by the head of the Steel Company that it intends to "meet competition" brings the unruly competitor back to the prices set by
the dominant corporation. The gasoline stations, though there are
many competitors and the business is overcrowded, charge the same
prices, and make the same changes in price, at the same time.

This is American Capitalism. It is an economic government of
bankers more powerful than the political government. Its sanctions
are not the physical force of the state—they are the more powerful
sanctions of credit, profit, and loss. The system looks like the old
"law" of supply and demand and like the economists' principle of
marginal utility. Competition still is free, but the sanction has been
changed from the economist's satisfaction of wants to the business
man's fear of bankruptcy. The little capitalists, who, in Italy or
Germany, furnish the popular recruits for Fascism, become in
America the disciplined followers of Banker Capitalism.

It is the clause in the Clayton Act enabling corporations to "meet
competition," that indicates a triumph of the lobbying power of
American Capitalism. J. B. Clark, with keen insight, had shown, in
1901, that if, when a corporation cuts prices in *one locality* in order
to kill off a small competitor who had only a local market, the law
should require that the corporation should make a similar cut in
prices in *all* its markets, then the corporation could not recoup its

profits in the other markets to compensate its losses in the cut-price market. The great corporation would be placed on an equality of bargaining power with its smallest competitors. But, though this insight of Professor Clark was supported by members of Congress when the law was enacted (1913), yet the lobbyists of the companies were able to insert the words "except in good faith to meet competition." Had the exception not been inserted, then the older ideals of free competition would have been retained on something like an equality between big and little business. But with this exception inserted, a mere threat to "meet competition" usually compels the small capitalists to restore prices and makes American capitalism distinctly a follow-your-leader capitalism.

Even with this exception in the law, why do the Banker Capitalists permit these little capitalists to survive? They are not always little and not always inefficient. They may be even more efficient than their big competitors. They are allowed to survive if they do not produce too much and do not pull customers away by cutting prices. This is the economic reason.

There is also a political reason. The integrated capitalist does not wish to be known as a monopolist. If he can point to small competitors who have the sympathy of the public, he avoids political attacks. The little capitalist is his political umbrella.

It turns out that this American method of voluntary follow-your-leader capitalism is much more powerful, flexible, and efficient than the legal compulsion of either the cartels of Germany, the Fascism of Italy, or the Communism of Russia. It is more powerful because it pays high salaries for executive ability. It is more flexible because it leaves the way open for a little capitalist to make a big profit if he increases his efficiency. Already the United States Steel Company has lost one entire branch of its industry, the pipe industry, because a relatively little capitalist of something like 20 million dollars developed a process far more efficient than the old-fashioned process of the Steel Company. The remedy is for the corporation to buy the little capitalist. The American system forces capitalism to establish immense scientific research departments. It may be that the Supreme Court is highly justified in rejecting syndicate capitalism and forcing America into Banker Capitalism.

Yet neither Syndicate Capitalism nor Banker Capitalism can overcome the menace of overproduction and unemployment in periods of extreme fall in prices. In fact it appears that fluctuations of overproduction and unemployment are more extreme with large corporations than with little employers. Further, it has been contended that business concentration in huge factories often increases the costs of marketing as much as it reduces the costs of production.

Equally important are the huge investment and overhead costs of equipment, and the overhead costs of the trained mechanics and managers who must be kept together even if the plant is idle and the other laborers are unemployed. The plant and managers are specialized for the particular product, and cannot be shifted to other products, as the older economists supposed. It may therefore be better to keep up production even though there is overproduction and the margin of profit has been wiped out by falling prices, if only the overhead costs can be covered. Or, a profit cushion can be set up for paying dividends without employing labor and producing an output for sale. Hence banker capitalism is a cause of even more unemployment than little capitalism. Little capitalism is neighborhood capitalism. Banker capitalism is world capitalism.

It is this situation that forces the managerial economists to the third stage of their philosophy—a National Economic Planning Council. Competition is ceasing to be competition between individuals in the same industry to undercut prices. The industry acts like a unit, whether it be fair trade, syndicate, or banker capitalism. Competition is becoming competition between industries to obtain possession of the consumer's dollar. The old idea of reducing prices becomes the new idea of high pressure salesmanship without reducing prices. Hence this Planning Council shall bring together all the capitalists of all industries and shall allocate capital and labor in the right proportions, not only between competitors within each industry which is done by Regularization, but between all industries of the entire nation, which is to be done by a council of all the industries. For the managerial economists this is not a dream. They point to two exhibits, the Supreme Economic Council of Soviet Russia and the new Corporate State of Fascist Italy.

But these exhibits are no longer voluntary capitalism. They are dictatorships. No Economic Planning Council can enforce its plans, either of regularization or national planning, without physical compulsion by the state, for it is a system of quotas and rationing. Not all individuals, or corporations, or industries, will voluntarily submit to it. If they can make a profit at the prices or wages recommended, they cannot be expected to withhold production within the quotas assigned to them. The Council must have the aid of the state to prevent overproduction. We see the beginnings already in the laws of Texas and Oklahoma prohibiting the drilling of oil wells or enlargement of output except on permission of an executive branch of government. Extend this sample to all industries and we have the managerial goal of a National Economic Planning Council backed by the executive dictatorship of the state.

This brings us to the ultimate problem of public policy and practical politics. Are democracy and representative government competent to manage these world-wide financial governments? Communism and Fascism have given their answers. They have frankly and avowedly abolished popular elections, representative government, freedom of speech, and freedom of association, and have substituted dictatorship and compulsory membership in regulated associations.

But Russia and Italy are countries of petty capitalism, peasant agriculture, low standards of living, and almost no experience with universal suffrage. American capitalism has high salaries, promotions for executive ability, high standards of living, the spread of investments to millions of voters, universal suffrage, and a Supreme Court.

The American problem, if we may derive it from comparison with Russia and Italy, is twofold: economic and political. We may take two things as fixed and certain for the future. On the economic side is the spread of banker capitalism; on the political side is the sovereignty of the Supreme Court. The things that are unfixed and uncertain are the future of legislatures and the future of voluntary private associations of laborers, farmers, small business men, and political parties. Both legislatures and voluntary associations have been abolished in Russia and Italy. Both, we can plainly see, are getting weaker and weaker in America.

Business men dread a session of the legislature or Congress. Mussolini's Black Shirts marched on Rome to put an end to an ineffective parliament. So do communists resent universal suffrage. Lenin's Red Army prevented the constitutional assembly from even assembling. The American Supreme Court declares the acts of legislatures and Congress unconstitutional and determines for itself the legality of corporations and their practices.

Legislatures are undoubtedly discredited in the modern world of universal suffrage and conflict of economic interests. In a sense the lobby is more representative than the legislature. It represents economic interests—the legislators represent miscellaneous individuals. Italy had adopted proportional representation, representing majority and minority parties in proportion to their votes. This permitted, for the first time, the peasants to get representation in parliament proportionate to their numbers. But this only served to increase the number of political parties and their deadlocks, each party representing different economic interests, and it furnished

Mussolini with his most persuasive argument for the suppression of the legislature.

On the other hand Prussia, for more than ten years, was successfully governed by a proportional representation of Catholics, Socialists, and Democrats, abolished, in the end by the military dictatorship of Germany.

We know that universal suffrage has broken down in the southern states and our biggest cities. These are the places from which the business and professional classes look with longing to a business man's government, which is our Fascism. Mussolini had been a syndicalist, who applauded the workers' possession of the factories. He had learned the psychology of mass violence. He was fitted to become the leader of the business and professional classes when he gained their confidence and turned to them for financial support.

His first acts, before reorganizing the legislature which had a majority against him, were the repeal of the inheritance taxes and the increase of consumption taxes. Soon his violence and suppression of opponents began to raise up opposition to him in the legislature. The opposition finally left the legislature altogether. He turned then to organizing all the wage-earners and peasants, as well as employers, into compulsory syndicates. It is these syndicates, representing economic interests for the nation at large, with their officers appointed by the dictator, that take the place of the older legislative system representing the plurality of individual voters by territorial districts.

The district system of elections to the legislature had worked well enough in England when suffrage was restricted to the propertied classes. At that time there could be only two parties in the legislature, the landowners from the country and the capitalists from the cities. But since universal suffrage came in, practically a hundred years ago in America and scarcely thirty years ago even in England, the legislatures began to split into blocks, deadlocks, log-rolling and debating societies, representing the new economic interests.

But when Mussolini abolished proportional representation in the legislature he abolished the only method by which modern legislatures can be made truly representative of all economic interests. Economic interests are no longer confined to county districts of a state, or to ward districts of a city, or to state districts of a nation. They extend across district lines. They have their state and national organizations. The problem which proportional representation attempts to meet is how to elect these leaders to the legislature and keep them there. Their leaders are men like Gompers of the trade unions, or men like Gary of the Steel Company, or men like

Lowden of the farmers' organizations, or men like Berger of the socialist organization, or men like Wiggins of the Chase National Bank. Such men have too many enemies. They cannot be re-elected continuously by plurality or majority votes in small territorial districts. But they could be elected continuously over wider areas by proportional or minority representation. As it is, only men without enemies can be elected, and the American political machine is the device by which "dark horses" are discovered and elected, who are unknown as representative leaders, because they have the minimum of enemies. It is afterwards discovered that they were well known to the insiders.

The city of Cincinnati has furnished an exhibit of what proportional representation can do towards making the legislative body representative and effective, and in other countries the system has slowly extended to state and national legislatures, abolished only when dictatorship takes hold. Only when legislatures can be made representative of economic interests through their own freely elected leaders, can it be expected that they will have the experience and ability to hold in check the high-salaried executives and political machines of American Banker Capitalism.

But the example of Italy confronts us. It was this very proportional representation that made the Italian parliament an ineffective debating society with its blocks and deadlocks. So it might be in America. The board of directors of a great corporation has but one economic interest to promote—profits. The legislature has a dozen or more conflicting and overlapping interests.

But American legislatures and Congress are learning to relieve themselves of the details of administration required by the modern complexity of conflicting interests. The railroad and public utility commissions, the tax commissions, the industrial commissions, the market commissions, are created to deal with the conflicts between railroads and shippers, between employers and employees, between classes of taxpayers, between big and little competitors for business. These commissions are semi-legislative bodies, and where they are most effective it is being found that they set up representation of the conflicting economic interests as advisory committees, curiously analogous to Mussolini's Fascist Corporations but with the difference that the interests are voluntary, electing their own representatives, while his are compulsory and the representatives are selected by himself.

Relieved of these overwhelming details, the modern legislature is learning to restrict itself to the field where it may be effective, notwithstanding and even because it represents conflicting interests.

Its effective field is general laws and general standards of administration. These general rules are matters of compromise between conflicting economic interests, and a deadlock merely postpones the compromise, while the semi-legislative administration goes on with details and execution of policies as before.

But far more important than other reasons for improving and retaining the legislatures is the protection they may give to voluntary associations. This protection is summarized in the Bill of Rights which comes to us from the English Revolution of 1689. Yet every generation must renew its bill of rights. They are the rights not only of free speech, free press, and free investigation, but most important, the rights of free association. They mean, in our day, trade unions, farmers' coöperatives, business coöperatives, political parties. It is these that are abolished in Russia and Italy because legislatures are abolished.

Even so, these voluntary associations have begun to learn that they also must restrict their activities to the fields where they can be effective. In the United States we have some experiments to go by. The early labor organizations, ending with the Knights of Labor, attempted by voluntary association to substitute coöperation and self-employment for capitalistic employment, on the democratic principle of one-man-one-vote instead of the capitalistic principle of one-share-one-vote. Their organizations broke down on the one issue of electing the managers by popular vote. Or, if they succeeded, they closed their doors to new members and hired non-members for wages, and so eventually became ordinary corporations and went over to the side of the capitalists.

Farmers' coöperatives have had a similar experience. For sixty years they have been breaking down on the democratic principle of one-man-one-vote. Small coöperatives seem to work well, where all have similar interests and are fairly well acquainted with each other. But where their membership is changing and there are differences in politics, religion, color, race, language, personalities, then factions spring up and internal politics elects the managers, regardless of managing ability.

The big corporations limit themselves to one activity, profits. American trade unions of the past forty years, unlike unions in other countries, have learned to limit themselves to just one interest—wages, hours, and working rules. They do not try to manage business—they try only to get as large a share as possible of the product of business.

The farmers are still in the stage of the labor organizations of forty years ago. The government comes to their aid to finance their

coöpertives and furnish them leaders. They have yet to demon-
strate that, on a large scale, they can elect their own leaders with
security of tenure, promotions from within, and adequate salaries
to deal with the big corporations. Already the main advice given
to them is to elect better managers and pay better salaries. Un-
happily it cannot be said, in general, that they show capacity to do
so. There are a few examples of merchandising coöperatives; but,
whatever field we consider, it is to the legislatures that we must
look for the protection of these rights of association, not by furnishing them leaders from above, but by protecting them against discriminations by powerful competitors from without.

I am told by an eminent exile from the dictatorship of Hungary
that all of this talk about the Bill of Rights is obsolete and that in
holding to it I am the Last Mohican of Liberalism. The world, as
he and other Europeans think, is inevitably pushing towards Communism or Fascism, and the liberals are gradually or violently
squeezed out. It is indeed a notable contrast that the Constitution
of the United States is based on Rights, but the Constitutions of
Russia and Italy are based on Duties. Duties become the ethics
of dictatorship. It is the change brought about during a hundred
and forty years from the rights of man of the French Revolution
to the duties of man of the Russian and Italian dictatorships. The
rights of man are his liberties; the duties of man are the denial of
his liberties. But the rights of man now are his rights of free
association.

This is the problem of modern economics, which is coming to be
known as Institutional Economics. An institution is merely collective action in control, liberation, and expansion of individual
action. It may be Communism, Fascism, or Capitalism. The economic philosophy of the French Revolution would have abolished
collective action. The economic philosophy now, the world over, is
the philosophy of collective action. That which deprives people of
economic liberty is unemployment and poverty. It is but a step,
and indeed a necessary one to prevent revolution, to deprive them
of *political* liberty. They retain liberty for themselves by collective
action, either by voluntary associations or political parties.

It may be that American capitalism is moving towards Fascism
under the guise of an Economic Planning Council. It has begun
by suppressing Communism and Syndicalism. But it cannot reach
the ultimate Fascist state until legislatures are discredited and
judges are appointed and removed by dictators. With these sup-
pressions are suppressed the civil liberties that make possible the
voluntary associations of labor unions, farmers' unions, business co-

operatives, and political parties. It is these associations, instead of the older individualism of free individual action, that are the refuge of modern Liberalism and Democracy from Communism, Fascism, or Banker Capitalism.

Yet it is doubtful whether, under modern conditions, a decision can be reached as to which is the better public policy—the Communism of Russia, the Fascism of Italy, or the Banker Capitalism of the United States. In the two European systems and others that are copying them, liberty is suppressed and the intellectuals, who include artists, inventors, scientists, engineers, editors, professors, are eliminated, not merely because they are physically suppressed but because individual originality and genius cannot thrive in a nation of fear.

Yet these are a small fraction of the population. The overwhelming majority are manual and clerical workers in all lines of manufacture, agriculture, transportation, and banking. To them liberty is an illusion under institutions which demoralize them on the upturn of prices, pauperize them on the downturn, and coerce them by lack of jobs. They do not miss liberty if Communism or Fascism gives them security at low wages.

Likewise with the personal thrift which became the basis of the small capitalism that displaced the wastefulness of feudal aristocracies, and attracted eagerly the endorsement of Turgot and Adam Smith. The inflation and deflation of a twentieth century Banker civilization scrapes off the cream of that individual proprietorship which hitherto had induced individual wage-earners and farmers to save, to economize, to take the risks which they had a chance to surmount, and to maintain the American Republic. Thrift is becoming the institutionalized thrift of corporate surplus and of Russian or Italian rationing, and those individuals who, under American capitalism, personally denied themselves enjoyments in order to save and invest for the future are the ridicule of those who enjoyed all they earned at the time and are now no worse off than those who denied themselves enjoyments which they could have had.

If these thrifty individuals are eliminated from the capitalist civilization by becoming a proletariat of wage and salary earners, then it is probable that, for the overwhelming majority, a communist or fascist dictatorship may be preferable to American Banker Capitalism. It will, no doubt, promptly eliminate academic liberty and a free press, but meanwhile the economists have, for the time being, a new equipment of experimental laboratories on three grand scales, in Russia, Italy and America, for a rough and tumble testing of their classical, hedonistic, and institutional theories.

CHAPTER REFERENCES

I. Communism

Ryazanoff, D., *The Communist Manifesto of Karl Marx and Friedrich Engels* (1930). Translation of the original and extensive collateral material.

Lenin, N., *The State and Revolution; Marxist Teaching on the State and the Task of the Proletariat in the Revolution* (1917, reprint by Marxian Educational Society, Detroit). The transitional character of the dictatorship.

Lenin, N., *Collected Works of V. I. Lenin*, 4 vols. (tr. 1930).

Hoover, Calvin B., *The Economic Life of Soviet Russia* (1931). Appreciative and critical.

Hindus, Maurice S., *Humanity Uprooted* (1929; 3d ed. 1930). The Russian psychology.

Hansen, A. H., *Economic Stabilization in an Unbalanced World* (1932), 324 ff., "The Convergence of Capitalism and Socialism."

Commons, John R., "Marx To-day: Capitalism and Socialism." *Atlantic Monthly*, August 1925.

The Soviet Union. American periodical under auspices of Soviet representatives, Washington, D. C.

Moscow News. Soviet publication for English readers.

II. Fascism

Estey, J. A., *Revolutionary Syndicalism* (1913). The French origins.

Villari, Luigi, *Italy* (1929). The ablest defense of Fascism.

Lion, Aline, *The Pedigree of Fascism, a Popular Essay on the Western Philosophy of Politics* (1927). Philosophical apology.

Howard, Milford W., *Fascism: A Challenge to Democracy* (1928). The Fascism of the Southern States.

Sturzo, Luigi, *Italy and Fascisms* (tr. 1926). The agricultural peasants' opponent of Fascism.

Bolitho, Wm., *Italy Under Mussolini* (1926). Critical.

Mussolini, Benito, *My Autobiography* (1928). "A Life for which I have a deep affection." The American Ambassador's introduction.

Salvameni, Gaetano, *The Fascist Dictatorship in Italy* (1927). By an eminent exile.

Schneider, Herbert W., *Making the Fascist State* (1928). A sympathetic American observer.

Haider, Carmen, *Capital and Labor under Fascism* (1930). Authentic account to date.

Battaglia, Otto Forst de, ed., *Dictatorship on Its Trial* (1930). Vivid articles by leading Europeans for and against the various European dictatorships.

Fowler, C. B., "The Fascist Labor Charter and Unemployment Insurance in Italy," *American Federationist*, February 1933.

Barnes, Major J. S., *Fascism* (1931).

Publications in English of *Minister of Corporations*, Rome.

III. MANAGEMENT

Scientific Management in American Industry. The Taylor Society (1929).

Matthaei, L. E., "More Mechanization in Farming," *International Labour Review* (March 1931), 324–368.

Rathenau, W., *In Days to Come* (tr. 1921). The Father of Rationalization.

Strukturwandlungen der Deutschen Volkswirtschaft, B. Harms, ed., 2 vols. (2d ed., 1929). Chapters on Kartelle und Konzerne.

National Industrial Conference Board, *Rationalization of German Industry* (1931); *Mergers and the Law* (1929). The inefficiencies of syndicate capitalism.

Michels, R. K., *Cartels, Combines and Trusts in Post-War Germany* (Columbia University Publications, 1928).

U. S. Department of Commerce, *The International Cartel Movement* (Trade Information Bulletin No. 566, 1928). Brief summary of German Cartels.

Handler, Milton, "Industrial Mergers and the Anti-Trust Laws," *Columbia Law Review*, XXXII (1932), 179–271.

Hamlin, Scoville, ed., *The Menace of Overproduction* (1930). A symposium by managerial economists.

Donham, W. B., *Business Adrift* (1931). National Planning Council.

Soule, George, *A Planned Society* (1932).

Long-Range Planning, Committee of the National Progressive Conference, *The New Republic*, January 13, 1932.

Taeusch, Carl F., *Policy and Ethics in Business* (1931). Legislative, judicial, and economic developments since 1890.

Beard, Charles A. and William, *The American Leviathan: The Republic in the Machine Age* (1930). Democratic optimists.

National Bureau of Economic Research, *Recent Economic Changes*, 2 vols. (1929). An American survey.

Wagemann, Ernst F., *Economic Rhythm: A Theory of Business Cycles* (tr. 1930). A statistician's world economics.

Patterson, Ernest Minor, *The World's Economic Dilemma* (1930).

Brookings, R. S., *Economic Democracy; America's Answer to Socialism and Communism* (1929).

Liefman, Robert, *International Cartels, Combines and Trusts* (1927). Leading German authority on cartels.

IV. BARGAINING

Clark, J. B., *The Control of Trusts* (1901, 1912). Potential competition.

Fisher, Irving, *The Purchasing Power of Money; Its Determination and Relation to Credit, Interest and Crises* (1911); *Stabilizing the Dollar; a Plan to Stabilize the General Price Level without Fixing Individual Prices* (1920); *Some First Principles of Booms and Depressions* (1932).

Cassel, Gustav, *Theoretische Sozialökonomie* (1921). Prices, credit, gold.

Hawtrey, R. B., *Currency and Credit* (1919, 1928). Banking and gold.

Keynes, J. M., *A Treatise on Money*, 2 vols. (1930). The "New Wicksellism."

House of Representatives, Committee on Banking and Currency. House of Representatives Hearings on H. R. 7895 (1927), H. R. 11806 (1928). Stabilization proponents and opponents.

Rogers, James Harvey, *America Weighs Her Gold* (1931).

Commons, John R., "Bargaining Power," *Encyclopedia of the Social Sciences* (1930), II, 459–462.

Perlman, Selig, *History of Trade Unionism in the United States; a Theory of the Labor Movement* (1928).

V. BANKER CAPITALISM

Gerstenberg, C. W., *Financial Organization and Management of Business* (rev. ed. 1932).

Ripley, W. Z., *Main Street and Wall Street* (1927).

Berle, A. A., and Means, G. C., *The Modern Corporation and Private Property* (1932).

Bonbright, J. C., and Means, G. C., *The Holding Company; Its Public Significance and Regulation* (1932).

Clark, J. M., *The Economics of Overhead Costs* (1923).

Frey, John, "Bankers' Domination," *American Federationist* (February 1933).

VI. Legislation

Commons, John R., *Proportional Representation* (1896, 1907). Machine politics.

Hoag, C. G., and Hallett, G. H., *Proportional Representation* (1926). The Hare system.

INDEX

Ability, and opportunity, 301–348; double meaning, 267.
Absolutism, 386–389.
Abstinence, and savings, 455; Jevons, 501; Senior, 307, 455.
Abundance, 182, 199, 224, 349, 506, 773; and liberty, 198–201; equivalent of beneficence, 37, 40; periods, 774, 779.
Abuse, right of, 664.
Acceptation, 471.
Accidents, insurance and prevention, 840–874.
Accounts, receivable and payable, 542–543.
Accumulation, 188.
Act of Settlement—1700, 28.
Activity, 19, 24 f., 55, 623 f.; and custom, 145; concerted, 342.
Adams Express Co. v. Ohio State Auditor, 53 n., 652.
Adler, E. A., cited, 781 n.
Administration, 470, 471, 649, 717, 847 ff., 856 ff., 862–863, 900–901.
Age of Reason, Malthus' refutation, 245, 846–847.
Agio, of consumption goods, 506.
Agriculture, 880 ff., 901.
Akeley, Dean L. E., 100 ff.
Alienation, right of, 405.
Allen, E. S. (and Hans Reichenbach), *Atoms and Cosmos*, cited, 17 n.
Alternatives, 504; inaccessible, 317–325; scarcity and abundance, 91.
Altmeyer, Arthur J., 849.
American Federationist, quoted, 550 ff.
American Federation of Labor, policy of, 531.
American Legion, 879.
Analogy, two meanings, 96–97; kinds, 120.
Analysis, genesis and synthesis distinguished, 99; and insight, 746; statical and dynamical, 456–457.

Anarchism, 369, 370; and coöperative movements, 769.
Andrews, J. B. (and J. R. Commons), *Principles of Labor Legislation*, cited, 39 n.
Antithesis, see Thesis.
Anti-trust laws, 343, 881; and holding companies, 53.
Aquinas, St. Thomas, 39 n., 110, 260.
Arbitration, 3 ff.; a rationing transaction, 759.
Assessments, special, 828.
Assets, contrasted with wealth, 74–77, 127, 132, 265, 288; tangible and intangible, 663–665; see Wealth.
Association, custom, 24, 327, 709; right, 343, 712; see Coöperation, 769.
Assumpsit, doctrine of, 46, 61 n., 64, 83–84, 193, 474, 477, 525, 743, 744.
Assumptions, classification, 698; ethical, 699; habitual, 697–714; proprietary, 699; technological, 698.
Atkins, W. E. and Others, *Economic Behavior, an Institutional Approach* (1931), cited, 69 n.
Averages, 214, 267–276, 670.
Avoidance, 19, 88.

Bank of England, 434–438, 476, 590, 597.
Bank of Sweden, suspension of specie payments, 590.
Bank credit and debit, 447, 450, 469, 479, 494, 508, 539 ff., 548, 560, 590 ff.
Bank rate, 451 ff., 596 ff., 606, 616.
Bankers, their rôle in transactions, 510 ff.
Bankruptcy, 558–559.
Bargaining Power, 67, 82, 198, 267, 306, 342–348; buying and selling, 391, 392; formula, 331; institution, 365, 368; liberty-exposure relation,

909

Powicke, F. J., 29 n.
Practices, 709; *see* Custom.
Pragmatism, 83, 107, 150–152, 642, 646–647, 654–655.
Precedent, in custom and common-law method, 72–73, 704, 705, 709.
Prices, and value, 589; economic backbone of history, 121–124; maintenance, 343; margin for profit, 576 ff.; measure of scarcity, 380–386, 516; nominal and real, 204, 211, 791; of waiting, 431, 500 ff., 597; rationing, 68; reasonable, 211, 332, 783; stabilization, 610, 621 ff., 789–805; transactions, 510–526.
Principles, 71, 80, 735, 749–754.
Privilege, 686–687.
Process, 513, 658, 674.
Product, cost of, 309; value of, 310–317.
Production, and bargaining, 289, 797; cost of, 263, 317, 327, 650; for sale or use-value, 451; lag, 552–553; marginal, 498, 499, 607–608; productivity and efficiency, 127, 129, 133, 184, 186, 187, 259, 284–285, 451, 493, 671; regulation of, 257; right to expand or withhold, 894–895; social, 613; technology, 290, 500, 532, 600 ff., 616; theories, 474.
Profit, and interest, 509–510; and wages, 208, 534–535, 865; discount, 433, 503, 506 ff., 538, 609, 617, 839 ff.; margins, 530, 560–590, 612, 793, 797, 806, 869–877; nominal and real, 613, 792; rate, yield, share, margin, 208, 526 ff., 561–562, 598 ff., 612, 617, 793; scarcity and efficiency profits, 280.
Promotions, 889–890.
Property, and due process, 75–77, 82–83, 89, 113, 466, 522, 854–855; and liberty, 34; and money, 35 ff.; and persons, 34; assets and wealth, 72, 74 ff.; corporeal, incorporeal, intangible, 3–5, 31, 51, 70, 75–77, 81–83, 163–170, 193, 197, 208, 237, 351, 368, 386, 400 ff., 420 ff., 522–523, 649–656, 658, 662, 668–670, 673–677; individual and corporate, 167–169; inheritance, 46; justification,

168, 191, 303, 816; proprietary economy, 497, 630–631; scarcity and futurity, 390 ff.; scarcity and rights, 40, 41, 141, 168, 196, 302, 393, 397 ff., 483–500, 672; schools of economists, 110 ff.; social classes, 27; sovereignty, 25, 136; taxation. 52 ff.; transferable, 402 ff.; transactions, 51; value, 591–592.
Proportional representation, 898–899.
Propriety, Adam Smith's meaning, 158, 166, 215.
Prosperity and depression, theories of, 526–527.
Protective tariff, 836 ff.
Proudhon, Pierre Joseph, 5, 52, 55, 112 ff., 123, 366–378, 394, 482–483, 591, 846, 877–878.
Psychology, four stages in economics, 337–338; institutional, 438–443; managerial transactions, 64 ff.; negotiational, 6 ff., 90, 105–106, 320, 333, 334, 443, 504, 520, 525; parallelism and functionalism, 17, 115, 174–179, 194, 483; place in economic theory, 521, 640 ff.
Public purpose, 325–329, 654.
Public utilities, 652.
Publicity, 713.
Purchasing power, 262, 269, 428, 479, 518–520, 531–532, 536, 541–544, 551–552, 556, 579.

Quantum meruit, 61 ff., 83–84, 193.
Quesnay, François, 36, 38, 41, 52, 111, 125–139, 183, 185, 188, 190, 272, 486, 489, 546–547, 616, 810.

Rates interest, 453, 455; rediscount, 594 ff.; turnover, 626 ff.
Rathenau, Walter, 893.
Ratio, 456.
Rationing, and rationing transactions, 67–69, 368, 754–763.
Real, *see* Nominal.
Reality, 152, 266, 523.
Reason, identified with Nature and God, 22, 38, 125 ff., 169, 227, 752; rule of reason, 826; *see* Reasonableness.

For Product Safety Concerns and Information please contact our EU
representative GPSR@taylorandfrancis.com
Taylor & Francis Verlag GmbH, Kaufingerstraße 24, 80331 München, Germany